Magic in tł

MW01135115

Blackwell Ancient Religions

Ancient religious practice and belief are at once fascinating and alien for twenty-first-century readers. There was no Bible, no creed, no fixed set of beliefs. Rather, ancient religion was characterized by extraordinary diversity in belief and ritual.

This distance means that modern readers need a guide to ancient religious experience. Written by experts, the books in this series provide accessible introductions to this central aspect of the ancient world.

Published

Magic in the Ancient Greek World
Derek Collins

Religion in the Roman Empire
James B. Rives

Ancient Greek Religion
Jon D. Mikalson

Forthcoming

Religion of the Roman Republic
Christopher McDonough and Lora Holland

Death, Burial and the Afterlife in Ancient Egypt
Steven Snape

Ancient Greek Divination
Sarah Iles Johnston

Magic in the Ancient Greek World

Derek Collins

BLACKWELL PUBLISHING
350 Main Street, Malden, MA 02148-5020, USA
9600 Garsington Road, Oxford OX4 2DQ, UK
550 Swanston Street, Carlton, Victoria 3053, Australia

First published 2008 by Blackwell Publishing Ltd

1 2008

Library of Congress Cataloging-in-Publication Data
Collins, Derek.
    Magic in the ancient Greek world / Derek Collins.
      p. cm. — (Blackwell ancient religions)
    Includes bibliographical references and index.
    ISBN 978–1–4051–3238–1 (hardcover: alk. paper)—ISBN 978–1–4051–3239–8
(pbk. : alk. paper)   1. Magic, Greek.   I. Title.

    BF1591.C57 2008
    133.4'30938—dc22

                                                            2007027073

A catalogue record for this title is available from the British Library.

Set in 9.75/12.5pt Utopia
by Graphicraft Limited, Hong Kong
Printed and bound in Singapore
by Markono Print Media Pte Ltd

The publisher's policy is to use permanent paper from mills that operate a
sustainable forestry policy, and which has been manufactured from pulp processed
using acid-free and elementary chlorine-free practices. Furthermore, the publisher
ensures that the text paper and cover board used have met acceptable environmental
accreditation standards.

For further information on
Blackwell Publishing, visit our website at
www.blackwellpublishing.com

Contents

Acknowledgments

It is a pleasure to thank those who have contributed in large and small ways to the development of this book. I will never remember everyone, for which I apologize in advance. But in particular I would like to thank Jan Bremmer, Radcliffe Edmonds III, Christopher Faraone, Michael Gagarin, Fritz Graf, Albert Henrichs, Richard Janko, Sarah Iles Johnston, Gregory Nagy, C. Robert Phillips III, William Race, and James Rives. Several of these scholars were not involved directly in the preparation of this book, but over the years have been involved either in helping me to publish my earlier research on Greek magic, or have in other ways generously lent their time and knowledge. In no way should any of these colleagues be held responsible for any errors or imperfections in this book.

Various portions of the research presented here began their life as lectures. I cannot name here all of the participants in those lectures whose stimulating comments helped me to sharpen my views, and correct my errors, so I will content myself by thanking their institutions. They include: Bryn Mawr College, the University of Chicago, the J. Paul Getty Museum in Los Angeles, the University of Michigan and its Institute for the Humanities, the University of North Carolina at Chapel Hill, Ohio State University, and Yale University. In 2003–4, I was a Junior Fellow at the Harvard Center for Hellenic Studies in Washington, DC, during which time I completed a substantial part of the research for this book. I would like to thank the Director and Staff for their tireless support, and the University of Michigan for granting me a leave during that academic year.

I owe a separate acknowledgment to the two anonymous readers of the original manuscript provided by Blackwell Publishing. They furnished me with astute and penetrating criticism, which has only helped to strengthen the final version. I am also especially indebted to Al Bertrand at Blackwell. The impetus for this book began with Al, over a cup of coffee at the annual meeting of the American Philological Association in New Orleans, Louisiana, in 2003. Were it not for his suggestion, and his patience over the intervening years, the book would not have seen the light of day.

Finally, I dedicate this book to my parents and my sons, Adam and Bryan Collins, who still cannot quite believe that their father *studies* magic as opposed to practicing it. Boys, may you never lose that sense of wonder.

Abbreviations

AJP	*American Journal of Philology*
ANRW	*Aufstieg und Niedergang der römischen Welt* (Berlin, 1972–)
ARW	*Archiv für Religionswissenschaft*
CA	*Classical Antiquity*
CML	*Corpus Medicorum Latinorum*
CQ	*Classical Quarterly*
DT	A. Audollent, *Defixionum tabellae* (Paris, 1904)
DTA	R. Wünsch, *Defixionum tabellae atticae, Inscriptiones Graecae* 3.3 (Berlin, 1897)
FGrH	F. Jacoby, *Die Fragmente der griechischen Historiker* (Berlin, 1923–)
GRBS	*Greek, Roman and Byzantine Studies*
HThR	*Harvard Theological Review*
IG	*Inscriptiones Graecae* (Berlin, 1873–present)
JHS	*Journal of Hellenic Studies*
LSJ	Liddell, Scott, Jones et al., eds., *A Greek–English Lexicon* (9th edition, with revised Supplement, Oxford, 1996)
MD	*Materiali e Discussioni*
MDAI	*Mitteilungen des deutschen archäologischen Instituts* (Athenische Abteilung)
OLD	P. G. W. Glare, ed., *Oxford Latin Dictionary* (Oxford, 1996)
PG	J. P. Migne, *Patrologia Graeca* (Paris, 1857–89)
PGM	K. Preisendanz and A. Henrichs, eds., *Papyri Graecae Magicae: Die griechischen Zauberpapyri* (2nd edition, Stuttgart, 1973–74)
RE	A. Pauly and G. Wissova, eds., *Real-Encyclopädie der classischen Altertumswissenschaft* (Stuttgart, 1894–)
REG	*Revue des Études Grecques*

RhM	*Rheinisches Museum für Philologie*
SGD	D. Jordan, "A Survey of Greek Defixiones not Included in the Special Corpora," *GRBS* 26 (1985): 151–97
TAPA	*Transactions of the American Philological Association*
ThesCRA	*Thesaurus Cultus et Rituum Antiquorum*
ZPE	*Zeitschrift für Papyrologie und Epigraphik*

Introduction

Something of the vitality and vibrancy in the study of ancient Greek magic can be found in the works that have appeared over the last two decades, and there is no end to the enthusiasm in sight.[1] As might be expected from a burgeoning field, excellent books and articles have been written on everything from the history of the term 'magic' to the range of Greek magical practices attested from Homer down to late antiquity. The present study seeks to contribute to the discussion in a way that is both accessible to non-specialists and challenging to specialists. Thus my aim in writing this book is twofold: first, it seeks to introduce non-specialists to areas of Greek magic with which they may not be familiar, and to convey an appreciation for its conceptual and practical complexity; second, each chapter aims to cover both the high points of scholarly consensus and to offer new interpretive frameworks for understanding select Greek magical practices. Not every type of Greek magic is treated – notably, amulets, although the study of amulets could be assimilated easily to one or another of the interpretive frameworks offered here. Nor are literary depictions of magical activity treated here in any great depth. Be that as it may, each chapter is meant to be readable and engaging – hence I have minimized the use of Greek and Latin and either translated or provided translations of all texts – and at the same time each chapter ventilates a definite argument for interpretation.

One of the longest-running debates in anthropology and the history of magic concerns the definition of 'magic' itself. Despite the lively and at times brilliant contributions to this debate, it will become evident already in the first chapter of this book that I think that debate is largely irrelevant, at least to the extent that it focuses on defining the meaning of the modern term 'magic', whether it be in opposition to science, technology, religion, or some other term. Ancient Greek terms for 'magic', including

Greek μάγος and the Latin terms *magus, magicus*, from which our modern term 'magic' itself derives, do have an interesting and culturally diverse history, which we will examine in some depth. But as I hope to establish early on, a focus on particular historically attested practices is a more productive way to explore ancient behavior, and doing so often draws into question what to earlier generations of scholars had seemed clearly to be, for instance, either magic or religion. From the point of view of this book, such a distinction is largely effete.

The heart of this book contains five chapters that consider the methodological approaches to magic in anthropology; the development of Greek magic in the classical period; binding magic, curse tablets, and erotic spells, including the use of figurines; incantations derived from Homeric poetry in late antiquity; and the long history of Greek and Roman legislation against magic reaching into the early Middle Ages. A treatment of Roman laws on magic may seem out of place in a book on Greek magic, except that the Romans inherited most forms of Greek magic and in their laws continued to seek Greek precedents to refine Roman magical terms. On more than one occasion in this book we will extend our study into the medieval period – naturally, because Roman law served as the basis for prosecuting magic in the Middle Ages, and the practices that were prohibited more often than not were essentially Greek in character. More rarely, we shall make excursions into the early modern period, if only to highlight the commanding place which Greek, and subsequently Roman, magical concepts and practices held for later Europeans.

In chapter 1, I offer a history of anthropological theories of magical behavior, from the nineteenth to the twentieth centuries, which derive for the most part from studies of non-Greek cultures. This chapter is required reading in order to make sense of my interpretations of the Greek material. Rather than a mere survey of anthropological approaches to magic, instead I outline key concepts of sympathy, analogy, agency, causality, and participation which inform my analyses of particular Greek magical practices. At the same time, by tracing the main approaches to magic in anthropology, I show where false steps were made and where underlying assumptions misled scholars to ask the wrong kinds of questions about magic. Every reader of this book will bring assumptions to the table about what magic means – and many of these I hope to explode in chapter 1 with the help of anthropology, starting with the nature of belief in magic itself.

In chapter 2, I outline a framework for understanding ancient Greek magic. Here we explore the development of Greek concepts of magic in the fifth and fourth centuries BCE, and their underlying basis in causal relationships between the mortal and divine worlds. Next I briefly survey the individuals most associated with magical practice, from Persian priests to itinerant ritual specialists for hire, and finally review the most common magical practices associated with these individuals. New arguments are advanced that Gorgias, who is the first to use the Greek term *mageia*, understood 'magic' to be essentially purificatory in character, in line with Empedocles and the Hippocratic physicians. Moreover, I argue that the Hippocratic author of *On the Sacred Disease*, who offers the most strident attack against 'magicians', misunderstood the relationship between his own subject matter, epilepsy, and magic. Instead, I demonstrate that epilepsy could be caused by magical binding, making the remedies offered by the notorious itinerant specialists peculiarly apt.

In chapter 3, I survey the varieties of binding magic, with a particular eye toward its development in curse tablets or *defixiones*, and erotic magic and figurines. Binding the gods in Greek myth is offered as a parallel to human binding, and the argument is made that binding produces a disability in its victim which inverts Greek notions of physical health. The accumulation of body parts in curse tablets is contrasted with the singling out of body parts in the Greek and Roman practice of manufacturing terracotta votives, which were deposited in temples and other sacred sites. Both practices incorporate an extensible notion of the body, which can be collapsed or distributed in time and space as needed. Examples of binding magic used in erotic spells are then discussed, which leads to a treatment of figurines in Greek magic generally, and in erotic magic in particular. I argue that magical figurines have to be situated within a broader understanding of Greek attitudes toward statuary – since figurines are tiny statues – that view them as social agents which exhibit some, but not all, human attributes. A discussion of Greek and Greco-Egyptian examples of animating Eros figurines to attract a beloved, with some attention paid to the theurgic animation of figurines within Neoplatonism, serves as a model of social agency and concludes the chapter.

In chapter 4, I explore the late antique phenomenon of using Homeric verses as incantations. Incantations (*epōidai*) have a long history in Greek magic, starting with references to their use within Homeric poetry itself. But between the first and fourth centuries CE in Greco-Roman Egypt we find that individual verses are used, sometimes by themselves, sometimes with accompanying rituals, to heal specific ailments or to engender specific changes in their users. The principles by which verses were selected and why are exposed, and attention is given to both prevailing medical and popularly understood theories of ailment to illustrate why certain verses were chosen over others. The practice of using Homeric verses for incantations is then situated within late antique Neoplatonism and theurgy, which I argue provides the most cogent rationale for why

Homeric poetry, and not the poetry of other prominent Greek (or Roman) poets, became the exemplary source for incantations.

In chapter 5, I explore the history of Greek and Roman legislation against magic. This chapter is the most extensive chronologically, beginning with Greek and especially Athenian laws against poisoning and magic as we can reconstruct them from real and hypothetical cases, and as they were envisioned in Plato's ideal republic. From here we move to a consideration of the Roman Twelve Tables and especially to the *Cornelian law on assassins and poisoners* as enacted by Sulla in 81 BCE. This law casts a disconcertingly long shadow over later Roman legislation against magic well into the sixth century CE. I examine several criminal cases for magic that were tried under the Cornelian law, with an in-depth examination of the trial of Apuleius of Madaura in 158/9 CE – a case that continued to puzzle commentators well into the sixteenth century, as it does to this day. We end with a review of fifth- and sixth-century legal positions taken with regard to magic in the *Theodosian Code* and Justinian's *Digest*, respectively, with a view toward the impact of the *Digest* on continental European legislation against magic in the Middle Ages.

Long introductions bore me to tears, and continuing further would tend to spoil the pleasure of discovery that I hope this book holds. A short conclusion at the end of each chapter summarizes the main points, and the book concludes with a brief, overarching summary in chapter 6 that offers some methodological considerations for future research.

CHAPTER 1

Magic: What Is It and How Does It Work?

᠊᠊᠊᠊

The two questions in the chapter title above are perhaps the most common ones asked by students of the history of magic. They are also arguably the two most difficult questions to answer, although I would venture to suggest that the first is easier to answer than the second. This is the case because in any given culture at any given time there is often a loose, notional consensus about what magic is, as well as who practices it. In the history of magic from Greek and Roman antiquity to the early Middle Ages, there were crucial shifts in the understanding of how magic worked, which ultimately resulted in the bifurcation of magic into a natural and demonic counterpart.[1] These were the only two available theories of magical operation from the Middle Ages to the Renaissance, according to which magical properties were either inherent in natural objects, such as gems and plants, or magic was accomplished through the intercession of demons.[2] But these theories were formulated by Church Fathers and theologians, as well as the occasional late antique dabbler, who were largely outside the mainstream practice of magic. If one were in the position to query magical practitioners themselves about how their magic worked, on the evidence of Greek antiquity alone I doubt there would have been much consensus. In fact, I am certain that all but a few magical practitioners would have been dumbfounded by such a question. Such things were understood, and the written record with rare exceptions leaves virtually no trace of any discussion by magical practitioners themselves of how magic worked. What was discussed openly were the claims made by certain magical practitioners about what problems they were capable of solving. What was not open to question, and therefore prompted no discussion, was a world view in which magic, even if disproved in the case of a particular individual, remained possible.

To understand what magic is and how it worked in Greece therefore requires us to extend our inquiry beyond the ancient written and material record and to incorporate other models of behavior, derived principally from perhaps the most productive academic field in magic, anthropology, because the material record is insufficient in itself. It is important to recognize that our understanding of ancient magic begins, but does not end, with the close examination of texts and objects. Yet magic also incorporated ritual behavior, which is all too often not directly described for us. However, it would severely understate the fullness of a magical event if no attempt were made to situate a magical object in its performative context, or a plausible ritual context derived from comparative evidence. I propose to approach these problems in an unorthodox way. Rather than rehearsing every theory of magic available in antiquity and those offered by anthropologists, instead I want to emphasize those approaches that help us to understand magic in particular instances. Some general characterizations are inevitable. But simply put, there is no one way to understand all magic across all instances even for one culture at one historical moment. Magic is a busy intersection, to borrow from a classic anthropological statement about ritual, and as such there are always different religious, social, cultural, and performative routes that have to be pursued in explaining it. We shall have many opportunities in what follows to observe cross-currents of ancient culture converging in the practice of magic.

Before we can define ancient Greek magic, let us begin the discussion by assuming that one does not believe it exists or that is has ever existed. Why any person with a nasty fishbone stuck in his throat, possibly gasping for air, would believe that by virtue of saying a verse of poetry the bone would come out makes no sense. Why anyone would mold a figurine out of clay or wax and stick needles into its eyes, mouth, and breast – as a means to attract, but not permanently harm, a beloved – should, one would think, be consigned to the trash bin of superstition. Everyone curses and some curse with art, but why anyone would take the time to write out a curse formula invoking underworld deities on a thin sheet of lead, roll it up and pierce it with a nail, then bury it in the tomb of an unknown dead person reaches the height of absurdity. Illness, disease, and bodily injury from accidents are common enough features of life. But why someone would fashion an amulet from haematite or bronze, etch it with a rider on horseback spearing creatures like lions and scorpions or a prostrate demon, then wear this around his neck seems at best only indirectly to treat the ailment. It might be artfully crafted, but how could such an object possibly prevent harm? It takes no imagination to suppose that headaches were as frequent in antiquity as they are today, yet why someone would invest their time acquiring a charm written on papyrus that quite literally commands the headache to leave, as if the headache could hear, defies rational explanation. All of these examples were easily recognized in antiquity as magic. Different explanations would certainly have been given as to whether any of these procedures was effective – indeed some would have been dismissed out of hand as superstition – and questions would have been asked about the ultimate purveyor of each magical aid. But there would have been general agreement that each procedure fell outside the realm of officially sanctioned cult activity, possibly had the taint of being illicit, and was certainly less than dignified, which were several criteria by which ancient commentators formulated a definition of magic. Yet if this was magic, one reasons, then something must have been gravely wrong, or the ancients let their imaginations run too freely. There seems to have been no understanding in the magical operation of how the world 'really' worked. Even the ancients had to have some rudimentary understanding of causality, we might suggest. After all, they built magnificent temples, ships, and weapons, and the Greeks in particular developed the early rudiments of science, mathematics, and medicine. How could magic coexist with these other domains of cultural achievement which would simply not have been possible if everyone thought magically?

Frazer and Tylor

One theoretical approach that has been advanced is to think that magic is false science, in the sense that a magical practitioner reasons wrongly from cause to effect. This view, which is attributed to Sir James George Frazer (1854–1938), allows us to introduce human error into the equation. Here magic is a vehicle cultures use to discover fundamental laws of cause and effect; magic 'works' only because the real relationship between causes and their effects has been distorted or misrecognized. Another approach derived from Sir Edward Tylor (1832–1917) and embraced by Frazer is to regard the connection a magical practitioner makes between an object he or she manipulates here, and the person over there who is the target of that operation, as based on a fallacious association of ideas. The clay image and the person it represents share outward similarities but have no actual relationship to one another in the real world. In this view, magic is an erroneous association of ideas based on analogy or, as Tylor famously put it, a mistaking of "ideal connexions for real connexions." Moreover, in order for there to be an actual, tangential relationship between a magical object or action and its target, there would have to exist some medium through which the effects on the object here could be transferred to the person over there. A third approach regards practitioners of magic as a whole as delusional – assuming they are not outright charlatans – since they apparently believe that they exercise some control over the behavior of others when in fact they do not. Magic exists, according to this view, because everyone believes it exists. Powerful support for this approach can already be found in antiquity among such authors as Plato (*Laws* 933a–b), who was on the whole not particularly interested in magic. These are just a few of many approaches, outside of the specifically medieval explanations mentioned earlier, that have been offered since antiquity to explain magic, and each offers a valid perspective. While they allow us to say that magic "exists," in the sense that people do magical things, nevertheless they prevent us from concluding that there is any real effect behind it. Accordingly, none of these views allows magic to "exist" in the sense that it has any impact upon the world.

One alternative then is to conclude that magic is fundamentally a psychological phenomenon, whether collective or individual. There are many strands to this approach; however, its basic premise is that magical operations satisfy the practitioner's need to accomplish something practical in the face of otherwise insuperable or uncertain events. Illness presents a good example here. A family member has been struck with a debilitating illness for some inexplicable reason, by which I mean the available avenues of explanation have either been found wanting or are unknown. A magical operation performed on behalf of the ailing family member may not be thought directly to resolve the problem, but it allows those involved to feel as if some action has been taken. Magical action is practical action, and however misguided it may be, it nonetheless gives concrete expression to the concern of the family members involved in caring for their ailing relative. Note, however, that in viewing magic this way, we have not asked whose psychology underlies the perceived magical efficacy. It seems that both collective and individual psychology are at work here: society governs the conventions and expectations of magic, and individuals respond to and operate within those conventions. But the problem grows more difficult when we try to isolate exactly what an "individual" response is in this context. What we may take to be an "individual" emotional response – for example, mere satisfaction or relief on the part of the sick person that a healing amulet has been made and placed around his or her neck – at bottom has already been "collectively" defined by the society that takes the efficacy of such healing amulets for granted. It seems that we cannot escape the way in which individual responses reflect collective representations.

Malinowski

Other psychological approaches to magic have more effectively made that break or, rather, emphasized the "individual" quality of magic in terms of it being a means to an end, in contrast with religion as a collective organization that functions as an end in itself. In Bronislaw Malinowski's (1884–1942) famous essay, *Magic, Science, Religion and Other Essays* (1948), based on his research among the Trobriand islanders, he draws an important distinction between "sacred" activities like religion and magic, which partake of symbolic forms and behaviors, and "profane" or pragmatic activity like science and technological accomplishments. Thus in one sense Malinowski avoids the Frazerian puzzle of whether magic was actually science in its infancy because these two activities are separate for him. On the other hand, he understood that magic was practical activity that was simultaneously interwoven with symbolism, not to mention what he memorably called its "coefficient of weirdness." There is no simple way to disconnect the two, even if we recognize a continuum with pure technical activity at one end unencumbered by prohibitions and, at the other end, technical activity hedged round by a series of metaphysical concerns and given a ritual stage for its enactment. What is often taken to be Malinowski's most important contribution to the study of magic – that magic begins where technology is insufficient – has been easily refuted,[3] but what endures is his stress on the instrumental quality of magical activity and its anticipatory nature. As a means to an end, magical activity reaffirms the expectation of achievement and success in a given endeavor. It is psychologically satisfying to the individual participants for that reason. But that is not all. Malinowski also asserted that individual memory played a role in the perceived success of magic. Thus for every magical operation that "succeeded," this was remembered by the community more readily and vividly than those that did not.[4] Together the anticipation of success and its outsize memory cannot be overestimated as factors that help to reinforce magical behavior.

Magic as Communication

There is another, perhaps more personal, illustration of the problem of what magic is that does not directly involve any prevailing theory, which I present in the form of a thought experiment. Imagine that you are coming home after work or school, just as you typically would. It has been an ordinary day and nothing particularly unusual has happened. When you get to your door, you find a small package sitting on the doorstep. You assume the package was delivered for you, so you open it and inside you find a bloody chicken heart with a nail stabbed through it. Sickening as that is, you realize the heart has been cut and inside the incision there is a sliver of paper, folded in half. You carefully pull the paper out, unfold it, and find it has your name written on it. Tucked in the paper's fold there are some fingernails and hair – *your* fingernails and hair.

Since you are not superstitious, or are but would never admit it, the rational side of your brain takes over. The whole thing, you say, is ridiculous – some stupid trick. Who would have done this? And then you start thinking: if it isn't a gag, does someone really hate me? Why didn't they just tell me they hated me rather than doing this? Even if it is a gag, what exactly are they trying to say? Did they think I would believe it or that it would have some effect on me? Did *they* think it would work, even if I don't? Who do I know that would believe in such nonsense, or go through such elaborate measures even as a joke? And where in the world did they get my fingernails and hair, let alone a bloody chicken heart?

This example, albeit contrived, is not meant to suggest that magic is "real" in the sense that its operation has a physical impact on the world. It is meant to suggest that magic is fundamentally a form of communication – and that communication, whatever shape it takes, can indeed impact the behavior of others. Note that this is not the same thing as saying that magic exists because everyone believes it exists. Rather, as in the example above, even if one does not believe in magic, one can nevertheless believe that a magical act was meant to convey a message. The weirdness of the action itself prompts a series of thoughts about what it might mean, and therein lies the rub. Even before deciding whether there is anything to magic, one is diverted into thinking about *who* might be behind it.[5] We can therefore separate the question of whether magic is real from the question of whether it can have an impact on others' behavior. Most critiques of magic in antiquity and even more recently miss this distinction entirely, focusing as they do on mechanical causal relationships in the magical operation itself that should be explicable in terms of observable natural laws, not invisible forces. But magic is always effective only within a social context whose network of relationships defines it and gives it meaning. Indeed, magic is quite unthinkable outside a social context. And it is within such a social context that we can say magic is "causal." If a magical act changes someone's behavior, then it has exerted a causal effect.

But we can be much more specific here, even without yet worrying about particular cultural milieux or historical forms of magic. Magical acts imply intention, which means that behind the individual act someone intends to convey a message. The message can be harmful or helpful, depending on the circumstances, but the magical act itself registers and publicizes someone's desire.[6] Who is capable of publicizing their desires in this way and how exactly they do it will depend on the culture being examined. But the important point to take away is that such intentionality, realized as magic, is fully structured as a social phenomenon. If magic is an act of communication, then the parameters for who can communicate and how they do so will be defined by the society in question. To give a clear example, if I am a late Roman Greek and wish to compose a curse tablet calling upon a *nekydaimon* 'spirit of a dead man', I write that tablet in Greek, not in Latin or Syriac. I take for granted not only that the underworld spirit will understand Greek, but that it has any understanding at all. Since I am effectively using the spirit of a dead man as a go-between to harm my enemy – say a prosecutor I wish to strike silent as he testifies against me in an upcoming trial – then I am also assuming this spirit understands how to operate in my world. In this sense the dead man's spirit is indistinguishable from a living person. Thus the entire chain of magical communication, from its interlocutors to the medium of communication to the anticipated action itself, is constituted in manifold ways by social convention.

Lévy-Bruhl

In order to better grasp the significance of this point, and to accord the last example with modes of ancient Greek thinking, we need to come to terms with a fundamental anthropological notion set forth by Lucien Lévy-Bruhl (1857–1959), who was originally trained as a moral philosopher. In contrast to the evolutionary trend of Victorian scholarship on non-Western societies – of the type, for example, typified by Frazer's model for the development of religion out of science, which in turn developed out of magic – Lévy-Bruhl instead argued that such societies were not "irrational," in the sense of misunderstanding the laws of cause and effect, but were organized according to their own coherent principles. Foremost among these was what he called the *law of participation*. In *How Natives Think* (*Les Fonctions*, 1910), Lévy-Bruhl writes that:[7]

> Primitive man, therefore, lives and acts in an environment of beings and objects, all of which, in addition to the properties that we recognize them to possess, are endued with mystic attributes. He perceives their objective reality mingled with another reality. He feels himself surrounded by an infinity of imperceptible entities, nearly always invisible to sight, and always redoubtable: ofttimes the souls of the dead are about him, and always he is encompassed by myriads of spirits of more or less defined personality.

There are two important strands to disentangle here. The first refers to the notion of living within two orders of reality. This is what Lévy-Bruhl means by "mystic," namely a belief in forces and influences that are invisible, and often imperceptible, but nevertheless real. Ancient magic operates within such a world, whereby the forces called upon, even when not explicitly defined by a personality, are invisible and imperceptible and can only be felt after they have taken effect. The implications of a mingled reality can be drawn out further, however, especially with regard to objects. Throughout the whole of Greek antiquity physical objects such as cult statues were treated as though they had human attributes: they were bathed and cleaned, dressed and worshipped, presented with food offerings and prayers, and were thought capable of movement. The counterparts of cult statues, figurines fashioned out of clay or wax, were treated with similar care and used in ancient magic. Lévy-Bruhl helps us to understand why statues and figurines were treated in this way, without resorting to a notion of irrationality defined (in our Western manner) by a failure to draw the proper dividing line between animate and inanimate objects. In Greece in particular, matter itself could have an ambiguous status. To give a specific example, for some highly educated thinkers such as the late seventh/early sixth-century BCE philosopher Thales of Miletus, stones that had magnetic properties were thought to contain souls (11 A 22 D-K = Arist. *de An.* 1.2.405a19–21). It is not hard to see how magnetic stones that attracted iron filings, in the absence of an available electromagnetic theory, could be thought to be animate – in other words to contain a soul. Reality as we know it in the mechanical, causal Western view, with its sharp dividing line between organic and inorganic matter, is collapsed in Thales' view of the magnet. Nor should it come as a surprise at this point to know that magnets also figured in various ways in ancient magic. As outsiders to cultures that think this way, it simply will not do to superimpose a rational/irrational distinction on their actions, as if by characterizing them this way we are implying that with further understanding of mechanical causality their magical behavior would change. Such a view neglects to observe that magic is "causal" within a social framework whose effects are real. The problem then is that an incomplete grasp of physical causes is embedded within a broader social framework for the understanding of cause – and the key is that the social framework is the more salient of the two.

Along these lines we can turn to the second dimension of Lévy-Bruhl's concept of participation, which is the notion that the mingled reality of the primitive world is peopled with divine beings, particularly spirits of the dead. The Greeks, as so many other cultures, took elaborate pains with burying their dead, largely as a way to ensure that the dead person's soul rested peacefully. The Greeks harbored many different beliefs about dead souls, and scaled them in different ways, from heroes who rested at their leisure in the Elysium fields and the Isles of the Blessed, to an altogether different sort of underworld community whose anger was beyond human appeasement. It is this community that interests us in particular, and it comprised three sets of dead: those who died without funeral rites (*ataphoi*), those who died in an untimely or premature way (*aōroi*), and those who died violent deaths, such as, in later times, gladiators and other murdered victims (*biaiothanatoi*).[8] A practitioner of magic who wished to curse his adversary had to pay court to these angry denizens and address them with his request for aid, especially the *aōroi* and *biaio- thanatoi*. The curse tablet itself was laid in their tombs, and sometimes in the skeletal hand of the deceased. For the moment, the crucial point to grasp is that the Greeks, as so many of the cultures under study by Lévy-Bruhl, inhabited an extended society in which the dead participated as much as the living. Lévy-Bruhl emphasizes the social dimension of this kind of world this way:[9]

> In short, without insisting on well-known facts, the primitive lives with his dead as he does with the living who surround him. They are members, and very important members, of a society with manifold participations, a social symbiosis in which the collective representations of his group give him his place.

It is quite natural for us to think of ourselves as members of a living community, with responsibilities and obligations to variously tiered groups and subgroups, and to define ourselves in different ways with respect to each of these groups. It is quite another thing entirely to include the dead among those with whom we interact *as if they were living presences*, more- over to regard our obligations to them as equally important as those to the living. When I speak of a social context for the practice of Greek magic, it is this more expansive community that must be borne in mind.

There are many examples from Greek literature that illustrate that the dead were a vital part of the living community. The plots of whole Greek dramas turn on that relationship, but it is not primarily the literary exploitation of the dead that interests us. Rather, we are interested in the received wisdom that certain of the dead are engaged in an ongoing scrutiny of the activity of the living, and more importantly that the angry dead continue to drive the living to distraction. Hesiod tells us, for exam- ple, in the *Works and Days* (109–26) that after the immortals brought the Golden Race of mortals into being and they had lived for a time, at death they were dispersed by Zeus throughout the world of mortal men as invisible *daimones*. Thenceforth hidden in air and wandering the earth they became guardians of mortal men and, in some versions, were particularly drawn to the surveillance of cases at law and unjust deeds. Much later in the fourth century Plato tells us that souls of the angry dead are dragged back into the visible world and hover about tombs and graveyards (*Phaedo* 81c–d). Elsewhere he notes that those done to death by violence harbor a particular animus against their assailants (*Laws* 865d–e), and Xenophon adds that these souls track the wicked with avenging powers (*Cyropaideia* 8.7.18–19).

This invisible half of the social community is not comprised solely of the dead. It goes without saying that a fundamental feature of Greek religion is that the pantheon of Olympian divinities, not to mention the various shades of Olympian divinities that are localized and specific to certain city-states, as well as the "lesser" divinities that occupy certain demes or districts, cult and boundary sites, can make themselves felt to mortals, sometimes in particular and personalized ways. Greek literature from epic to tragedy and comedy, often an indispensable source for our understanding of Greek religion, is preoccupied with dramatizing such interactions, especially those involving the Olympian divinities. In day-to-day practice, however, the connection is rarely personalized to that degree, so that for instance a response from the Delphic oracle is literally, through the medium of the Pythia or priestess, the voice of Apollo. But Apollo's personality and individual proclivities, such as those discussed in the Homeric *Hymn to Apollo*, are hardly that manifest in his actual responses. In magic there are several underworld divinities – Persephone, Hekate, Hermes, Selene in her magical aspect, as well as a plethora of anonymous *daimones* – to whom practitioners of magic can address themselves. There are certain prescribed conventions of address here, for instance a victim in a curse is said to be bound in the presence of these underworld figures who are in turn invoked by epithets that refer to their binding capacity. But beyond this there is nothing particularly distinctive about the personality of the divinity being addressed. Nonetheless it would be a mistake to regard these conventions of address as rhetorical only. Nor are these invisible entities any less significant for the fact that their personalities are less well defined. This is because personification, or anthropomorphism more generally, of invisible forces cannot be used by itself as a measure of how *felt* these invisible forces are to members of a given community. That can only be measured by the degree to which that community's behavior is governed or modified by them. Thus Lévy-Bruhl's concept of participation helps us to see how, in the particular Greek context, the souls of the dead, divinities, and mortals all partake of the same reality, the same physical space and, in the case of magic, share responsibility as agents for the realization of someone's desired aim.

Evans-Pritchard

A landmark contribution to our understanding of how magic operates within a society was made by the justly famed British social anthropologist Edward E. Evans-Pritchard (1902–73) in his study, *Witchcraft, Oracles, and Magic Among the Azande* (1937). The impact of Evans-Pritchard's research has reached well beyond his field of social anthropology to the historical study of magic and witchcraft, both in antiquity and premodern Europe and beyond, however sometimes in ways that distorted the rather specific cultural findings he advanced. In brief, Evans-Pritchard demonstrated in thorough detail how among the Azande,[10] a people who live in central Africa along the Nile–Congo divide, magic, witchcraft, and oracles were "like three sides to a triangle."[11] By this he meant that the three practices were tightly interlocked, and depended on one another for mutual reinforcement. Witchcraft (*mangu*) for the Azande was in essence a psychic emanation from someone that could harm another person, and the Azande believed that witchcraft was localized as a material substance in the body that could be discovered by autopsy. Witchcraft could emanate from such a person without their knowledge or conscious effort. Magic (*ngua*), on the other hand, for the Azande involved techniques to achieve some purpose that incorporated medicines, spells, and rituals. Magic is always consciously undertaken. The Azande use oracles – of which the three most prominent in Zande society, with each progressing in prestige, were the termite,[12] rubbing-board,[13] and poison (*benge*)[14] oracles – to diagnose witchcraft in particular instances, which in turn sometimes demand magic as a remedy.

In a typical case of misfortune, let us say that a co-wife is suspected of cheating on her husband with another man, one or more oracles are consulted and a diagnosis of witchcraft is found. The witchcraft may be attributed to a different co-wife or a neighbor who is thought to harbor ill intentions toward the accused cheater, and the witchcraft is used to explain why the co-wife cheated. Sometimes the oracles are used mutually to confirm each other, with "lesser" oracles such as the termite oracle being confirmed by the rubbing-board, the rubbing-board is then confirmed by the poison oracle, and so forth. The diagnosis itself is always socially relevant because it points toward another member of the community as the agent responsible for the witchcraft. By diagnosing a social origin for misfortune, this allows intervention and action to be taken that can determine future behavior. So for instance at this point in our example the accused co-wife may undertake magical remedies, such as drinking and spitting water to cool off the witchcraft inside her, to remove the witchcraft. What has really happened, however, is that a stage has been set to enact a change in social relations. If the suspect agrees to undertake a magical remedy for her witchcraft, she is in effect acknowledging publicly the harm she has done and at least ostensibly promising to do what she can to avoid it in the future. More dramatic shifts in social relations can happen as well, such as when a suspect steadfastly denies any responsibility and as a result relations with that suspect are severed. But by virtue of the fact that witchcraft was not consciously undertaken, and that rules under British law at the time prevented direct retribution from being taken against confessed witches, an individual's responsibility for injury was diffused in such a way so as to encourage admissions of guilt. In other words, if witchcraft was performed unconsciously, the sense of personal guilt was correspondingly lessened.

It is impossible to do justice to the care with which Evans-Pritchard examines the wealth of Zande witchcraft and magical practices in such a short order. However, it is not a detailed examination of Zande witchcraft or magic in particular that I want to pursue. Rather, in our effort still to come to terms with some key features of what anthropologists used to call a magical world view,[15] especially to think about the ways in which individuals who exhibit such a world view explained their beliefs both to themselves and to outsiders, Evans-Pritchard offers some insightful evidence about the Azande. Having inherited the concern since Frazer and Lévy-Bruhl about whether non-Western magical practices could be reconciled with a "rational," which is to say causally based, view of the world, Evans-Pritchard took great pains to examine exactly how the Azande justified witchcraft, oracles, and magic to themselves and to him. He showed for instance that if the Azande partially accounted for misfortune in terms of mystical (in the Lévy-Bruhl sense) relations, they were also quite aware of their own role in such misfortune, as well as of the usual haphazards of everyday life. Witchcraft was invoked not as a general explanation of misfortune, but rather to explain how on a particular occasion, all other things being equal, misfortune happened. The attribution of misfortune to witchcraft imposes a moral framework on events, because the social dimension of witchcraft enables such events to be given an actionable meaning. It is my contention that Greek magic was also located within such a framework by its practitioners, although one must grant due consideration for the substantial differences between Zande and ancient Greek society.

One of the most significant examples of a Zande explanation in this regard reported by Evans-Pritchard is the following:[16]

> I found it strange at first to live among Azande and listen to naïve explanations of misfortunes which, to our minds, have apparent causes, but after a while I learnt the idiom of their thought and applied notions of witchcraft as spontaneously as themselves in situations where the concept was relevant. A boy knocked his foot against a small stump of wood in the centre of a bush path, a frequent happening in Africa, and suffered pain and inconvenience in consequence. Owing to its position on his toe it was impossible to keep the cut free from dirt and it began to fester. He declared that witchcraft had made him knock his foot against the stump. I always argued with Azande and criticized their statements, and I did so on this occasion. I told the boy that he had knocked his foot against the stump of wood because he had been careless, and that witchcraft had not placed it in the path, for it had grown there naturally. He agreed that witchcraft had nothing to do with the stump of wood because he had been careless, and that witchcraft had not placed it in his path but added that he had kept his eyes open for stumps, as indeed every Zande does most carefully, and that if he had not been bewitched he would have seen the stump. As a conclusive argument for his view he remarked that all cuts do not take days to heal but, on the contrary, close quickly, for that is the nature of cuts. Why, then, had his sore festered and remained open if there were no witchcraft behind it?

In this account witchcraft is not invoked as a general explanation of misfortune. Instead, witchcraft explains how particular conditions came together, not contrary to but in conjunction with natural causes, to bring someone into relation with events such that they sustained injury. Hence it would be incorrect to suggest that because the Azande believe in witchcraft they do not have an understanding of natural causation. Witchcraft is one among several causes that explain an event, and its relevance derives both from the moral framework for responsibility to which it has reference and from its ability to account for deviations from an otherwise normal state of affairs that results in injury. To the extent that magic involves mystical or invisible powers, Zande explanations for magic are essentially the same as for witchcraft.[17] That there was a person who consciously undertook the magical rite, as distinct from the unconscious activity of witchcraft, goes without saying. But the feeling among the Azande that in both witchcraft and magic events are determined by invisible and visible action, and that explanations for situations of failure must thereby entail both natural and mystical causes, is about as close as an outside observer can come to a coherent account of their beliefs.

Finally, it is worth noting a rather important implication of Evans-Pritchard's attempts to engage the Azande about their witchcraft and magic beliefs. Part of the difficulty he encountered is that the typical Zande informant "actualizes these beliefs rather than intellectualizes them," and "their ideas are imprisoned in action and cannot be cited to explain and justify action."[18] These remarks tell a cautionary tale that reaches well beyond the anxiety that the classicist, as a student of ancient culture, has no direct access to living subjects like the anthropologist. Even granted that access, magic and witchcraft in both ancient and contemporary cultures are responses to misfortune and failure realized as action. Yet this action may only admit of reflection by the members of those cultures to a limited and, perhaps to our minds, unsatisfactory degree. Thus while we as observers attempt to understand how magical practices are constructed within a given society, and further to draw out the implications of those practices as far as they imply a set of premises for how the world works, we must be prepared to accept that our explanations might have seemed incomprehensible or even bizarre to the subjects under investigation. Were we actual members of that society, on the other hand, we may well not be interested in explaining magic at all.

Sympathetic Magic

Although we have already mentioned Frazer's position that magical activity rests on a mistaken relationship between real causes and their perceived effects – a view that indispensably relies on Edward Tylor – we have not yet confronted his most significant contribution to the study of magic. It is easy to exaggerate the importance of Frazer's insight into the nature of magical operation. But for more than a century anthropologists, classicists, and scholars in related disciplines have been unable to displace his fundamental notion of sympathetic magic, even if they have legitimately criticized and largely rendered effete the assumptions upon which it rests. In *The Golden Bough* (1890), a Herculean effort that eventually filled twelve volumes, Frazer sketched an overarching view of magical behavior that he called *sympathetic* and which branched in two directions: "first, that like produces like, or that an effect resembles its cause; and, second, that things which have once been in contact with each other continue to act on each other at a distance after the physical contact has been severed."[19] The former idea Frazer called *homeopathic* or imitative magic, since it was based on the association of ideas through similarity; the latter he called *contagious* magic, since it was based on the association of ideas through contiguity. These two forms of magical thinking are ideal types, and Frazer correctly recognized that in practice they are often combined. So for example to fashion a figurine out of clay and pierce it with needles is homeopathic magic, if I expect my victim to suffer injury on his person at the points where I stick the needles. If I incorporate some of my victim's hair, nail parings, or a piece of his clothing into the figurine, I am using contagious magic. Because it is very common in many cultures to do both operations at the same time in fashioning a figurine, care must be taken in analyzing it in such a way that does justice to both sympathetic principles.

Both homeopathic and contagious magic imply a notion of sympathy that can be more closely analyzed. As an example, the magical operation that is performed often mimics the results desired. If I pierce a lead curse tablet and construe my act of piercing it as a binding action – in other words, piercing the tablet here means to transfix it – and I anticipate the transfer of such a binding action to the target of my curse – binding my victim in the sense of preventing him from speaking or acting – then I am acting sympathetically. This is essentially the idea behind homeopathic magic. However, the sympathetic relationship between my magical action and its intended effect implies that the effects must be transferred or communicated to my victim at a different point in space and a later point in time.[20] How this process is understood by magical practitioners varies from culture to culture. The Azande, for instance, attribute the transfer to what they call the *mbisimo* or 'soul' of magic and witchcraft.[21] This is a psychic property of persons and things that can invisibly transfer itself through space and time, and it is this property which in their view accounts for how magic or witchcraft can realize its effects at a distance in space and time. Contagious magic relies upon a related but different notion of sympathy. Effects are similarly transferred through space and time; however, in this case the magical operation itself is directed toward a victim's possessions or body parts. A Greek witch burns her victim's hair or clothing, for instance, as a way of transferring the fire of erotic emotion to him. Lévy-Bruhl understood contagious magic to imply his concept of participation, in the sense that there was a special connection between a person and his things:[22]

> The things that a man has used, the clothes he has worn, his weapons, ornaments, are part of him, *are* his very self, (construing the verb "to be" as "to participate"), just like his saliva, nail-parings, hair, excreta, although to a lesser extent. Something has been communicated to them by him which is, as it were, a continuance of his individuality, and in a mystic sense these objects are henceforward inseparable from him.

Magic and the Extended Person

More fundamentally the very existence of contagious magic implies an extended notion of 'personhood'. This is what anthropologists in other contexts have called the *distributed* or fractal person, which we can apply to magical practice in a narrower sense than that which they employ.[23] I use the term also to mean that a person's possessions or body parts can be distributed throughout his environment, and that in some sense these accoutrements and parts can be thought of as replicating him. Magic capitalizes upon the belief that acting on the distributed parts will still affect the whole (*pars pro toto*). The sympathetic relation guarantees that the part of the person being acted upon magically stands for the whole person and that this connection holds true at a distance in time and space. In some cultural contexts, the notion of personhood can be expanded much further. For instance, within medieval Catholic tradition, not merely reliquaries, containing the body parts, bones, teeth, and blood of saints, were thought to convey power, but also holy oil poured onto their tombs and kept afterwards in vials or even grave dirt extracted from around their tombs and kept in tiny parcels. In these latter instances, the saint's person is distributed throughout the material that comes into contact with his tomb or sanctuary, and conventions have been reached by the community in question as to how far the saint's personhood extends. In one instance, the painted eyes of Saint Peter on a fresco in a thirteenth-century Bulgarian church have been scratched out and saved, implying that the paint scrapings themselves can be thought of as extensions of Peter's person.[24] Moreover, we have numerous examples from other cultures of 'sacred geography' – another example of participation – which refers to the way in which a saint is identified with a village or his cult site. The extensions of his person in these instances may reach not only to the physical geography of his site, but also to the rituals performed in his honor, the dreams he conveys to those who incubate at his tomb, as well as to the whole array of communicative acts that take place between him and his devotees on their pilgrimages.[25]

It is also interesting to consider how a culture conceives of personhood as illustrated specifically in their magical behavior, which may or may not conform to other social or institutional forms of personhood. A different kind of distributed personhood can be found in fourth-century BCE Attic curse tablets. Many of these tablets single out in a stereotyped way the hands, feet, tongue, and soul of their intended victim for binding. This binding action is more broadly understood to cause a halt to the victim's activity, whether it be their day-to-day commercial activity or whether it be to secure and hold their erotic interest after turning it away from another. In some fundamental way, then, the magic captures the essential person parts for its action to be complete. Sometimes the body parts that are targeted are relevant to the aim of the magic – as an example, the tongue and minds of prosecutors are bound by a worried defendant since these are the faculties most relevant to their profession – but at other times the same faculties are bound in a more general formula to restrain a business competitor.[26] In any case, to bind these parts is to bind the whole person. And while there is variation in the formula, which sometimes expands to include a person's breast, heart, and, rarely, genitalia, some person parts such as the ears and nose are left out entirely. It may be that all of these sensory functions are subsumed under the mention of the soul (*psychē*) in the tablets, but this is not clear. And yet every Greek had a more ample notion of personhood from daily experience, social, political, religious, and familial relations, childbirth, and so forth. Moreover, no Greek in daily life ever addressed his family or fellow demesmen by reference to these isolated body parts. Thus the question we have to answer is why in Greek magical practice the person is in some sense dislocated and reduced to a handful of fractured yet apparently essential parts.

Magic and Analogy

The preceding discussion has carried us somewhat further afield from Frazer, but it illustrates in various ways how some of the key assumptions that underlie his sympathetic principles have been productively, if rather differently, amplified. There is, however, one assumption implied in Frazer's sympathetic principles that we have not addressed, and this concerns the problem of *analogy*. In homeopathic or imitative magic, an analogy is created between the magical behavior and the effects desired. Frazer had described this as an incorrect association of ideas that like produces like and that an effect resembles its cause. As a cardinal example he had unearthed a flurry of cross-cultural examples of image magic or the creation of figurines, on which for the infliction of harm cultures never seemed to tire of exercising their imagination. Stabbing, burning, pricking, piercing, shooting, ripping, tearing, burying, and stomping were all acceptable activities exercised on figurines that manifested a variety of emotional attitudes toward the intended victim, although one must be careful to contextualize each of these actions with emotions that are relevant for the culture under consideration. Hence stabbing or piercing do not necessarily imply anger, as we might be inclined to think from our own cultural experience, and in the case of Greek magical figurines in particular piercing may not even imply pain.

The first order of problem with analogy that we have to consider is the notion of the copy in homeopathic or imitative magic. According to Michael Taussig, Frazer (in the vein of Edward Tylor before him) implies in his extensive treatment of image magic that the images are copies that represent their intended victim. So much, one might say, seems straightforward. But Taussig draws attention to the idea that for this kind of magic to be effective, the copy must affect the original to such a degree that the representation shares in or acquires the properties of what is represented.[27] To him this is a disturbing notion because a copy implies an original and at least ostensibly suggests that in fact it needs to resemble that original to some degree. So he asks, "How much of a copy does the copy have to be to have an effect on what it is a copy of?"[28] The problem is that, as many scholars since Frazer have noted, image magic can often employ "copies" that in no way resemble the human beings who serve as their targets. In Greek examples that we shall consider later, clay or waxen images at times are lumpy and unshapely, at best rude examples of persons they are supposed to represent. Moreover, many cultures including Mediterranean ones also employ stones, wood, bones, dough, barley-meal, earth, plants, clothing, precious metal – virtually any imaginable material – to make magical effigies, leaving open the question of how a "copy" is meant to resemble its "original," let alone how that copy comes to be invested with the properties of the original. There is no simple answer to these questions, because image magic depends to a large extent on cultural conventions of representation that have to be examined in a broader context. We can also put the problem another way by asking what are the strategies of representation employed by a given culture such that a piece of wood or stone can be used in image magic.

This brings us to the second order of problem with the notion of analogy, namely the very idea of representation itself. It seems difficult when studying magic to avoid grappling with some notion of representation, insofar as a given magical act – for instance in weather magic, as when one stirs a bowl of water with a finger to create inclement weather – seems to encapsulate in miniature its intended consequences. Many scholars assume, therefore, that magic uses symbolism as its strategy of representation. Image magic is again the classic example. But what does the term *symbolism* in the context of image magic mean? For instance, do we mean that an image is 'symbolic' to the participants themselves or only to outsider observers? The distinction is important because if it is not kept carefully in view, it is all too easy to attribute symbolic meaning to behaviors that from the participants' perspective are not indirect, but direct, immediate, and efficacious acts of communication. For example, Greeks and Egyptians left food offerings for the images of their gods, but if we as outsiders call this behavior 'symbolic' we will overlook the fact that these are *"real physical interactions"* with divinity, in the words of Alfred Gell.[29] Images in the form of temple statues offered the Greeks channels of access to their divinities, and there is ample evidence that from their perspective there was nothing at all 'symbolic' about their behavior toward them. In other words, it is not by offering food to a statue that the Greeks were representing how a statue might eat, *as if* it ate in some other way which the food offering was meant to symbolize. Instead, one offered food because that was how a statue ate – in other words, we have to accept that to Greeks statues were physically capable of eating. This is not to say that idols and images are not at times used symbolically as aids to religious piety. But where such idols function as vehicles of divinity and where, as in the Greek and Egyptian worlds, statues and figurines explicitly embodied divinity, it is inappropriate to analyze the behavior toward them as 'symbolic'. The sense of agency exhibited in magical behavior, in the formulation of John Skorupski, is 'literal' not symbolic,[30] and failing to take adequate account of this point risks mischaracterizing magical behavior as something akin to acting or impersonation. Moreover, to describe an action as symbolic implies some underlying will to representation – as if there were some moment at which the culture in question collectively agreed that thenceforth a stone carving was going to stand for or represent a divinity – whereas in actual practice ritual action of this type always involves inherited behavior and understanding. And as Evans-Pritchard showed, despite his best efforts to engage the Azande on precisely these points, such an inherited understanding may not be susceptible to discursive reflection. If contemporary parallels to ancient behavior are any indication, I daresay few ancient Greeks would have understood the question of whether a divinity's statue was a symbolic rather than a real agent, capable of actually interacting with humans, because the inherited understanding of divine statuary already guaranteed that the latter was possible. We as outsiders begin from the assumption that statues cannot have genuine agency and mobility, making symbolism a rational alternative to explaining how other cultures interact with them. However, these cultures *live the reality* that statues are animate, not only rendering our symbolic interpretation irrelevant but also calling into question our causal understanding of human action, according to which the motivation for human behavior that we do not share is reducible to a set of intellectually defensible propositions.

None of what has been said up to this point removes the problem of analogy in magic. Indeed, analogical thinking in one form or another in my view lies immovably at the heart of ritual behavior in so many different cultures that it is arguably its most characteristic feature. Magical behavior in this respect is no exception. However, we must take extra care that when we use a term like analogy in the context of magic, we do not at the same time allow our own discursive notions of representation or symbolism to come into play when they are unwarranted.

Beyond Frazer

If Frazer's legacy has led to a productive consideration of sympathetic magic by generations of scholars, in other ways some of the underlying assumptions of those sympathetic principles have now been superseded. For example, to the extent that homeopathic and contagious magic were premised on a misunderstanding of natural law, Frazer's theory has largely been proven wrong. Many investigators, among whom the philosopher Ludwig Wittgenstein ranks in the forefront,[31] have argued that magical practice is not fundamentally concerned with the discovery of natural law. Magic may incorporate ways of thinking that depend upon a society's view of how the natural order works, as it does technology, as Malinowski showed, but magicians are not scientists *in utero*. Thus Frazer erred insofar as he took the causal understanding of natural law to be the main aim of magical practice. In the view of some critics, Frazer erred more profoundly by suggesting that a misunderstanding of (mechanical) cause lay at the heart of magic in the first place. However, as we have seen for instance in the case of the Azande, magical practice does not exclude an understanding of mechanical causation, nor is mechanical cause the only causal system with which magic operates. If read too narrowly, Frazer's model for magic implies an irremediable human error, as Wittgenstein argued, and wrongly suggests that at bottom magic is a response to a scientific hypothesis about how the world works. But not only does this approach fail to account for a certain ceremonialism in human nature – which we might call ritual for ritual's sake – it also does nothing to help us understand why particular forms of magic hold good for a given culture at a given time. Frazer used the particulars of magical practice from hundreds of ethnographic accounts – an extraordinary and largely unparalleled feat to this day – to justify his model of magical principles. Yet every culture's magic has a history that cannot be fully explained by reference to those principles alone.

Tambiah and Persuasive Magic

In rounding out our survey of anthropological approaches to magic we have finally to mention the work on performance by Stanley Tambiah.[32] Tambiah's research brings attention to the performative dimension of magic – the rituals and spells and their enactment – that help to create a magical event. Tambiah's work largely amplifies several lines of thought proposed by Malinowski, especially as found in his *Coral Gardens and Their Magic* (London, 1935), and Evans-Pritchard in his *Witchcraft, Oracles, and Magic Among the Azande* (Oxford, 1937). At the risk of oversimplifying Tambiah's careful rereading and elucidation of Malinowski and Evans-Pritchard, we can roughly summarize his findings as they apply to the *form* and *function* of magical acts. First, relying on examples taken from Evans-Pritchard, Tambiah shows how the form of magical acts and objects often is conceived within detailed metaphorical and analogical schemes whereby desirable properties of one object or action are transferred to another. The power of analogy, as we have already discussed, is brought out fully within magical action, but before the action can be analyzed, it is crucial for the observer to understand what properties a given object or action are thought to possess within a culture. Only then can the point of a given analogy deployed within magic be grasped. Here is one example taken from the Azande, which deals with their magical treatment of epileptic fits, that Tambiah elucidates:[33]

> Epileptic fits are associated with the red bush monkey, which is thought to display certain movements resembling epileptic symptoms. Before sunrise this monkey seems to be in a torpor, but as he comes out of it under the warm rays of the sun, so does the epileptic slowly recover when placed in the warmth of a fire. One of the remedies for epilepsy is to eat ashes of the burnt skull of the red monkey. Superficially considered, it seems inconsistent and absurd that the ashes of the skull of the "epileptic" monkey can cure an epileptic man. But in fact the analogy moves in two steps, exploiting the fact that although the monkey's movements resemble epilepsy, yet it is a normal occurrence for the monkey to revive daily from its torpor under the warm rays of the sun, and the same recovery is desired in the patient. It is this capacity of the monkey to revive daily that is persuasively exploited by the rite of eating the ashes of the monkey's skull.

Several analogies are at work here. The Azande associate epileptic fits with the movements of the red bush monkey. This association allows further analogies to be drawn, so that the monkey's daily "recovery" seems applicable to an epileptic patient, who is also known to be capable of recovering in a similar way after being placed near a fire. What remains is to effect a transfer of the monkey's ability to recover to the patient, and this transfer is enacted quite directly by having the patient eat the ashes of the monkey's skull. What Tambiah's research shows is that it is above all critical to understand the network of analogical and metaphorical tax-onomies a given culture like the Azande has created for the objects, animals, plants, colors, geography, and so forth, in their environment. Every culture imposes on its physical environment some kind of classification scheme, whether it be deployed practically to distinguish helpful or harmful plants[34] and animals or whether, as in magical or ritual action, the positive values in that scheme are exploited to solve some practical problem, such as a physical ailment.

In the words of Tambiah, the rite "persuasively" exploits the monkey's desirable qualities, and to understand what he means by this we turn to his work on Malinowski. The essence of Tambiah's interpretation of Trobriand magic, as first presented by Malinowski, is that a magical act is inextricably bound up with speech and ritual actions. But this is not as transparent a proposition as it at first seems. For the Trobriands, magic involves sacred speech, originally handed down to men from their first ancestors and culture heroes, which has the defining characteristic of being able to influence events in the world. Ritual action not only taps sacred myth – in other words ritual action incorporates mythical imagery and narrative – it has its own "grammar," according to which its nonverbal acts can be organized. This approach to ritual is characteristic of anthropologists who have made what is sometimes called the "linguistic turn," meaning that they have found analogies from historical linguistics and textual language to be helpful in explaining ritual action. For our purposes what is significant is that for Tambiah ritual action, just as language, is a sign system that can be used to exploit metaphors and analogies inherent in a culture's system of meaning. Conversely, relying on philosophy of language theory proposed mainly by J. L. Austin's *How to Do Things with Words* (Cambridge, Mass., 1962), Tambiah shows that under certain socially determined contexts and conditions words are equivalent to action. To take just one non-magical example, when an American jury pronounces a verdict of "Guilty" or "Not Guilty" before the judge and court, it not only makes an evaluative judgment about a defendant, it simultaneously changes the status of the defendant's relationship to the court and society. These words, uttered at the socially appropriate moment, actually bring a new reality into being. Although Tambiah perhaps lays more stress on ritual language than on magical action in his overall analysis of magic,[35] he recognizes that it is fundamentally the two together that create a magical event. The conglomerated action is "persuasive" partly because it anticipates future events, as Malinowski first suggested, and attempts to bring into existence a state which is not yet achieved. More importantly it is persuasive because the analogical nature of magical action implies a desired transfer of positive or negative qualities or properties. As we have already noted, in broad terms magic publicizes someone's desire to influence events, often in a ritually emphatic way, but both magical objects and magical actions are structured through analogy, imitation, simile, and metaphor (themselves forms of analogy) – all of which Frazer generally subsumed under the term *sympathy* – that depend for their efficacy on invisible, but nonetheless real, relationships between the magic and its intended target.

It is within the wider scope of ritual action generally, and with attention to the effect of ritual on its participants, that Tambiah offers this succinct characterization:[36]

> Thus, it is possible to argue that all ritual, whatever the idiom, is addressed to the human participants and uses a technique which attempts to restructure and integrate the minds and emotions of the actors. The technique combines verbal and nonverbal behavior and exploits their special properties. Language is an artificial construct and its strength is that its form owes nothing to external reality; it thus enjoys the power to invoke images and comparisons, refer to time past and future, and relate events which cannot be represented in action. Nonverbal action, on the other hand, excels in what words cannot easily do – it can codify analogically by imitating real events, reproduce technical acts, and express multiple implications simultaneously. Words excel in expressive enlargement, physical actions in realistic presentation.

Because magical action is ritual action we can readily apply Tambiah's view to all of the magic we will encounter in this book. Note first his emphasis on the human participants as the audience for ritual or magical action. This refers to the indispensable social framework within which ritual and magic take place. We can actually extend this notion further and suggest that even when an individual performs magic alone or in private, it is nevertheless within an imagined social framework that it becomes effective. In other words, because magic is aimed at influencing behavior, whether of human beings or even of demonic agents such as illnesses that threaten to attack, magic always becomes efficacious within the community of agents that are understood to have influence in the world. In my view, Tambiah's most important contribution to our understanding of magic is in recognizing how verbal and nonverbal action interpenetrate one another. If ritual imitates a realistic presentation – stabbing a doll to cause pain in a victim – at the same time that it can exaggerate or telescope that presentation, then spells complement and enlarge upon the ritual action by invoking further comparisons and contrasts. The series of analogies created by the combination of words and action is not then fundamentally reducible to one interpretation. This is a key point, because it means that magic is expansive – new metaphors realized through action or language can be created and old ones can continually be reinvoked – and this helps to explain the adaptability of magic to new circumstances, new contexts, and even to new cultures over time. The very fact that image magic is attested for over two thousand years in cultures in the Mediterranean basin and European cultures farther north, which continued to be influenced by Greco-Roman practices, cries out for such an explanation. This could only have happened if the practice of image magic continued to retain a certain authority derived from its antiquity on the one hand, while on the other being open to newer interpretations consistent with the changing institutional and religious realities of later times. Indeed, Greco-Roman magical practices actually form the basis of later medieval and early modern perceptions of witchcraft.

Conclusion

There are several specific questions worth emphasizing in light of our review of the major, mainly anthropological, theorists of magic. Our survey has not been exhaustive, but it has touched upon the most significant directions researchers have taken in their investigations of magic. For any given magical object or instance of magical action, we have to bear in mind the fundamental question of *agency* – which means we have to ask how the magic works, or what or who makes it effective. Since magic relies on invisible forces, we have to ask what those forces are and how are they perceived. Since we know that magic operates within analogical frameworks, we must pay particular attention to the metaphors, similes, and imitative acts that are involved, while being careful to separate truly imitative acts from those that are instead real or lived physical interactions. Finally, to understand why magic looks the way it does for a given culture, we have to ask rather straightforwardly why it looks that way and not some other way. In other words, we have to investigate its history as magic – for instance were certain ritual actions always considered magical by the culture in question, or did a given object that was not formerly magical become so at some point in time? If we ask these kinds of questions, without getting too bogged down in our own preconceived definitions of magic, we have a better chance of grasping something of what Greek magic was in action. As we shall see in a moment, the Greeks used many often interchangeable terms for magic and had their own ideas about what it was and how it originated. However, what the Greeks called magic is often indistinguishable from their officially sanctioned cult practices – what we, but not even they, would call their "religion."[37] It therefore does an outsider no good to regard, for example, one form of purification as "magical" and another "religious," if both fall under some commonly understood framework for what makes purification effective, or what makes it interesting or necessary to do. Those are the things that our questions ought to seek to answer because they bring us closer to what magic was for the Greeks.

At the same time, it is important to recognize that both the terms *magic* and *religion* have limited value insofar as they artificially divide practices that for all intents and purposes can be the same. The distinction between magic and religion, still employed by many Western scholars even today, emerged as early as the fourteenth century CE, and took firm hold in the sixteenth, when Reformation Protestant theologians began prop-agandistically to label Catholic sacramentalism and church ritual as magic as a way to distinguish their own practices from those of the medieval church.[38] These writers well understood that, for instance, the inherited terms *magia, magicus, maleficium, maleficus/a, veneficium,* and *veneficus/a* had original, pagan Roman meanings, which were in turn further defined in the works of Saint Augustine (354–430 CE) and especially in the law codes of the late antique emperors Theodosius II (401–50 CE) and Justinian (ca. 482–565 CE). Moreover, all of these Roman terms harked even further back into Greek pagan antiquity, leaving open the question of how relevant they were already in the fourteenth, let alone in later centuries. But their immediate concerns were to reformulate a new definition of (Protestant) Christianity that was emphatically not based on the seven Catholic sacraments (baptism, confirmation, marriage, the Mass, ordination, penance, extreme unction). Because these sacraments looked like magic they called into question the Catholic church's cardinal distinction between magic, which was relegated to the Devil and his servants, and miracles, which were alone reserved for God and his agents. Hence Protestant writers tendentiously employed the ancient Roman terms, along with a host of newer medieval creations, to attack their Catholic adversaries. This complex and fascinating history, which need not directly concern us and which has been explored in massive detail by the historian Keith Thomas[39] and more recently by Stuart Clark,[40] was crucially important to the distinction between magic and religion embraced by both Tylor and Frazer. Although this history is not of immediate concern in the present work, it should encourage us to keep separate the terminological distinctions of magic and religion and their unique history from the investigation of ritual practices. In antiquity, ritual practices often go without explicit labels or bear labels that shift at the convenience of an ancient critic.[41]

This does not mean that we will always find completely satisfactory answers to our questions about magical practices, and here is where comparative approaches can be of help. The particulars of a given cultural context will always be definitive in any interpretation of magic, and comparative approaches often tell us what to look for to help frame that interpretation. As we look more closely at examples of Greek magic, we will have many opportunities – especially in cases where we lack evidence for how a given magical act was performed – to draw out some plausible implications for how it was understood to work by its practitioners. There is a good deal here that for readers familiar with the scholarship on ancient magic, I hope, will be new. Some of the best current research on ancient magic tends too cautiously to be descriptive and authors hesitate to advance interpretations that cannot be supported by textual evidence. Unfortunately, Greek magic involved non-textual objects and ritual action that were not always directly described. But this does not mean that we cannot offer, in line with comparative approaches, a plausible if at times provisional interpretation. Indeed, beginning in the fifth century BCE the outlines of what we might call a theory of magic become fairly well defined, giving us an important basis from which to start. Nevertheless, we must always bear in mind the caveat that the average Greek users of magic, as against their elite and literate social counterparts who had a vested interest in controlling it, probably gave little thought to how magic worked. They just knew that it did.

CHAPTER 2

A Framework for Greek Magic

꒰꒱꒰꒱

Our task in this chapter is to present an intellectual framework for Greek magic in the fifth and fourth centuries BCE that will provide a theological and causal basis for understanding how it was perceived to work. Only after we have come to terms with such a framework can we then proceed to examine particular kinds of magic. The central dilemma for any student of Greek magic is that the Greek term *mageia* (Latin *magia*) from which we derive 'magic' only emerges in the latter half of the fifth century BCE, while the evidence for practices and substances that were understood to be magical, as well as for individuals who were thought to be magicians, existed prior to the birth of the term. From the point of view of practices, this state of affairs should not present a dilemma. Moreover, even as we may attempt to use native Greek terms to define magic with precision, Greeks in the fifth century and later were not themselves completely consistent in their use of this or other related terms. By keeping our focus on practices, we avoid the overly textual approach of some scholars who claim at bottom that unless there is an available term for magic, then practices that are, from a later point of view, indistinguishable from magic are not magic.[1]

Magic and the Gods

A couple of examples from Homer will illustrate the problem. In book 11 of the *Odyssey*, a work whose composition can possibly be dated to the eighth century BCE but in any case non-controversially to before the sixth, we find the hero Odysseus venturing into the underworld to summon the spirits of dead noble heroes and their wives and mothers. He does this by digging a pit and filling it with honey and milk, sweet wine, water, and sprinkled barley meal. Then he sacrifices sheep and lets their blood run into the pit. After his sacrifices and prayers, the dead begin to come forward to drink the blood so as to be able to communicate with him. By the fourth century BCE, if not the fifth, individuals who claimed the ability to summon the dead and communicate with them were widely regarded as magicians engaging in necromancy. But in the description of Odysseus, no such words for magic or necromancy are used – in fact, the Greek term for summoning the dead, *psychagōgia*, is post-Homeric and first occurs in the first quarter of the fifth century.[2] Nevertheless, no Greek living in the fifth century would have thought twice about considering Odysseus' ritual actions to be necromancy and to have had magical connotations.

A different sort of example involves the adventures of Odysseus and the goddess Circe. On the way to Circe's palace in book 10 of the *Odyssey* to retrieve his companions, the god Hermes descends to warn Odysseus about the dangers of this powerful goddess, who is explicitly called by the epithet, *polypharmakos* 'skilled in many drugs/medicines'. Hermes then offers Odysseus a 'good medicine' *pharmakon esthlon*, which he says is called *mōly* by the gods but which men have difficulty digging up. *Mōly* is a plant with a black root and milky flower that later botanical authors occasionally identified as garlic, though it is unclear from the Homeric text what the plant originally was.[3] Hermes explains to Odysseus that when he arrives at Circe's palace, she will make him a drink and put *pharmaka* (plural, singular *pharmakon*), this time meaning 'drugs', into it, which without the *mōly* would turn him into a pig, as she has already done to Odysseus' companions. The *mōly* Hermes says is a good medicine that will protect Odysseus from the transformative effects of her *pharmaka*, which in fact it does. (The moment at which Circe offers Odysseus her drugged drink is represented on the cover of this book, in the 1891 oil painting by John William Waterhouse.) Again we have the problem that both Hermes' *mōly* and Circe's unnamed *pharmaka*, from the point of view of the fifth century and later, were considered magic. Indeed, *pharmaka* 'drugs/medicines' are one of the hallmarks of Athenian magical practice in the fifth century and, by the fourth century, Circe along with other literary figures like Medea became synonymous with magical practice. There is nothing to distinguish what Hermes and Circe do with their *pharmaka* from what later practitioners do, except for its effects of turning those who ingest them into swine, and yet the term *pharmakon* existed well before the term *mageia*. We would be remiss to dismiss the evidence in earlier texts from consideration, not least because we could not then account for why later Greeks were so willing to recognize magic in them.

Moreover, one may legitimately ask whether we should distinguish in any substantive way between magic as practiced by Greek gods and goddesses, and magic as practiced by mortals or heroes like Odysseus. From the point of view of our main focus on practices, the answer is clearly no. However, Theodor Hopfner,[4] a distinguished nineteenth-century scholar of ancient magic, was once criticized for taking this approach to the extreme. Hopfner adduced many examples from Greek mythological literature of deeds accomplished by the gods and objects in their possession which he considered magical, such as Hermes' famous golden staff that mazed the eyes of men, but which other scholars believed fell clearly outside the realm of magic.[5] Somehow, the argument seemed to run, the divine world needed more clearly to be marked off from the mortal one, since in respect of other religious activity the Greeks themselves sharply differentiated between divine and mortal behavior. In the case of Hermes giving the drug *mōly* to Odysseus, our text makes clear that this herb is called *mōly* by the gods and it is hard for mortals to dig up. Hermes must point it out to Odysseus, explain to him how to take it properly, and even further how he should approach Circe once he has taken it. From a Greek mythological point of view, this kind of divine insight into the mortal world is standard fare. We are told in numerous places that the gods even have a separate language to describe things in the natural world that are not fully understood by mortals. But every Greek in the fifth century understood that *pharmaka* 'drugs' could be used by physicians practicing medicine as well as by magicians hawking them as specialized products. It would not have occurred to them to discount Hermes' *mōly* somehow as a categorically different kind of drug. Accordingly, we should also be able to examine the effects of *mōly* on Odysseus and his companions to gain insight into how this kind of pharmaceutical magic was perceived to work.[6]

The case of the goddess Demeter's magical treatment of the mortal infant Demophoön presents an even clearer example of why a differentiation between divine and mortal magic is problematic. In the *Homeric Hymn to Demeter*, which is datable to the mid-seventh to mid-sixth centuries BCE, the goddess has come to earth in disguise as an old woman and been taken into the household of the king of Eleusis, ostensibly to serve as the nursemaid for the king's newborn son, Demophoön. When Demeter boasts of her abilities to do the job, she singles out her knowledge of magic in particular (227–30):

> I will raise him, nor do I expect a spell or the Undercutter
> to harm him through the negligence of his nurse.
> For I know a charm more cutting than the Woodcutter;
> I know a strong safeguard against baneful bewitching.[7]

There are several peculiar terms used in the original Greek in this boast that relate to witchcraft and magic. First, the term she uses for 'bewitching' *epēlusiē*, which literally means 'to come upon/over one', occurs only in this poem and in the *Homeric Hymn to Hermes* (37) in a parallel expression, but is not among the common words for witchcraft in fifth-century usage. Whatever the exact frame of reference encompassed by *epēlusiē*, it would be a mistake not to see it as fitting within a broad understanding of witchcraft or magic that comes to be described by other terms at a later period.

The terms for "Undercutter" and "Woodcutter" in the same passage have also puzzled scholars for at least a century.[8] One influential interpretation has it that these are names for human agents who might try to harm the baby through drugs or noxious herbals. This view was based on the fact that herbalists who cut roots for magical purposes were well known in the classical period and went generally under the name *rhizotomoi* 'rootcutters'. A more recent and very plausible interpretation has shown that because the Greek terms for Undercutter and Woodcutter have parallels in later magical texts, they instead refer to supernatural or demonic forces that attack the gums of teething babies through cutting.[9] If this interpretation is correct, it shows us that we cannot in any intellectually defensible way distinguish Demeter's magic from that of mortal practitioners. On the contrary, the *Hymn to Demeter* might well preserve for us one of the earliest references to this kind of teething or cutting demon. Moreover, Demeter's boast itself is reminiscent of the actual form of some of these charms to protect against cutting demons, making it plausible that the anonymous author(s) of the *Hymn* knew of such charms and put them into the mouth of the goddess. It is often the case in Greek mythology that gods and goddesses are represented as the first practitioners of an otherwise human tradition, especially ritual traditions that address themselves to the gods. This is a classic example of myth operating as a *charter* for a culture, which refers to a general theory of myth outlined originally by Malinowski. Such may be the case with Demeter and her knowledge of teething magic: her actions and words were preserved as an example to later Greeks, and the ritual performance of her *Hymn* by generations of Greeks – especially those concerned with initiation into her mysteries at Eleusis, which is the main focus of her *Hymn* – further preserved and disseminated such magical knowledge. But however that may be, on no account are we justified in claiming that, either on the grounds that Demeter is a goddess or on the grounds that more common terms for magic emerge only after the composition of her *Hymn*, her knowledge of witchcraft and magic is not fully worthy of the same consideration we extend to magic of later periods.

Divinity and Nature

That the gods and goddesses of the Greeks should practice magic touches upon another, more abstract, way in which divinity figures crucially in the framework for Greek magic that we are developing. I am referring to the relationship between divinity and nature, especially as conceived by philosophers and physicians of the sixth and fifth centuries BCE. Our most important critics of Greek magic emerge in the late fifth and early fourth centuries in the writings of the Hippocratic physicians and Plato (ca. 429–347 BCE). These authors give us much direct insight into the range of magical practices known in their day and the claims made by their assorted practitioners. The most striking thing about their critiques, however, is that the possibility of magic is never plainly refuted. A modern reader might expect that to be their first point of attack but, instead, their critiques turn on moral or logical contradictions in the claims and practices of the magical practitioners. For them the question of whether magic is possible at all seems not to be directly at issue, and is clearly of less relevance than whether a claim to be able to practice magic implies some unwarranted control over the gods. The reason for this is that, as I have shown elsewhere,[10] the attacks on magic and magical practitioners assume a basic, largely Presocratic, view of the world in which nature and divinity were inseparable. By implication, if nature is divine, then exploiting nature's properties in magic in some sense implies a mastery of the divine. Some eight hundred years after the Presocratics the naturalist writer Aelian tells us that nature (*phusis*) is a witch (*pharmakis*),[11] but this kind of statement entails a shift of thinking that now regards the wonders of nature as something largely separable from divine influence. In Athens of the fifth century such a statement probably would have constituted a charge of impiety (*asebeia*), under which rubric individuals could be exiled or sentenced to death.[12] On the other hand the dividing line between the effects of divine and the effects of magical causes in the fifth century was not altogether clear. How was anyone to know, for instance, in a given case of illness or misfortune, whether the causes were divine or mortal? Answering this question was critical because it determined the correct ritual or medical responses which could then be undertaken to heal the illness. It became all important, in other words, to know what magic could and could not do, and how its effects were different from divine causes. Until that dividing line between magic and divinity was more clearly drawn, the critics of magic were not in a position, it seems to me, to attack magical practices in a way that could actually invite criticism of divine agency itself. And as we shall see in a moment, the ability to manipulate divine agency appears to have been a central claim of fifth-century magicians.

The key position about nature among philosophers who lived before Socrates with which we have to come to terms is that divinity was inherent in nature. It is not a question here of particular, anthropomorphic divinities like Demeter and Hermes, but rather that the natural elements themselves were divine. Because the Hippocratic physicians and Plato were direct heirs to this tradition, we must first briefly examine at least its broad outlines to understand why they framed their critiques of magic in such a particular way. Thales of Miletus (late seventh/early sixth BCE), for example, whom we have already met in connection with magnets and the souls they contain, actually took a much broader view of ensoulment. For Thales was reputed to have said that everything was full of divinities, which he called *daimones*.[13] In this context we can consider a *daimōn* to be a divine force capable of producing motion, but which is otherwise not clearly defined. Thus Thales' first principle, water, out of which everything in the universe was generated, would also be divine. Anaximander of Miletus (d. after 547 BCE), according to later sources, developed the principle that the universe was unlimited – what he called the "Infinite" – and that the "Infinite" itself was divinity.[14] In his footsteps Anaximenes of Miletus (fl. 546–525 BCE) made air (*aēr*) his first principle, and the idea was also attributed to him that all things present, past, and future, as well as gods and divinity, generally emerged from air.[15] Heraclitus of Ephesus (fl. ca. 500 BCE) grounded the emergence of the universe in fire, in direct reaction to the Milesian system of Anaximander and Anaximenes that had placed air at the center, but similarly felt that the elemental powers constitutive of everything were full of *daimones*.[16]

The long-standing tradition among the Presocratics that the whole universe was divine can be complemented by the equally pervasive view that astronomical phenomena were also divine. Aristotle tells us that Alcmaeon of Croton (fifth century BCE), like Thales, Heraclitus, and Diogenes of Apollonia (fl. fifth century BCE), wrote that "all divine things also always move continuously: the moon, sun, stars, and the whole heaven."[17] Reflecting a similar viewpoint the comic poet Epicharmus claimed that the winds, water, earth, sun, fire, and stars were gods.[18] And Empedocles (ca. 492–432 BCE), a Presocratic philosopher whom we shall encounter later owing to the strong claims he made about his own magical abilities, maintained that his four elements or roots – fire, earth, air, and water – were also gods.[19] These, then, are some examples of the complex attributions of divinity to nature made by the Presocratics. Their views about nature and astronomical bodies lead directly to the form of critique found in the most significant attack on magic that we have from the late fifth to early fourth centuries.

The Hippocratics: Magic, Divination, and Epilepsy

Arguably the most influential attack on magic ever made in antiquity appears in this period in the Hippocratic treatise, *On the Sacred Disease*. The treatise is addressed to the rival healers of the Hippocratic school of medicine, who have not been identified with certainty but whose views seem to include both popular ideas about medicine and elements of the more sophisticated Presocratic philosophers like those briefly examined above. Nevertheless, the attacks made in this treatise were considerably less influential in their own day compared to the use to which they were put almost two millennia later.

The fundamental arguments made in *On the Sacred Disease* against the false claims of magical practitioners, as far as we can tell, had no discernible impact on the behavior of its Greek contemporaries. This is a significant point to bear in mind as we proceed through the author's arguments, because they speak strongly against his influence in his own day and against the sometimes exaggerated importance ascribed to his views by scholars. Nevertheless it is quite remarkable that in 1563 the German court physician to Duke William of Cleves, Johannes Weyer, writing toward the middle of the major phase of continental European witch trials, published what is now regarded as a landmark in the emergence of skepticism toward witchcraft with the publication of his *De praestigiis daemonum* (*On the trickeries of demons*).[20] Sigmund Freud regarded Weyer's book as among the most important in the history of psychiatry, and situated prominently in Weyer's chapter on "Magicians of Ill Repute" are none other than the excerpts on magic from *On the Sacred Disease* to which we are about to turn.[21]

The author or authors of *On the Sacred Disease* defend an approach to the treatment of epilepsy – for the Greeks epilepsy was a divinely sent or sacred disease – that does not involve recognizing the immediate manifestation of divinity, especially in anthropomorphic form, but rather looks to a set of more naturalistic or physical causes as the basis for the disease. I hesitate to call such causes *natural*, because as we shall see even this Hippocratic author operates within the basic Presocratic framework that attributes divinity to nature and its phenomena. In the author's effort to distinguish the approach he will set forth, he needs, it seems rather desperately, to refute the claims made by a host of penumbral religious specialists who are apparently able to cure epilepsy through variegated interactions with divinity. In the opinion of our author, those who first called the disease of epilepsy 'sacred' did so in order to conceal their own inadequacy. Should their proposed remedies fail, the author suggests, these purveyors could easily blame the gods and avoid taking responsibility for failure themselves. He adds:[22]

> that those who first consecrated this disease are the same people who even today are called magicians (*magoi*), purifiers (*kathartai*), beggar-priests (*agurtai*) and charlatans (*alazones*); the very same who pretend that they are particularly pious and know much. Accordingly these individuals, by hiding behind divinity and setting it forth as a pretext for their helplessness, make use of it so that, not knowing anything, they are not exposed; thus they called this illness 'sacred'. By choosing suitable words and prescribing purifications and spells (*epōidai*), by advising abstinence from baths and from many foods unsuitable for the sick, they made their healing method safe for themselves.

In our author's view the whole array of services offered to heal epilepsy is one endless subterfuge, behind which the so-called specialists can hide through their appeal to divinity. Their practical advice is hollow and even their proposed dietary regimen is designed falsely to produce results: the implication is that the foods from which the patients are advised to abstain are already harmful to them; it does not take much imagination to speculate that such foods might in fact have been given to sick patients just to "prove" the effectiveness of refraining from them. But the claims made about divinity in this passage also emerge as problematic, in a way that has drawn little attention from scholars, as the author proceeds with his critique.

The main problem with calling epilepsy 'sacred', which thereby entails certain indefensible claims on divinity, is that in the author's view doing so falsely distinguishes epilepsy from other diseases. However, epilepsy is no different than other diseases insofar as they *all* have divine and human components. The author proceeds to describe this state of affairs in accord with the Presocratic view outlined earlier that the elements of nature are divine:[23]

> This so-called 'sacred' disease comes from the same causes as others, from what comes to and goes from us, from the cold, the sun, and the changing and never-ceasing winds. For these things are divine, so that it is not necessary for one distinguishing to consider the disease more divine than the others, but all are divine and all are human. Each has a nature and force of its own, and none is unmanageable and without remedy.

Thus the causal agents of disease in this account are the natural elements that have their own properties and unique effects. Diseases are both divine and human inasmuch as the divine elements are ultimately responsible for their occurrence, and they are human inasmuch as each disease has its own nature and course which can be manipulated by the physician.[24] We might have expected our author to deny any divine origin to epilepsy except that, on the contrary, in many Hippocratic treatises and in popular tradition the acceptance of a twin origin for many diseases from both divine and human causes was conventional wisdom. The divine origin of epilepsy stood out in particular because there were famous myths such as the madness of Herakles, depicted for example in Euripides' play of that name, which actually described the onset of epilepsy. So well known was this story that, in addition to the term the 'sacred' disease, epilepsy could also be called the 'Heraklean disease'. In any case, what our author mainly decries is the false claim that because epilepsy is more divine than other diseases, it thereby requires magical or religious specialists who are wont to exaggerate their credentials in piety. His aim is as much to discredit this group as it is to provide a different basis on which to treat epilepsy.

The magical and religious specialists singled out for the author's ire offered services and claimed knowledge that extended well beyond healing epilepsy. In the most famous passage from *On the Sacred Disease*, we are told that their abilities fundamentally involved changing the course of nature which, in light of our author's Presocratic assumptions with regard to the divine elements of nature, was tantamount to impiety (*asebeia*):[25]

> If they claim to know how to draw down the moon and eclipse the sun, to make storms and fair weather, rain and drought, the sea impassable and the earth barren, and all other things of such kind – whether they claim to know these things from rites or from some other knowledge or practice – by making this their business they seem to me to be impious, neither believing that the gods exist nor that they have any power, and in so doing fail to refrain from extremes, since the gods are as nothing to them.

The implications of these claims bring us face to face with what our author finds so objectionable. As a good Presocratic, he regards the moon, sun, weather, and sea as features of the natural world that all partake of divinity, if they are not divinities themselves. When our magical specialists claim control over these elements they imply that mortals can somehow control divinity. But rather than insist on the transcendence of divinity at this point – in the sense that mortals can never control divinity

– instead our author concludes that these naturally divine powers cannot really be divine if the specialists' claims are true but mortal, since mortals control only what is mortal (1.31). In effect, he reasons, our specialists are then denying the existence and power of divinity and these denials constitute impiety.

There is no question that our author has advanced an attack against his adversaries on mainly logical and rhetorical grounds. Recent research confirms this impression and has shown the Hippocratic authors to be well versed in the sophistical arguments and rhetorical strategies of their day.[26] But a rather glaring contradiction in his argument remains. On the one hand, our author says that the magical and religious specialists use the supposed divine origin of epilepsy as an excuse to absolve themselves from criticism when their remedies fail. This suggests that they are appealing to their ultimate inability to control divinity, even if they offer the hope of influencing it. On the other hand, the specialists' claims of drawing down the moon and eclipsing the sun suggest to our author that, if it were possible to do such things, the gods could not exist nor have any power. Now our author cannot have it both ways: at one moment his adversaries' actions are based on the assumption that they cannot control divinity, at another on the assumption that divinity does not exist at all. We have no way of knowing whether the weakness of arguments of this kind was exploited, since no evidence remains of how, for example, the opponents of our author responded to it. As Geoffrey Lloyd has shown,[27] the Hippocratic writers are competing not only against one another, but also likely against ritual practitioners of temple medicine at cult sites like the famous one at Epidaurus for Asclepius, for medical business, in addition to the obvious competition coming from the magic and religious specialists named in *On the Sacred Disease*. At least some of the remedies on offer at local healing cult sites seem to have been meant specifically to counter the remedies suggested by physicians. On that point, there was a saying frequently quoted in antiquity to the effect that when the remedies of the physicians failed, everyone resorted to sacrificers, seers, spells, and amulets to solve their problems.[28]

How the magical specialists actually diagnosed epilepsy provides some insight into their techniques and treatment. It ought first to be said that the naturalistic explanation of epilepsy offered by the author of *On the Sacred Disease*, utilizing as it does a typology of illness due to imbalances in the humours phlegm and bile, turns out to be as fanciful as those offered by the magical specialists.[29] The author's arguments are purely speculative and show no evidence of real anatomical understanding, but this is probably to be expected at a time when human autopsy was still more than a century from being readily practiced.[30] His treatment regimen for epilepsy is allopathic, meaning that because the imbalances in phlegm and bile in turn suggest too much dryness or moisture, and cold or heat in the body, remedies that reversed those dispositions at the right moment should cure the disease. As has been noted by Lloyd, in effect all our author does is substitute one set of invisible causes for another. Nevertheless, in his own mind he is clear that the magic (*magia*) and purifications (*katharmoi*) offered by the ritual specialists to cure the disease are ineffective, as he says at the very end of his treatise.[31]

The shocking and bizarre nature of an epileptic seizure, as every Greek who knew of Herakles' own sufferings could attest, was so extraordinary that it almost begged for divine explanation. But to the Greeks, the fact that a divinity could invade a human body was a familiar experience, most famously illustrated in the case of the Pythia at Delphi being invaded by Apollo who thereby provided her with an oracular voice. In this case Apollo's divine visitation was invited and controlled and unlike a sudden epileptic seizure, where it was not even clear which divinity might in fact be present. Our author describes the epileptic's symptoms this way:[32]

> [The patient] becomes speechless and chokes, foam runs from the mouth, his teeth lock together, his hands contract, his eyes twist about, and they lose consciousness; in some excrement also passes.

In the description of Herakles' epileptic seizure, a goddess of madness, Lussa, invades Herakles' body, and Euripides actually describes the onset of the madness in terms remarkably similar to these.[33] The Greeks construed an epileptic seizure in terms of divine invasion, and in anthropological terms this kind of cultural phenomenon is called *possession*.[34] The issue now for the patient, however, according to the author of *On the Sacred Disease*, was to determine which divinity was responsible for the possession. As we might expect, the terms in which these actions are described are pejorative, but we need to be careful to distinguish the logic of the ritual specialists' actions from the logic attributed to their actions by our author. We are told that if the patient imitates a goat, roars, or suffers convulsions on his right side, the ritual specialists claim the Mother of the Gods is responsible. If he utters a loud and sharp cry, he is likened to a horse and Poseidon is made responsible. If he passes excrement, as our author has already explained is a common occurrence, the goddess Enodia is named. If the patient's cries are more frequent and higher-pitched, like birds, Apollo Nomius (pastoral) is responsible. If he foams at the mouth and kicks, Ares is the cause, and if he has fears and terrors that strike at night, driving him out of bed, Hekate or the heroes are responsible. To our author all of these attributions are absurd, and bespeak the lack of proper naturalistic reasoning to which he anticipates his audience will appeal. However, in his effort to discredit the ritual specialists he mischaracterizes their responses as illogical when, in fact, there is a coherent logic behind them.

The first point our author seems to miss is that the diagnoses of divine origin for epilepsy are in effect a form of Greek divination. There are many different types of Greek divination, and of course it would take us too far afield to explore them all here. However, the homology that is created in the diagnosis between the various 'signs' a patient exhibits and the divinity who is best characterized as the originator of those signs is in accord with standard Greek views of divination. Indeed, the functionally imitative relationship between the sign and the divinity responsible for it is *sympathetic*, in the reconsidered terminology of Frazer that we explored in chapter 1. In ornithomancy or bird divination, for example, the flight patterns and cries of birds are interpreted to determine which divinity is responsible for the sign and what the message might be.[35] Certain birds are associated with particular divinities, such as the crow and Apollo, making it reasonable to associate higher-pitched birdlike cries with him, as in the example of Apollo Nomius above. Although it is true that the cries and convulsions here are exhibited by the patient, we have no evidence outside the report of our author to suppose that this form of divination was viewed as illegitimate. Given the sheer variety of what the Greeks considered to be legitimate, humanly manifested divine signs – including chance utterances, involuntary bodily motions such as sneezing, tingling in the hand, and ringing in the ear – we cannot as confidently as our author judge the actions of the ritual specialists to be perverse. Instead, I would suggest that we actually have here another form of Greek divination which, because of its context in *On the Sacred Disease*, has not been for the most part seriously examined by scholars.[36] This interaction between divination and magic should also remind us of the Azande, for whom divination was the means used to determine the source of a given bewitchment or magical affliction.

The second and more important point that our author overlooks will bear directly on how we understand certain aspects of Greek magic to operate. It concerns the conceptual relationship between the epileptic, who is described in Greek as being held by the disease, and the dominant metaphor of binding or being held down that animates the magic of Greek curse tablets. The connection between epilepsy and binding magic has not been fully explored by scholars, although almost a century ago at least one scholar suggested a connection.[37] Part of what has been missed lies in how the author of *On the Sacred Disease* mocks the ritual actions undertaken by the specialists to cure epilepsy, which he describes in the following way:[38]

> For they purify those held (*tous ekhomenous*) by the disease with blood and other such things as though they have some pollution, an avenging spirit, or were bewitched (verb *pharmassō*) by men.

In the author's view purification is an illogical response to epilepsy because by definition, the author argues, purification implies a prior defilement (*miasma*), blood guilt (*alastoria*), bewitchment (*pepharmakeusthai*), or some other unholy deed (*ergon anosion*), none of which is relevant to epilepsy. Moreover, the author derides the fact that epileptic victims are not taken to the temples of the gods thought responsible for the attack, nor are the offscourings from purification dedicated to those gods. Instead, the offs-courings from purification are hidden in the earth, dumped into the sea, or carried into the mountains so as to prevent anyone from touching or stepping on them. To our author each of these actions illustrates the wrong ritual response because each fails to acknowledge in a ritually appropriate manner the supposed responsible divinity. My concern is with the author's comparison that these purificatory actions are undertaken 'as though they have some pollution, an avenging spirit, or were bewitched by men'. Our author clearly does not accept these explanations because they do not accord with his own understanding of epilepsy's causes. But his remarks suggest that the specialists did, in fact, treat epilepsy as the outcome of pollution, avenging spirits, and bewitchment. And it is the magical dimension here that most interests us. It is hard to understand why the specialists would treat epilepsy as if it derived from bewitch-ment unless it was believed that epilepsy itself could be motivated by magic.

A common type of magic in the fifth century and later involves the metaphor of binding or holding down someone, as a way to thwart their ambitions, activities, or even their powers of perception. In curse tablets, for example, the written curses frequently depict a speaker who says in the first person 'I bind down' (*katadō*) or 'I hold down' (*katekhō*) such and such a person, and his or her attributes, works, companions, and so forth. We shall have an opportunity later to examine some of these tablets in detail. For the moment, suffice it to note that this same metaphor of holding down, and the same verb *katekhō* and its cognate forms, are used to describe in the broadest terms the Greek phenomenon of possession. And we have just seen epileptics described in terms similar to these, especially in the phrase 'those held (*tous ekhomenous*) by the disease'. Despite the use of the simplex form *ekhomenous* in the description of an epileptic seizure in *On the Sacred Disease*, speechlessness, choking, clenching of the teeth and hands, must have visibly illustrated to the magical specialists as well as to an ordinary bystander the very definition of the compound forms *katokhos* or *katekhomenos*, which mean 'possessed' or literally 'held down'. The additional features of losing consciousness and having one's eyes twist about – which the Greeks described as having one's normal mode of awareness replaced by a different one – are also important to the general Greek understanding of possession. In later medical literature (Galen, second century CE), the term *katokhē*, another cognate from the same verb *katekhō*, still refers specifically to a disorder like catalepsy, in which there is a loss of consciousness and complete rigidity of the body, although by this time the divine origin of this family of afflictions had been largely discarded.[39] Possession in the fifth and fourth centuries BCE was literally a matter of being overtaken by a divinity or divine power, and epilepsy seems to have been thought of as a particularly strong form of divine possession. But the disposition of possessed persons, who appeared visibly bound or held down, also dovetailed exceedingly well with the prevailing conception of binding magic. Thus contrary to the views of the author of *On the Sacred Disease*, our ritual specialists were altogether logical in ritually treating epilepsy as if they were counteracting magic, because magic was regarded as one possible cause.

There is still further confirmation of this view to be found if we look again at the particular divinities named as examples of those thought responsible for epileptic attacks.

Several of the divinities mentioned by the author of *On the Sacred Disease*, including the Mother of the Gods,[40] Ares,[41] Hekate, the heroes,[42] who are commonly figured in Greek thought as *daimones*, are invoked by name in known curse tablets. Some of these tablets are dated as early as the fourth century BCE, but our earliest tablets reach to the beginning of the fifth century. According to the typical curse formula, these divinities are the ones in the presence of whom a victim is magically bound and they also function as the agents who will realize the aims of the curse. It was Ganschinietz[43] who long ago suggested a connection between the state of being *katokhos* 'possessed' and the frequent use of the verb *katekhō* 'I bind' in the Attic curse tablets. But not even he, I believe, fully realized the implications of his suggestion. Moreover, in the curse tablets the chthonic or underworld divinities Hekate and Hermes are frequently called by the epithets *katokhos* and *katokhē*, terms which reinforce their role as the divinities most responsible for overseeing the binding action envisaged in the tablets. Recall that the author of *On the Sacred Disease* also mentions that the specialists' ritual actions suggest to him that they are purifying someone from an 'avenging spirit' (*alastoria*). In Greek thought this term was reserved for actions that were explained by divine vengeance, and we have other confirmation outside *On the Sacred Disease* from Plato[44] and later Aesop[45] that refer to magic used specifically to avert divine anger. Clearly one form which that divine anger could take was an epileptic attack, and such an attack in turn could be brought on by a binding curse. We have then, in contrast to the view of our physician author, every reason to believe that the magical specialists whom he criticizes were offering remedies aimed at appeasing the divinities invoked as agents in a binding curse. This is not to say that all instances of epilepsy were diagnosed by these specialists as the result of magic. It is rather to say that because the author of *On the Sacred Disease* is so determined to discredit his adversaries' logic, he misconstrues in fact how consistent their ritual solutions were when cases of divine anger as a result of binding magic were actually diagnosed. Moreover, the whole divine taxonomy of symptoms developed by these specialists provided a framework in which to judge the crucial question of which divinity was responsible for the attack. The degree of specificity required by that framework further testifies to how important it was to identify the correct divinity. We are no longer in the world of myth when characters can appeal to the gods generally for aid. In the realm of magic, with the possibility of specific divinities being invoked as magical agents, a specialist whose job it was to counteract that magic had every interest in getting his diagnosis exactly right.

To our author the main sticking point is that, in his view, it is illogical to suggest that a divinity could be a source of pollution. Rather, it is more plausible to expect the divinity to be a source of purification and sanctification.[46] This view is quite wildly at odds with what we might consider the popular Greek view, in which it was taken as a tenet of Greek religious behavior that angered divinities could cause pollution in human beings. Such a difference in understanding again gives us evidence that our author does not appreciate the religious rationale of his contemporaries. Note clearly that our author does not call divinity into question, only the claim that it could be a source of impurity. Furthermore, according to him, the specialists' remediation involves purification with blood, which was normally regarded in Greek religion as impure. As Robert Parker[47] has suggested, the specialists need blood not because it defiles but because it is a token of the defilement or pollution that was to be removed. Earlier Greek thinkers, such as Heraclitus of Ephesus, famously took issue with the logic of ritually purifying with blood, and claimed that it was contradictory, 'as if one who stepped in dirt washed himself off with dirt'.[48] Our author seems to have inherited the same Presocratic viewpoint. But both of these criticisms fail to acknowledge that the purification was aimed at reversing magical attacks that harnessed divine anger, which as we have seen was accepted by the Greeks as a common enough cause of illness and disease, or even madness. It was therefore quite consistent that the offscourings from purification had to be disposed of completely, with no possibility of further human contact. By criticizing where the specialists deposited the remnants of their purifications, the author of *On the Sacred Disease* again misunderstands the common practice, for instance, of disposing offscourings in springs, marshes, and fountains to dissolve the "pollution through contact with the purest forms of matter."[49] In other words, the specialists seem to have known what they were doing; our author, by failing to acknowledge this, comes close to running afoul of his own conventional, religious norms.[50] This leads him to make a very curious admission at this point in his attack against the specialists' purificatory actions:[51]

> Indeed divinity purifies and sanctifies and is the thing that cleanses the great-est and most unholy of our sins. We ourselves mark the boundaries of the sanctuaries and sacred precincts of the gods so that no one will traverse them unless he is pure; when we enter we besprinkle ourselves, not as defiling our-selves, but to wash away any defilement that we have previously acquired.

Thus it is not the principle of purification that disturbs our author nor is it, given the common practice of using bloodshed in certain types of puri-fication ritual, the medium through which purification takes place. Instead, as this passage suggests, it is the specialists' practice of purification out-side the boundaries of civic cult, signified here by the mention of temple precincts and sanctuaries, which is most offensive to him.[52]

Plato and Greek Psychology

This concern is amplified in a similar way in the fourth century by Plato, who shares with the author of *On the Sacred Disease* a deep distrust of the cast of characters – magicians (*magoi*), purifiers (*kathartai*), beggar-priests (*agurtai*), and outright charlatans (*alazones*) – who unscrupu-lously foist their magical services on their clients. What neither author directly addresses, unfortunately, is why these clients have apparently found the services offered by civic cult to be inadequate. Like the Hippocratic author, Plato's writings offer much insight into the types of magical ser-vices offered by specialists, although Plato's own views about the efficacy of magic, as distinct from his contempt for its itinerant purveyors, are harder to pin down. For instance, Plato can cite approvingly the example of midwives who excite or relieve the pains of childbirth through drugs (*pharmaka*) and spells (*epōidai*),[53] and the arsenal of physicians that includes simples, cauteries, incisions, and spells (*epōidai*),[54] but at the same time he can condemn 'those that evoke (*psukhagōgein*) the souls of the dead, claiming to persuade the gods as if by bewitching them with sacrifices, prayers, and spells (*epōidai*)'.[55] Paradoxically, it is not the efficacy of spells that is in question here, nor evocation of the dead – much as the author of *On the Sacred Disease* stopped short of denying the efficacy of purification – but rather the individuals whose religious services, in his view, do not serve the public interest. He reserves his most stinging criticism for the begging-priests (*agurtai*) and seers (*manteis*), the latter of which were not explicitly identified by the author of *On the Sacred Disease*:[56]

> [and how] begging-priests and seers go to rich men's doors and persuade them that, having acquired a power from the gods through sacrifices and spells, with pleasures and festivals they can cure any misdeed by a man or his ancestors, and if a man wants to harm his enemy, for a small cost he will be able to harm just and unjust alike, persuading, as they say, the gods to aid them through spells (*epagōgai*) and binding magic (*katadesmoi*).

The begging-priests and seers in this passage, as well as the magicians, purifiers, and charlatans mentioned in *On the Sacred Disease*, have recently been extensively examined by Matthew Dickie. In his research, Dickie shows that although the names differ, there is substantial agreement in the ancient sources that members of these groups are, on the whole, self-proclaimed religious specialists, self-employed, itinerant, and socially inferior, although each group does have its peculiar characteristics that ought not to be left out of account.[57] That these individuals are motivated by self-interest alone is an assumption which Plato and the Hippocratic author make – since their pecuniary needs are singled out by both authors – but which we perhaps should not take so readily for granted. On the whole, Plato seems more interested in restricting the private nature of this group's activities and in sentencing the ones who have specialized knowledge of magic to severer penalties than those who do not have such specialized knowledge.

It is in the context of sentencing the religious specialists who practice magic (*pharmakeia*) in his ideal state that Plato offers what amounts to a theory of magic. He first divides magic into two categories. The first involves harm caused by drinks, foods, or unguents, and owes its efficacy to 'harm by means of matter against matter according to nature'.[58] His main point here is that these substances have known effects on the body and Plato seems to allow that, call them what you will, these effects are basically biological. Poisoning someone, for example, for the purposes of erotic magic owes its effects to the toxins harmful to the body, Plato would argue, not to any "magical" attributes the substances were believed to contain. The second type of magic (*goēteia*) is based on the anxieties and fears produced in its victims and it operates primarily on psychological grounds:[59]

> The other type is that which, by means of enchantments and spells and so-called bindings, persuades those attempting to harm their victims that they can do so, and persuades the victims that they really are being harmed by those capable of bewitching (*goēteuein*). With respect to this and all such matters, it is neither easy to recognize what has happened, nor, if one knows, is it easy to persuade others. With regard to men's souls, it is not worth trying to persuade those who are suspicious of one another about such things, if some of them see molded wax images either at their doorways or at the places where three roads meet or on the tombs of their ancestors themselves, nor to admonish those who do not have a clear belief about all such things to make light of them.

Plato's catalogue of magical practices is not random but includes the most common forms of magic in the classical period, and we shall engage with each of them in later parts of this work. His characterization of magic, basing its efficacy as it does on a mistaken belief about causes and implying that it would disappear if only its practitioners understood physical causality, might almost be said to make Plato modern in his outlook. Insofar as people perform spells and binding charms, place wax images at doorways or on tombs, Plato concedes that his fellow Greeks practice magic, although he stops short of claiming that their activities exert anything other than psychological effects.[60] He further adds that such activities also reinforce the practitioner's belief in his own powers – a statement that might have come right out of the writings of Frazer, Malinowski, or Tambiah.

Magic and Causality

The impression from Plato that, apart from its psychological effects, this second type of magic exerts no real effect in the world brings us to the consideration of Greek *causality*. Our notions of causality are not the same as for the Greeks. The causal systems at work in classical Greek culture, to the extent we can reconstruct them, along with the types of inferences which they believed were derivable from them, are not intuitive and must be examined carefully. If the cross-cultural research we reviewed in chapter 1 suggests anything, it is that cultures operate within their own, unique frames of reference when it comes to causes and effects, especially when the causes are invisible. As we saw with the author of *On the Sacred*

Disease, the question before the physician was not whether there was an invisible network of causes, but which were the proper ones to diagnose in a given case of illness. So it is with magic in general.

The general problem of causality in situations of illness or injury was a topic of considerable interest to fifth- and fourth-century Greek intellectuals, including tragedians, historians, orators, and physicians.[61] Their explanations are revealing because they demonstrate that the determination of the cause of an event could imply competing and, at times incompatible views of agency. Nevertheless, multiple causes could determine the same event, but which to us would appear as inconsistent. It is noteworthy that in Plato's view, he locates the causes of his second type of magic entirely with the individual practitioner, and identifies the efficient cause of magic as his or her ability to persuade themselves and others that their actions produce real effects. At the same time, in other writings of Plato he seems to take the efficacy of spells, when issued by midwives and physicians, for granted, just as he takes pharmaceutical "magic" for granted, making it unclear exactly where he stands on magical activity as a whole. He is not alone, however, in this ambiguity. We have already seen the author of *On the Sacred Disease* wrestle with the similar dilemma of denying the efficacy of his adversaries' remedies, without denying their efficacy in principle. There are several reasons for this: first, magical causation was difficult to distinguish from divine agency, and before Aristotle intellectuals' attempts to rationalize the cause for an event typically included divinity as one possible factor. Second, like divinity magic operated according to the principle of *actio in distans* 'action at a distance', which is a medieval scholastic term that, I think, metaphorically captures the ancient reality. As an example, a binding curse tablet could be buried in a grave or well and cause an orator in court – at a distance in time and space – to lose his memory and voice. This means that even when other, more immediate causes for an event, such as loss of memory, can be found, it is nearly impossible to exclude magic as one possible cause, especially when there is already a cultural expectation that some types of events can be caused by magic. Third, Greek magic like most magic was based in volition, which means that a person used magic to achieve a desired outcome, and by doing so prompted a sequence of events toward fulfilling that desire. Volitional cause, as we shall see below, is often overlooked and can subsume within it what we might take to be more proximate, visible, and physical causes.

For many contemporary readers, what we take for granted in our causal thinking is largely the product of hundreds of years of social and legal deliberation. It is not inevitable, for example, that events perceived to be out of human control enjoy the legal status of 'acts of God', differently defined under contract and tort law, but rather the result of centuries of institutional disagreement that has worked out when breach of contract or liability should ensue. It is no easy task to come to terms with how differently ancient Greeks interpreted such phenomena. In antiquity an 'act of God', such as a natural disaster or a lightning storm, might not only have had divine causes, but the humans who suffered during the event might well have been regarded as morally responsible for it themselves. When we inquire into the causes of an event, assuming we have first stipulated what the 'event' itself is, we are confronted with many possibilities which grow as a situation is analyzed into its constituent parts. As one example, in contemporary Anglo-American jurisprudence, the proximate cause – meaning a necessary cause near enough to the target event (e.g., damage, injury, loss, etc.) in space and time to be considered a sufficient one – is often singled out to help guide the court in the determination of moral responsibility. However, proximate cause relies on a spatial metaphor that has long been recognized as inadequate to serve as a main criterion of responsibility.[62] In antiquity the argument of proximate cause was even less relevant than it is today because human agency and divine agency could overlap in the explanation of a given event.

We can see how this works by relating the famous late fifth-century case of the javelin-thrower.[63] An athlete practicing one day threw a javelin and killed another youth who ran into its path. Plutarch (ca. 50–ca. 120 CE) reports that Pericles (ca. 495–429 BCE) and the philosopher Protagoras (ca. 490–420 BCE) spent an entire day discussing whether the javelin, the athlete who hurled it, or the judges of the contests ought to be considered the cause of death 'in the most correct sense'.[64] It might at first strike readers as odd that the javelin itself could be considered a cause of injury, but in Athens there was actually a separate court for the trial of inanimate objects.[65] Inanimate objects could, on the contrary, be held legally and ritually responsible for murder in Athens. We shall look further at this phenomenon later when we discuss the use of figurines in magic in chapter 3. For now, suffice it to note that the discussion between Pericles and Protagoras gives some indication of how complicated the determination of cause could become. A similar case is at issue in Antiphon's *Second Tetralogy*, a prepared but not a real speech, where the further possibility is considered that the deceased himself was responsible because he ran into the path of the javelin.[66] An additional factor that is raised, but not considered in any depth, is that the youth's trainer might be responsible, because he had called the youth onto the field at the fatal moment. A further possibility beyond human action is then considered, and it is this possibility that we need to highlight. In the deliberation, the father of the dead youth remarks that it would not be just to acquit the javelin-thrower merely because of the misfortune of his error, because it is not clear whether the misfortune has occurred with or without divine influence. He says that if the misfortune occurred without divine influence, then the javelin-thrower should be punished for his error. But if divine punishment is at work in these events and has fallen on the youth because of some (unknown) impious action, then it is just not to hinder divine retribution – in other words, the javelin-thrower should not be punished.[67] Thus the consideration of empirical causality does not exclude divine influence. The possibility of divine influence in human action creates a situation in which mere human error may be implicated in an invisible network of divine retribution, and the effects of human error and divine retribution (the youth being run through by the javelin) may appear the same.

Although this example has not been exhaustive, it should give ample indication of the flexible system of causality available in Greece, whereby an event can be determined by factors human and divine, visible and invisible, present and past, as well as proximate and remote, both in a spatial and temporal sense. These considerations can be paralleled in Greek dramatic literature, which can sometimes exaggerate the realities of what was believed for effect. But in the remarks of a Phrygian slave in Euripides' *Orestes* we find the same array of alternatives when he is asked whither his mistress, Helen, had disappeared. He replies that it was either through magic (*pharmaka*), the arts of magicians (*magoi*), or that she was stolen away by the gods (1497–98), and it is important to see that these alternatives are not mutually exclusive. Like the religious specialists criticized in *On the Sacred Disease*, if I am confronted with an epileptic patient I now have to ask whether the seizure is due to human or divine causes, none of which may be visible, and if divine whether it is due to divine retribution for some impious act, or to divine retribution that results from magic, both of which could have happened in the past, or to some bewildering combination of all of the above. And because these causal conditions are not mutually exclusive they might all hold true for a given event at the same time.

Magic adds another dimension, namely volitional cause, because magic can be understood as an expression of intention and, in some cases, as a visible register or marker of intention. Although Plato does not discuss this directly, he does seem at least partially aware of how it works. Recall that in his mention of spells, binding curses, and wax figurines on one side of the equation these reinforce to the practitioners that they are in fact capable of harming their victims, while on the other side they reinforce to the victims that they really are the victims of harm.[68] We have a good deal of direct evidence from later sources of magic, such as the Greco-Egyptian magical papyri, which amply testify to the volitional nature of magic. Many spells begin with the assertion "If you desire (*ethelō*) to do such and such," then follow such and such a procedure. But apart from later evidence, it is a quite straightforward observation to say that spells and curses are the expression of someone's intention to harm or otherwise influence their victim. What Plato acutely observes is the reinforcement mechanism of magic as it pertains to intention. If I see a wax figurine on the tomb of my ancestor, whether I believe the figurine to be efficacious, I nonetheless now know that some enemy of mine intends to harm me, perhaps through evoking the soul of my dead ancestor. What I do not know is exactly how, beyond the physical evidence of the magic, my enemy's intentions will manifest in my affairs, and that is where the crux lies.

One of the most perceptive recent analyses of volitional cause as it applies to magic has been made by the anthropologist Alfred Gell. In the following quirky example, Gell explains how volitional cause can subsume, for instance, multiple physical causes, and still emerge as the socially salient explanation for a given event:[69]

> Magic is possible because *intentions cause events to happen in the vicinity of agents*, but this is a different species of causation from the kind of causation involved in the rising and setting of the sun, or the falling of Newton's apple, etc. For instance: here before me is this boiled egg. What has caused the egg to be boiled? Clearly, there are two quite different answers to this – (i) because it was heated in a saucepan of water over a gas-flame, or (ii) because I, off my own bat, chose to bestir myself, take the egg from its box, fill the saucepan, light the gas, and boil the egg, because I wanted breakfast. From any practical point of view, type-(ii) 'causes' of eggs being boiled are infinitely more salient than type-(i) causes. If there were no breakfast-desiring agents like me about, there would be no hens' eggs . . . no saucepans, no gas appliances, and the whole egg-boiling phenomenon would never transpire and never need to be physically explained. So, whatever the verdict of physics, the real *causal explanation* for why there are any boiled eggs is that I, and other breakfasters, *intend* that boiled eggs should exist.

Greek magic, whether in the form of Plato's figurines and spells or the religious specialists' acts of purification, is performed with the intention of realizing the practitioner's aims. But it is not sufficient in analyzing magic, as Plato implies, to recognize 'what has happened' in terms of physical causes and leave it at that, because physical causes can ultimately follow from intentional causes. In Plato's example the molded wax figurines are visible reminders to 'those who are suspicious of one another about such things' that harmful intentions have been expressed. Multiple causes, which can be visible and invisible as well as separated in space and time, have the potential to overlap to produce the same event.

This means that when some misfortune does occur for the person who believes himself to be the target of the figurine, other visible, immediate, and physical causes of the misfortune may be compatible with and explicable in terms of the harmful intentions of the adversary who made the figurine or had it made.

This point is worth stressing: magic in the Greek world is possible because physical causes are not excluded by intentional causes. Because intentional explanations are socially salient and therefore more relevant in the determination of responsibility, they can, on the contrary, subsume physical causes. A good example of how this works can be found toward the end of the Roman Republic in Cicero's *Brutus*, in which the effects of a basically Greek binding spell are described.[70] The event happened during a trial in the 70s BCE after Cicero had finished his defense of a woman named Titinia. He recalls that the opposing counsel, a man named Gnaeus Sicinius, suddenly forgot his entire case and blamed his lapse of memory on the spells (*veneficia*) and incantations (*cantiones*) of that same Titinia.[71] The point to stress here in this example is that the socially relevant explanation of Titinia's magic takes precedence, even when a more obvious physical explanation, such as fatigue or some other immediate and visible cause, might have been found.

Greek Magicians

It is within this kind of complex aetiological framework that we have to situate the activities of our veritable cast of Greek magical characters, the magicians (*magoi*), purifiers (*kathartai*), beggar-priests (*agurtai*), seers (*manteis*), and outright charlatans (*alazones*) named by the author of *On the Sacred Disease* and Plato. Much light has recently been shed on this group and the research shows that, with the possible exception of the *magoi*, apart from what has already been said, there is no clearcut way to distinguish their magical activities. Indeed, it is not even clear from the Hippocratic and Platonic descriptions that the terms for these individuals were used exclusively, since seers could perform purifications like the purifiers and magicians, and all of these individuals were apparently itinerant and scrappy in generating their own business interests like the beggar-priests. Frankly, they might all be characterized as religious entrepreneurs, offering their services to rich and poor alike who were looking to solve problems they otherwise could not through traditional temple cults and physicians.

The term 'charlatans' (*alazones*) described any number of quacks and braggarts, boasters and false pretenders in the ancient world, but apart from the general characteristic of deception it offers nothing distinctive to magic. In the context of *On the Sacred Disease*, the term is pejorative and general. The beggar-priests (*agurtai*) form an interesting category of mendicant vagabond, often from Asia Minor, who sometimes claimed prophetic ability. In Aeschylus' *Agamemnon*, for example, the Trojan princess Cassandra, who has been granted the gift of prophecy by Apollo but who is forever condemned to have her advice ignored, in some ways typifies the stereotype of the *agurtēs*. Although adorned with the professional garb of the seer (*mantis*), she frets that she may be a false seer (*pseudomantis*), that she is called a wandering *agurtēs*, a beggar going from door to door trying to hawk false visions.[72] Other groups of *agurtai* (known technically as *mētragurtai* and *mēnagurtai*) who may be relevant are the devotees of Rhea or Cybele, the Mother of the Gods, whom we have already seen could be invoked in Attic curse tablets. These groups originated in Phrygia, moved in bands, and were known for their ecstatic ravings and the tintinabular sounds emanating from their raucous worship of the goddess.[73] In the few accounts that survive of these worshippers, however, there is little that we can discern having directly to do with magic, although as cult devotees they no doubt proclaimed some privileged relationship with the Mother of the Gods herself.

Seers or *manteis* form another heterogeneous group, but in the classical period *manteis* who were attached to temples and to armies formed a professional class of seer.[74] The Pythia or priestess at Delphi, for example, was a *mantis* who inherited her position at the temple and occupied it for life. Military seers such as the famous Tisamenos and Hegesistratos from Elis, over whom Spartans struggled to obtain their services,[75] are also standard examples of the professional seer. These military seers were known for their ability to interpret the entrails of sacrificed animals, especially those of oxen, sheep, and goats, with the aim of announcing whether the gods favored a course of military action or not. As might be expected, the manner in which this was done was complex and involved interpreting signs on animal livers, such as any deformation of the lobes or discoloration, interpreting the health of the entrails generally, divining from the flow of the animal's blood after sacrifice, and placing the animal's bladder in a fire to divine the god's intentions from the manner in which it inflated and burst.[76] There were other forms of divination in which these professional *manteis* engaged, such as interpreting the flight patterns and cries of birds, but their sacrificial expertise is what principally defined them. It is important to recall here that purification through bloodshed was one of the *manteis'* activities which aggravated the author of *On the Sacred Disease*. Whatever the rationale behind their use of bloodshed in purifying epileptic patients, it is consistently to their facility in sacrifice and divination from the sacrificial animal's innards and blood toward which the evidence for *manteis* points.

The professional class of seer is sometimes difficult to distinguish from the itinerant *mantis* who wandered from city to city offering their services for hire, but it is generally the latter group in whom we are most interested. About these itinerant *manteis* we hear occasionally that they misappropriated their lineage in an attempt to distinguish themselves, as in the example of Deiphonus from Ionian Apollonia, the seer who sacrificed on behalf of the Greek forces at Mycale before a battle in 480 BCE.[77] Deiphonus was said to be the son of a renowned seer, Euenius, from Apollonia, but Herodotus reports that, according to what he has heard, Deiphonus' parentage is suspect and that he has gained work all over Greece owing to this false claim to be the son of Euenius. It is hard to infer from the evidence whether this sort of career was typical, but the balance of historical and literary evidence suggests that itinerant *manteis* were resourceful and unscrupulous, and that they preyed upon the gullible. However, despite the fact that some of our sources (such as Aristophanes) stereotype and ridicule the traveling *manteis*, they seem nevertheless to have carried on an active trade and to have made themselves indispensable even to the wealthier strata of society. Contrary to the impression that our sources sometimes give of their illegitimacy, it is almost certain that these *manteis* had a modicum of education and could read, since sources like Plato attest that they used texts containing oracular poetry of the kind ascribed to Musaeus and the mythical poet Orpheus.[78] It is probably to be inferred therefore that, in the face of limited Athenian literacy, the itinerant *manteis* were able through their privileged access to arcane material to exert some hold over the imagination of their clients.[79]

The purifiers or *kathartai*, like the *manteis*, also formed a group that can be divided into those who enjoyed professional status and those who, less legitimately, emerged in the midst of crisis to offer their services. Several of the more dignified *kathartai* were quite famous, and stories both historical and mythological abound of their purifying individuals of illness and madness, and of purifying whole cities in the aftermath of sacrilegious activities. Melampus, a famous archaic age seer, was known for having cured the mythical Proetus and his daughters using a squill, sulphur, pitch, and seawater.[80] In the latter half of the seventh century BCE, the Athenian nobleman Cylon along with some of his friends seized the Acropolis in Athens with a view toward tyranny. The Athenians attacked and, although Cylon himself escaped, some of his friends were killed at an altar, which violated the sacred immunity granted to suppliants seeking refuge at altars. Hence arose the famous curse (*agos*) and pollution on the Athenians, which the prestigious Epimenides of Crete was brought in to remove.[81] Epimenides was known to have purified several city-states, and it was said that he could purify people through rites from any damage whatsoever, physical or mental, and that he could even determine the cause of the damage. There is also evidence that Epimenides was a seer,[82] a point that once again reinforces the care that must be taken with the sometimes hazy boundaries such terms as 'seer' and 'purifier' denote. The activities of one easily bleed into those of another. In any event, unlike the *kathartai* mentioned in *On the Sacred Disease*, our evidence for Epimenides is on the whole without taint of illegitimacy or amateurism.

The purifier Empedocles of Acragas (ca. 492–432 BCE) deserves a special mention. He too was above the moral reproach reserved for the itinerant purifiers in *On the Sacred Disease* and in the historical record. Born of a distinguished family, accomplished in rhetoric, and ardently democratic, Empedocles composed the poems *On Nature* and *Purifications* (*Katharmoi*), presumably the remains of one poem,[83] and a prose work on *Medicine*. His magical feats (*goēteia*) were said to have been witnessed by perhaps his most famous student, Gorgias of Leontini, whose own thoughts on magic we will encounter later.[84] Empedocles' poetry in particular attests to a dignified reputation as a healer. To give some idea of how publicly well known his poetry was, we hear from more than one source that his *Purifications* were performed by a rhapsode at the Olympic games,[85] and that during this visit no one was more talked about than him in social circles.[86] Strikingly, though, within his poems he claims to be capable of transforming the natural order in virtually the same terms as the itinerant purifiers in *On the Sacred Disease* are said to have done. We recall that the Hippocratic author described the claims of the religious experts in the following way:[87]

> If they claim to know how to draw down the moon and eclipse the sun, to make storms and fair weather, rain and drought, the sea impassable and the earth barren, and all other things of such kind – whether they claim to know these things from rites or from some other knowledge or practice . . .

In one of the most famous fragments of Empedocles, he writes:[88]

> You shall learn all the remedies (*pharmaka*) that there are for ills and defense against old age, since for you alone I will accomplish all this. And you shall stay the force of the unwearied winds which sweep over the earth and lay waste the fields with their blasts; and then, if you wish, you shall bring back breezes in requital. After black rain you shall cause drought for men in due season, and then after summer drought causing air-inhabiting and tree-nourishing streams. And you shall bring from Hades the life force of a dead man.[89]

Both of these descriptions of abilities involve reversing or changing the order of nature, to the extent at least that making storms and fair weather, drawing down the moon, or drawing back the life force of a dead man[90] involve altering nature's course. It turns out that astronomical magic of this sort was also the stock-in-trade of magical stereotypes on the Athenian stage. In Aristophanes' *Clouds*, for example, it is said that anyone can readily purchase the services of a witch (*pharmakis*) from Thessaly, a region in northern Greece that was famous in antiquity for being the birthplace of, and commercial center for, witches. Their services include drawing down the moon and creating an eclipse, and Aristophanes regards this upset state of affairs as an opportunity for the unscrupulous to avoid paying their burdensome debts.[91] Empedocles' magical claims in the passage above, especially his knowledge of *pharmaka* that defend against old age and the returning of a man's life force from Hades, are somewhat out of line with the claims made by the itinerant specialists. But on the other hand, it is important to bear in mind that our evidence for their claims depends almost exclusively on the author of *On the Sacred Disease*, Plato, and literary sources. If it is argued that Empedocles' claim that he knows how to lead back the 'life force of a dead man' is another way of saying that he can 'evoke the souls of the dead' (*psukhagōgein*), as Plato reports about the itinerant specialists,[92] then together with his weather and astronomical magic, and above all his expertise in purification, Empedocles may reasonably be regarded as an exemplary religious specialist, perhaps on the order of a shaman.[93]

Nor did Plato and the Hippocratic authors regard Empedocles as merely one among the rabble of itinerant religious specialists. To the contrary, both drew from his writings on nature and Empedocles' four 'roots' (earth, air, fire, and water – themselves embedded in the excerpt of his poetry above in the references to the earth, winds, summer drought, and rain and streams[94]) formed the basis of humoural theory in Hippocratic medicine. This is quite a striking state of affairs, actually, because we have at least one report that Empedocles treated a patient named Pantheia whom the physicians were unable to treat successfully.[95] There are thus clear hints of rivalry between professional physicians and the religious specialists who, if we are to believe our sources, as a rule garnered a lesser repute. But apart from his social and intellectual status, there is no clearcut way to distinguish Empedocles' self-proclaimed magical abilities from those of the anonymous, wandering specialists.[96] Nor is it quite right to see in the earlier, archaic age purifier/seer, of the type exemplified by Melampus and Epimenides, a more ample repertoire of which only the 'manipulative' aspects of purification were inherited by the specialists decried in the writings of the Hippocratic author and Plato.[97] As we have seen, the specialists' procedures for divining the god or goddess responsible for an epileptic seizure are fully worthy to be called mantic. Moreover, Empedocles himself was considered a *mantis* and he is said to have earned this reputation when he sent away a dead woman alive. In a later account attributed to Heraclides of Pontus, we are told that for thirty days Empedocles kept a woman breathless and in a trance, her body without pulsation – and therefore to all intents and purposes 'dead' – and then he revived her.[98] For that reason he earned the name of *mantis*, in addition to that of physician. We might add that such a feat also clearly resembles shamanic activity as found, for example, in Central Asia.[99] It is not quite clear on the basis of which activity he earned the title of seer, except to the extent that *manteis* were known to communicate with the dead and evoke their souls (*psukhagōgein*). We have then in the accounts of Empedocles evidence for a set of technical skills which, while extraordinary, are not radically different than those of the anonymous and less socially distinguished religious specialists also called seers and purifiers.

Magoi

The one name to which Empedocles did not lay claim, despite the reports of his nearly divine status and his own suicidal efforts to confirm that reputation by diving into the fiery craters of Mt. Etna, was that of *magos* (μάγος) or magician.[100] The term and its family derive from the Old Persian name for priest *magu-* (nom. *maguš*) and is etymologically related to Avestan *moγu-*, which seems to have meant '(member of a) tribe'.[101] *Magos* and its sphere of application have received much attention from scholars because it is the basis, by way of Latin *magus*, of our term 'magic'.[102] Properly the term *mageia* refers to the activity of a *magos*, *magikos* is the related adjective, while the terms *manganeuein* 'to use of charms/trickery', *manganon* 'charm/philter', *mageuein* 'to be a *magos*/ use magic arts', *mageumata* 'charms, spells' and related terms are all derivative. Given the range of Empedocles' activities and the fluidity of all the terms considered so far, there is of course no very good reason why he should not have been called a *magos*, since his knowledge of weather magic and reported ability to evoke the dead make him remarkably similar to the skills attributed to Persian magi, who comprised from the viewpoint of the Greeks a significant and respected group of religious specialists.

The central problem with the philological history of the term *magos* and its derivatives is that they tell us little to nothing directly about the activities performed by this kind of individual. Moreover, when the Greeks were not speaking explicitly about Persian *magoi*, who were the servants of the Persian king and his empire and from whom the Greeks borrowed the term *magos*, their use of the term in the fifth century BCE regularly connotes charlatanry and deception, usually for personal gain. To give some idea of this unhelpful state of affairs, let us turn to the often-quoted first instance of *magos* in Greek. The attestation in question is found in Heraclitus of Ephesus (late sixth century BCE) but because it is reported by a later author, Clement of Alexandria (early third century CE), it is unclear how much of the passage is original. According to Clement, then, Heraclitus is reported to have prophesied that a punishment by fire awaited 'those who wander in the night: *magoi*, bacchants, maenads, initiates'[103] because these individuals improperly initiated others into the mysteries. There are anachronisms in the wording here of the terms for Dionysiac worshippers, bacchants and maenads, that have caused some scholars to doubt the authenticity of the fragment, but Heraclitus' characterization of *magoi* is clearly negative. It is not as clear whether the *magos* in this passage refers to Persian *magoi*, although that may be a reasonable inference given that Ephesus was under Persian control in the time of Heraclitus and Persia already had, by the middle of the sixth century BCE, begun to expand west into Asia Minor.[104] But the main problem from our point of view is that, even if we accept that *magoi* were associated with private cults and performed initiations that were out of line with mainstream civic cult, as Heraclitus suggests, we still learn next to nothing of what they actually did.

It is above all in fifth-century Greek tragedy where we find references to the dubious, non-Persian *magos* known stereotypically for his skull-duggery and avarice. Some of this evidence accords remarkably well with what we find in *On the Sacred Disease* and Plato. The most common example comes from Sophocles' *Oedipus Tyrannos*, datable toward the last quarter of the fifth century. When Oedipus begins to suspect that Creon and his court seer, the famously blind Teiresias, are collaborating to over-throw him, he denounces Teiresias as a *magos*, a weaver of plots, and a crafty beggar-priest (*agurtēs*) who only has sight when it comes to profit.[105] The association between *magos* and *agurtēs* is exactly that made by the author of *On the Sacred Disease*,[106] which attests in my view to the wide nature of this stereotype. It is also in this context that Oedipus men-tions the 'envy' or 'malice' (*phthonos*) of Teiresias[107] as the driving force behind his presumed political ambition. This term, *phthonos*, is often asso-ciated in Greek literature with magic and has led at least one scholar to argue that envy is therefore its principal motivation.[108] I am very sympa-thetic to this view, inasmuch as rivalry and personal ambition are frequently associated with certain types of magical accusations, such as those involving curse tablets, although it reveals next to nothing about why magic takes the shape that it does for the Greeks. However, recognizing that envy, malice, or ill-will (all covered by the term *phthonos*) play an important role in magical accusations gives us another way to demonstrate how magic is situated within an intentional context, defined by social relations. There are other examples of *magos* and related terms deployed within Greek tragedy with the same range of associations as those in the *Oedipus Tyrannos*. None of these references adds anything substantial, however, to the view that these so-named individuals were suspected of abusing their privileged relationship with divinity for private rather than public gain.

The deceptive uses to which magic was put by *magoi* in tragedy have little in common with the activities of Persian priests, or the magi proper, who worshipped fire, sacrificed, chanted, sang theogonies, interpreted dreams and solar eclipses, and performed numerous other religious rites. Our source for most of these references to the early Persian *magoi* is Herodotus, but there are important if scattered references in other historians and philosophers of the fifth and fourth centuries BCE.[109] With the exception of three ritual events mentioned by Herodotus, the balance of evidence suggests that the Greeks regarded the activities of this Persian priestly class as more or less legitimate in contrast to how they viewed the activities of a Teiresias or an anonymous beggar-priest. But the meaning of three ritual events appears less transparent to Herodotus, and may give us insight into where Greek notions of religious piety diverged from Persian. First, in a passage that describes the march of the Persian king Xerxes and his forces westward to the river Strymon in Thrace, Herodotus tells us that the Persians paused there and the *magoi* made a blood sacrifice of white horses to obtain good omens.[110] This sacrifice is on a par with the typical activities of the Greek military seer, although the context and the language used by Herodotus do not permit us to say with accuracy whether divination from horse entrails or some other type of divination was involved. The Greeks, for instance, did not divine from horse entrails. What is interesting is that Herodotus refers to this sacrifice by the verb *pharmakeuō* (from *pharmakon* 'drug, spell'), which is used elsewhere regularly in Greek to connote 'magic' in the sense in which, for example, the author of *On the Sacred Disease* and Plato criticize magic.[111] It is not clear whether Herodotus is unconvinced of the religious legitimacy of this rite, or whether he employs the verb because he is influenced by his own preconceptions about Greek magic. But his next example appears to raise further questions.

After the sacrifice at the river Strymon, the Persians passed over to an Edonian town named the Nine Ways. Learning that this was the name of the town owing to the number of bridges thrown across it, the *magoi* then for some inexplicable reason buried alive there nine boys and maidens taken from among the people of the country.[112] It must have struck Herodotus that this rite would appear unusual to his Greek audience, because at this point he says that burying people alive is a Persian custom. However, there is no confirmation from elsewhere that the Persians buried people alive.[113] Herodotus then proceeds to tell a story he has heard that when Xerxes' wife Amestris reached old age, she buried fourteen sons of notable Persians as a thank offering on her behalf to the god of the underworld.[114] The Greeks themselves had their own, largely fantastic, ideas about human sacrifice, but it remains an open question whether Herodotus regards the sacrificial rites of the magi in this instance as suspect. Nor can the veracity of Herodotus' account be taken for granted, since it appears that these sacrificial acts called for some qualification.

Finally, there is the account of the violent storm produced by the north wind, which the Greeks called Boreas, that lasted three days and shipwrecked the Persians near the promontory of Sepias, on the coast of Magnesia in Thessaly.[115] Herodotus reports that this storm destroyed upward of 400 ships, and the wreckage caused so much merchandise – including corn, gold and silver drinking cups, and many other Persian treasures – to be cast ashore that the Persians built a high fence around their spoils to protect them. After three days of the storm with no relief, the *magoi* sacrificed to the dead (*entoma*) and sang incantations (*kataeidontes*) to appease the wind with the help of magicians (*goēsi*), then they sacrificed to the sea nymphs Thetis and the Nereids. As far as incantations to control the wind and sacrifices to divinities who control the sea, the Persian magic seems similar to what we have seen with the religious specialists in *On the Sacred Disease* and Empedocles. But the *entoma* or sacrifice to the dead deserves further exploration. Herodotus uses the term *entoma* in one other place in his work, in a context similar to this one, when he tells the story of Menelaus' visit to Egypt and the storm there that prevented him from leaving. To overcome the bad weather, Menelaus committed an unholy act: we are told that he surreptitiously took two Egyptian children and sacrificed them as an *entoma*, or offering to the dead, to control the weather.[116] Although we cannot be sure that the Persian *magoi* performed human sacrifice at Sepias, their apparent proclivity for it as we have seen in other accounts at least supports the possibility.[117] Whether any of this Persian magic was effective is then called into question by Herodotus. He says that on the fourth day the storm ceased, or 'perhaps it abated of its own accord'. In these three instances, then, which all involve sacrifices not considered typical by the Greeks, Herodotus hints that he may not be entirely convinced of the legitimacy of Persian magic. Such a view is, of course, quite different than openly assuming that *magoi* of the likes of a Teiresias or an itinerant specialist are charlatans, and clearly for

Herodotus most of what the Persian *magoi* do is above reproach. On the whole, throughout antiquity the Persian *magoi* were positively valued by the Greeks as religious experts who practiced magic. But they do not really emerge as a group in whom the Greeks are particularly interested for their magical affiliations until after the Persian War of 480 BCE, and they do not become firmly branded as magicians by the Greeks until the final decades of the fifth century.[118]

Gorgias, Mageia *and* Goēteia

The term *mageia*, meaning on the one hand the 'activity of a *magos*' and, on the other, 'magic' in the looser sense defined by the author of *On the Sacred Disease* and Plato, first emerges in the fifth century. But when not used directly of Persian *magoi*, such as the famed Zoroaster, the term *mageia* is surprisingly devoid of any distinctive meaning in itself. In turn, what we are able to say about *mageia* depends on the magical activities, such as sacrifice, purification, and incantation, which are apparently covered by that term. The earliest known instance of *mageia* can be found in the latter half of the fifth century in Gorgias of Leontini's (ca. 485–380 BCE) *Encomium of Helen*, a work that attempts to rehabilitate Helen's reputation for treachery in the Trojan War. Gorgias was a very influential rhetor and sophist, whose oratorical style commonly lent itself to parody by his contemporaries, but he interests us mainly because of his pedigree in magic. Gorgias was said to be the pupil of Empedocles, and he is said to have witnessed the magical feats (*goēteia*) of his teacher.[119] These experiences must be held to account as we look more closely at Gorgias' own conceptualization of magic.

In the *Encomium of Helen*, Gorgias offers several reasons for Helen's deception and betrayal of the Greeks when she absconded with the Trojan prince, Paris. It could have been caused, he argues, by fate, the will of the gods, the decrees of necessity, or that she was carried off by barbaric force. But if it was speech that persuaded her, then this calls for an altogether different explanation. Speech in Gorgias' view – and we shall not miss his rhetorical interest here – persuades the soul, and words are incantations (*epōidai*) that can produce pleasure and avert grief. Filled with divinity, words can deceive and compel the soul to do things it otherwise would not through magic (*goēteia*). He then says that two types of magic have been invented, *mageia* and *goēteia*, both of which are errors and deceptions of the soul. The term *goēteia*, which we have already seen used several times earlier in the passages on magic from Plato and in reference to Empedocles' practices, technically refers to the activity of another common Greek term for 'magician', *goēs*. The philological history of *goēs* suggests that originally the term referred to a specialist in one type of lamentation for the dead, called *goös*.[120] It has been plausibly suggested that the *goēs* was skilled precisely in invoking the spirits of the dead, and although this characteristic cannot always be felt, in some authors such as Plato a good case can be made that such a distinction is still relevant.[121] Later sources seem to take for granted that *goēteia* refers exclusively to invocation of the dead.[122] But in Gorgias there is nothing to suggest that he understood invocation of the dead to underlie *goēteia*, rendering it altogether possible that already in the latter half of the fifth century, at least in some contexts, no such distinction in meaning was relevant. Both *magos* and *goēs*, moreover, are roughly interchangeable terms of abuse in Greek rhetoric, approximating something on the order of 'scoundrel'.[123]

As he develops his case for how the soul is influenced by speech, Gorgias appeals to another magical analogy that is revealing for its connection to Empedocles in a way that has not been noticed by scholars. He describes this in the following way:[124]

> The power of speech over the disposition of the soul is like the disposition of drugs (*pharmaka*) over the nature of the body. Just as different drugs drive out different humours from the body, and put an end either to disease or to life, so with speech: some words produce harm, others pleasure, others fear, while still others can embolden their listeners. Or again, by means of some harmful persuasion, words can bewitch (*pharmakeuein*) and thoroughly cast a spell (*ekgoēteuein*) over the soul.

The term *pharmakon* (plural *pharmaka*) to which Gorgias refers was notoriously ambiguous in Greek, because its range of meaning covered helpful 'medicine', harmful 'poison', as well as magical 'drug' or 'philter', all of which were plant-based concoctions with sometimes active psychotropic ingredients.[125] In the context of magic, it is the *pharmakon* and its effects on the body to which Plato referred, as we saw earlier, when he mentioned the drinks, foods, or unguents that cause 'harm by means of matter against matter according to nature'.[126] The noun *pharmakon* gave rise to several other terms in Greek related to magic, including the noun *pharmakeia* 'magic' and the verb *pharmakeuein* 'bewitch' above, that we will encounter in due course. For the moment suffice it to note that, in the context of Gorgias' remarks, he clearly intends the basic, medical meaning of *pharmakon* as well as the magical one.

What has been overlooked in this passage, however, is that Gorgias' pharmaceutical analogy for how the persuasion of speech works comes directly from the realm of purification, complete with a reference to the humours that are driven out from the body in the process. In the

Hippocratic treatises more than one theory of the humours was in circulation. However, the four basic humours (Gr. χυμοί, Lat. *humores*) – blood, phlegm, yellow bile, and black bile – which in turn corresponded to Empedocles' four 'roots' or elements – earth, water, fire, and air – are probably what Gorgias has in mind here.[127] For this perspective Gorgias has either his education under Empedocles to thank, or perhaps his teacher's writings such as the *Purifications*. The purification analogy is fleshed out by Gorgias in other remarks in the *Encomium*, when he compares how the soul is impressed by sight, just as it can be impressed by speech. Whatever is in the soul prior to a frightful sighting, for example courage, at the sight of an enemy in war is displaced or driven out by fear as if the danger were already present.[128] We are to infer that words and their ability to generate powerful emotions operate on the soul in an analogous way.[129] Although we cannot be absolutely certain on this point, I am suggesting that the basic procedure of purification was intrinsic to Gorgias' notions of magic. Along these lines, it may be of some interest that although Gorgias uses three different terms for magic, *pharmakeia*, *goēteia*, and *mageia*, the term *pharmakeia* and its related terms *pharmakon* and the verb *pharmakeuein* are regularly used in Hippocratic medical vocabulary specifically to refer to purgatives and purgation.[130] Purificatory remedies that involve purgation are central to the overall theme in Hippocratic medicine that recognizes purification as an essential restorative process for the body.[131] The Hippocratic term for 'purification' is *katharsis*, and its verb *kathairein* 'to purify' is from the same root that gives us the term for the itinerant purifier, *kathartēs*, who was so ardently attacked by the author of *On the Sacred Disease*. Thus there is an inherent ambiguity in both the *pharmakon* and *katharsis* family of terms between medical and magical purgation and purification, and this ambiguity could well be at the crux of the Hippocratic author's professional disagreement with the religious specialists.[132] In other words the conflict arises over the correct aetiology of epilepsy, not over the conventional practice of purification.[133] In any case, Gorgias' analogy between the effects of speech on the soul and magic works only if it is purificatory magic that is at issue. And he is as likely to share his understanding of purification with the author of *On the Sacred Disease* as he is to share it with the experience and writings of his teacher, Empedocles.

Other Magical Terms

In terms of our understanding of magic, Gorgias' *Encomium of Helen* demonstrates that by the late fifth century BCE, no fundamental distinction was made between the terms *pharmakeia* (as instanced by his use of *pharmakon, pharmakeuein*), *mageia*, and *goēteia*.[134] This is why it has been so important in developing a framework for Greek magic to emphasize the practices and implements associated with it rather than to rely on terminology alone. If anything, it is the fluidity of the whole range of Greek magical vocabulary that draws attention, although some terms retained a certain classical flavor more than others. The balance of terminology that we have yet to consider can be dealt with in fairly short order. From the ambiguous term *pharmakon*, in its magical not medical aspect, we derive in Greek the nouns *pharmakis* 'witch', *pharmakeus* 'sorcerer' (both of which terms simply refer to practitioners of magic who are female and male, respectively), the abstract noun *pharmakeia*, and the verb *pharmakeuein*. In many of the passages that we have seen, beginning with *On the Sacred Disease*, magical practitioners are said to cast spells or incantations (*epōidai*, singular *epōidē*). The term *epōidē* 'charm/incantation' literally means a 'song sung over or against', and in turn this very common word for incantation gives rise to the verbs *epaeidein*, *kataeidein*, both of which mean basically 'to charm', and the noun *epōidos* 'enchanter'. Although used mainly of magical practitioners, we have seen for instance in Plato that even physicians can occasionally have incantations at their disposal.[135] But in some contexts, as we might expect, *epōidos* can be used interchangeably with *goēs* in the abusive sense of 'charlatan'.[136] And *goēs* in turn, as we have seen, can be used interchangeably with *magos* to denote a fraud or deceiver. The term *goēs*, whatever its original association with invocations of the dead, is the one term that well into the Roman imperial period continued to connote charlatanry, even as it connoted magic. As has been pointed out by others, there is some late evidence that *goēs* and *goēteia* were considered more Attic – in other words more classically Greek – than *magos*.[137] This perception in conjunction with the generally positive reputation enjoyed by Persian *magoi* may explain why the complex of *magos*-related terms never achieved the same currency among Greeks in later centuries as its borrowed forms did among Romans.[138] The Romans did not share this same prejudice and, as a result, used the terms *magus/a* 'magician', *magia* 'magic', *magicus* 'magical' with much greater frequency.[139] As examples, Catullus (ca. 84–54 BCE)[140] and Cicero (106–43 BCE)[141] first use *magus* to refer to the Persian magi. Vergil (70–19 BCE) first uses the adjective *magicus* in his *Eclogues*[142] and uses, in his great epic the *Aeneid*, the more imaginative term *magicae artes* 'magical arts'.[143] This term *magicae artes* 'magical arts' is adopted by many authors in late antiquity, the Middle Ages, and the early modern period as a term of art. Although its underlying conception changed rather dramatically over that time, our modern term 'magic' owes its origin to the Latin forms used in this stretch of Roman history between the late republican and early imperial periods.

Conclusion

In rounding out our framework for understanding Greek magic primarily in the classical period, it is important to emphasize the balance that must be struck between the philological history of the most common terms for magic, and the few descriptions we have of actual practices. These descriptions include purification, blood sacrifices, invocation of the dead, the writing of curse tablets and binding spells (*katadesmoi*), the use of charms (*epōidai*) and drugs (*pharmaka*), and the fabrication of wax figurines. Claims attributed to magicians, on the other hand, are much broader and include drawing down the moon, eclipsing the sun, controlling the weather, and, in the unique case of Empedocles, resisting the onset of old age and drawing back the life force of the dead. The most transparent descriptions of magical practices from this period are in *On the Sacred Disease* and Plato; however, in both cases the descriptions are partially clouded by the authors' own biases against the legitimacy, largely on theological grounds, of magic. More specifically, it is the implied theology of the magicians, as Fritz Graf[144] originally showed, that is under attack by the Hippocratic author and Plato, according to which the magician's actions apparently entail control over divinity. But as I hope to have shown, in the case of *On the Sacred Disease* the author actually misconstrues the degree to which the specialists' ritual diagnoses and responses to an epileptic invasion by a divinity are appropriate – and appropriately deferential. Such an implied errant theology was further skewed away from conventional religious thinking in the works of Empedocles, who, unlike the itinerant specialists with whom he can readily be compared, actually claimed he was a god.[145] For whatever reason, what would probably have been considered borderline heterodoxy from a traditional Greek religious point of view did not prevent either the Hippocratic authors or Plato from adopting Empedocles' theory of the basic four cosmological elements. Nevertheless, we owe to this clash of perspectives in the late fifth and early fourth centuries between the physicians and philosophers and their magico-religious adversaries whom they chose to attack the first attempts to define Greek magic as an intellectual construct. The attempts are tendentious, to be sure, and it is still not altogether clear whether it is magical practices *per se* that are under scrutiny, or the specialists operating outside the mainstream services offered by official civic cult and academic medicine who should properly bear the brunt of their criticism.

In contrast to the intellectual defense of religious piety, Plato also proposes a psychological theory to explain the perceived efficacy of magic. While his views offer some insight into the mindset of his contemporaries, they seem to do little justice to the complex causal view which the Greeks held, according to which divine and human causes could produce identical effects in the world. Because sudden, unpredictable events could have multiple and invisible causes, and certain types of magic such as purification or curse tablets actually relied on divine intervention for their efficacy, it was difficult to know in any given circumstance the exact combination of divine and human causes that were responsible. In this respect, the invisible world was more important to the Greeks than the visible one, and misfortune for which an immediate and tangible cause could be found did not necessarily take precedence over an invisible and magical one. Moreover, the causes of magical action that were perceived as salient were primarily social, as Plato already realized. Magic expresses social tension by other means, and although it incorporates physical causes within it, magic is fundamentally given meaning by a network of social relations. 'Social' here needs to be broadly understood to include not only the living, but, as Lévy-Bruhl showed, also the extended, invisible community of divinities, *daimones*, and the dead with whom the living interact and participate. As we shall see next in the case of curse tablets, as long as the intentions of the living can be made to converge with those of the divine, daemonic, and dead, magic remains a vital avenue for the achievement of practical aims.

CHAPTER 3

Binding Magic and Erotic Figurines

꒰꒱꒰꒱

Among the most widely employed kinds of magic in Greek and, later, Roman antiquity is binding magic. The majority of the evidence we will survey in this chapter is culturally Greek, but because binding magic extends chronologically from the classical period to later Roman antiquity, it will be important also to consider material dated throughout the Roman imperial period. A brief consideration of Roman curses will help us to distinguish the implied forms of torture in Greek and Roman spells. Finally, we will consider the role of figurines in binding and erotic magic, and I will attempt to contextualize the use of erotic figurines within wider Greek and Roman attitudes toward statuary.

Binding magic takes two forms: (1) a binding spell or curse, written on a variety of media, including wax, potsherds, and commonly thin sheets or tablets of lead, which are then rolled or folded and sometimes pierced with a nail; and (2) a figurine, often made of wax, clay, wool, occasionally lead and bronze, and very rarely marble, roughly approximating the form of a man or woman whose limbs can be bound or twisted. The figurines sometimes have nails or needles pressed into them, or are sometimes buried in "coffins" made from thin sheets of lead. The term *binding* refers to the Greek term κατάδεσμος 'binding curse' (*katadesmos*, plural *katadesmoi*) used by authors such as Plato to label this kind of magic.[1] Scholars often use the Latin equivalent, *defixio* (plural *defixiones*), to refer to binding spells written on tablets.[2] The notion of binding can also be found in the language written on the tablets themselves, which often expressly state the desired action through the use of verbs such as *katadein* 'to bind' and *katekhein* 'to restrain'. Furthermore, the metaphor of binding can be visibly illustrated by the folding, rolling up, and piercing of the commonly found lead tablet. In the case of the figurines, the metaphor of binding is achieved through the literal twisting, binding, and piercing of the figurines with nails. Although a basic binding formula is standard, the binding spells have been divided by scholars into thematic groups that deal with competition in the realm of athletics, drama, forensic affairs, or business;[3] with erotic matters including sex and marriage; and with pleas for revenge or justice.[4]

The earliest binding spells found in the form of lead tablets date to the beginning of the fifth century BCE. They are found throughout Greek and Roman antiquity for the next thousand years, from areas such as Roman Britain to Sicily, Greece, North Africa, Egypt, the Levant, and Antioch. In addition to the most common medium of lead, binding spells have been found inscribed on potsherds, limestone, gemstones, papyri, wax, and ceramic bowls, but by far the preferred medium was lead or lead alloys.[5] To date upwards of 1,700 curse tablets have been found, most of which are written in Greek with a smaller number written in Latin. The usual process for fashioning a lead curse tablet involves pouring molten lead into a mold, then hammering or scraping it into a thin sheet with a smooth surface. The sheets are then cut into smaller tablets onto which the curses are inscribed with a stylus made of bronze or some other hard metal. Because the range of handwriting on the tablets varies considerably, from the more controlled and elegant to the semi-literate, it has been plausibly suggested that both professional and amateur scribes were responsible for writing tablets – with a tilt toward professionalism especially during the Roman period (first through sixth centuries, CE).[6]

As a rule many of the earliest tablets in the fifth and fourth centuries BCE, found for example in Attica and Sicily, list only the names of the intended victim, with no additional verb for binding and no mention of any of the divinities or *daimones* that figure more prominently in later tablets. Often the names are written in the Greek nominative (or subject) case, whereas on other tablets the names appear in the accusative (or object) case, which implies that a verb – one presumably to reference the action of binding – was understood. Some scholars have speculated that the verb of binding was recited in an oral rite early on, which may have accompanied the deposition of the tablet, and then only later written down, but the evidence is silent on this hypothesis.

Recent research has suggested a connection between the earliest, single-named tablets and the Athenian practice of ostracism in the classical period.[7] Athenians could decide to hold an ostracism once a year, in which case the names of the persons who would be exiled were written on potsherds or ostraca that were then cast into a designated spot in the agora or central marketplace. If at least six thousand votes were cast, then the individual who obtained the most votes was exiled from Athens for a period of ten years. The fact that many Attic curse tablets contain the names of well-known politicians, including Demosthenes, Lycurgus, Xanthippus, Phrynichus, and many others, strongly suggests that, in addition to being the targets of ostracism, they were also the targets of curse tablets.[8] Morever, we know of several binding curses from the classical period that were written on ostraca.[9] Much later in antiquity, spells written on ostraca are somewhat more common and there are examples in the Greek magical papyri (*PGM*)[10] which advise writing certain types of spells on ostraca.[11] Further research is needed to identify the exact relationship between curse tablets and ostracism, but their possible connection may indicate a magical dimension to ostracism as well as a political and democratic dimension to curse tablets, at least in Athens. Caution is in order here, however, since most ostraca do not present the name of the potential exile in a backward script, as is common in curse tablets, nor can we easily generalize the practice of ostracism in Athens to other city-states and regions.

As an example of an early and relatively simple tablet, consider the following Attic tablet, 4 by 1 cm in dimension:[12]

Σ Η Δ Ε Λ Κ Ι Σ Ω Σ
s ē d i e l k i s ō S

The lettering spells the name of "Sōsikleidēs" backwards from right to left, and although the name is spelled backwards, the Greek letters themselves are not reversed as in a tablet from Patissia,[13] in which both the name and each letter are backwards. When both the name and letters are backwards, we get a mirror image of the name. At first glance it is not clear what the intended effect is of mirroring a victim's name. Literate Greeks often wrote in a manner called boustrophedon, which referred to writing alternately from left to right and then continuing from right to left, as in the furrows dredged by oxen in plowing. The phenomenon of backward writing, moreover, is also observable in Greek vase painting, where the names and speech of individuals represented on the vase can be spelled backwards, in accordance with whatever design is aesthetically pleasing to the painter. Thus there are several non-magical precedents for backward writing. Be that as it may, this does not mean that magical connotations could not have developed around the metaphor of backwardness or reversal.[14] It has been suggested, for instance, that writing backwards reflects the reversal of fortune the practitioner wishes his victim would experience. This is certainly plausible, except that there are variations in the reversals that do not seem to have any rhyme or reason, at least none that has been detected so far. Another Attic tablet, for instance, reads, in English translation that imitates the Greek spelling:[15]

esehT
all
I bind
sēppihkrA
sēteniapE, etc.

'These all I bind: Arkhippēs, Epainetēs, etc.' Here, however, the Greek for 'these' is spelled backwards, 'all' and 'I bind' are spelled normally, while the names of the victims, not all of which are represented above, are all spelled backwards. The metaphor of reversal here may have visual connotations as well. The act of binding could be conceived as a twisting around or a reversal, as if one were binding another person with rope and moved over and under their body, forward and backward. For example, we have two late Roman curse tablets datable to the fourth century CE with drawings of a human entwined by ropes.[16] It is virtually certain that the individuals portrayed on these tablets represent the victim of the curse, which suggests that the act of binding was, at least by these tablet authors, conceived as binding with rope or bands. However, these are late tablets and we must be cautious not to assume that in our earliest exemplars the same type of binding action was envisaged.

Another visualization of reversal is illustrated in the famous example of the clay Louvre figurine[17] whose arms and legs are bound behind its back (discussed further below), and there are many figurines with their hands or feet pressed together, although not necessarily twisted backwards. Many orthographic variations from the Attic tablet cited above exist in other tablets, and this does not make it altogether easy to determine the rationale for reversing some words and not others, or some letters and not others. In later, imperial Roman tablets, palindromes become popular, some of which are quite elaborate and contain only partially intelligible names, but which suggest a collapsing into one of writing forwards and backwards at the same time. What we have, then, in the backward and mirror writing is a loose affiliation of ideas of reversal, which as always in magic admit of creative variation and elaboration over time.

Binding the Gods

The more immediate question concerns the meaning of the metaphor of *binding* in general. The tablets spell out fairly clearly the intentions of the user, and what they intend to change in their adversary through the binding of their person, perceptual abilities, and works, as we shall see in more detail below. But why is the metaphor of binding used and not some other metaphor such as being cut, hanged, trodden upon, or drowned? All would seem in principle to work. There are no definitive answers here, but in Greek mythology a very common feature associated with divinities is that since they cannot kill one another, they seek alternative means such as imprisonment and binding to restrict their adversaries' movements.[18] However, some divinities are recognized as divinities precisely when humans attempt to bind them and cannot. So for instance, after the god Apollo is born, nectar and ambrosia are poured for him and we are told:[19]

> But when, Phoebus, after eating the immortal food
> then golden bands did not hold you as you struggled
> nor did bonds (δεσμά) restrain you, but all their ends came loose.

Apollo's inability to be bound is a mark of his divinity. The plural noun δεσμά (sg. δεσμός[20]) comes from the verb δεῖν 'to bind', which in turn gives us the most common verb for binding in the curse tablets, καταδεῖν 'to bind down'.

The most striking instance of a divinity who cannot be permanently bound is Dionysus. After suddenly appearing on shore as a beautiful young man, Dionysus was captured by pirates, who thought he would bring a good ransom and so we are told that the sailors:[21]

> wanted to bind (δεῖν) him with painful bonds (δεσμοί),
> but the bonds (δεσμά) could not hold him, and the withies fell
> far away from his hands and feet

At this point the helmsman of the ship recognizes that this young man is in fact a divinity and exhorts the other sailors, in vain as it happens, to return him to shore. This passage is also interesting because it shows that the binding of Dionysus' hands and feet was attempted, which corresponds to the very common request in the curse tablets that the hands and feet (or arms and legs, χεῖρας, πόδας) of a victim be bound. Again it is the inability of a divinity to be bound that both marks him as divine and signals the limitation of human ability to exercise control over a god.

Several Greek myths make clear, on the other hand, that divinities can bind other creatures as well as one another. In the *Homeric Hymn to Hermes*, for example, after Hermes returns from having stolen the cattle of Apollo, his mother says that surely Apollo will come and bind his hands (or arms, χερσί) around his ribs as recompense.[22] Later, after Hermes takes Apollo to the cave where he had hidden the cattle, Hermes retrieves them and to prevent them from leaving he fashions bonds (δεσμά) for their feet, which miraculously take root and graft the cattle to the spot.[23] Given these stories, it may not come as a surprise that by the fifth century BCE Hermes, along with Hekate and Persephone, are the underworld divinities most closely associated with binding magic and are among those most often mentioned in the Attic tablets. The most powerful divinity that was bound by other divinities was Zeus, whom we are told in the *Iliad* was once freed by Thetis after Hera, Poseidon, and Pallas Athena had bound him in shackles (δεσμοί).[24] Nearly as famous is the story of Zeus' wife, Hera, whom Zeus once bound with a golden bond or chain (δεσμός) and hung from the heavens presumably for some treachery, and threw the other gods who attempted to help her from Olympus.[25] But it is the Titan Prometheus whose binding in the Caucasus mountains at the command of Zeus most visibly depicts the limits of even Zeus' power to overcome a divine adversary. In Aeschylus' *Prometheus* our namesake refers in his opening lines to the 'shameful bond (δεσμός) put upon him'[26] by Zeus, and the shackling of Prometheus generally can be taken to epitomize the limits of divine power. The reasoning here seems clear: since divinities cannot kill one another to achieve their aims, restraining them through binding is the next best measure to control their will or restrict their movements.

Stories that depict the early accomplishments of young divinities, as in the *Homeric Hymns*, furthermore employ the image of the inability of these gods to be bound as a trope and a distinguishing marker of their otherworldly status. It is more than likely then, even in the face of little or no direct evidence, that the figurative and literal use of binding in curse tablets reflects the widespread notion that this action in particular was associated with the realization of divine power. Of course the curse tablets are written by humans to control other humans, but they rely already in the fifth and fourth centuries BCE on the intervention of named and sometimes unnamed divinities to achieve their purpose. In later curses, the speaker of the curse sometimes claims that he actually is a divinity. While these examples from Greek myth do not prove that the notion of binding in magic comes from the association of binding with divinities, binding is a metaphorical precedent in Greek religious thinking with regard to constraining or otherwise controlling a divinity. The practitioners of binding magic can then be seen to adapt that archaic notion to serve their own mortal purposes.

Divine Agents

Because curse tablets as a rule require the cooperation of underworld divinities and powers for their execution, they were placed in wells, springs, hippodromes in the case of athletic curses, theaters in the case of curses between dramatic performers, and in the sanctuaries of underworld divinities, but most commonly in the graves of young people who had died early (*aōroi*) or violently (*biaiothanatoi*). More rarely those who died 'uninitiated' (*atelestoi*, literally 'incomplete') are invoked.[27] All told, these 'restless dead' are characterized by anger and implacability, and it is these qualities which the magical practitioner hopes to channel to bring his curse to fruition. The myriad ways in which archaic and classical period Greeks interacted with their dead have been recently surveyed by Sarah Iles Johnston.[28] I want here only to point to a few key features of the dead, especially as they bear on the shift in Greek attitudes toward them between the archaic and classical periods.

That the dead can be restless, for example, we see from as early as Homeric narrative when Odysseus visits the underworld. There he first encounters his companion, Elpenor, who had died apparently without Odysseus' knowledge after he and others departed from Circe's island. Elpenor is restless in the underworld not because he had gotten drunk, fallen asleep on the rooftop of Circe's palace, and then fallen and broken his neck, but because no one was there to bury and mourn his death properly. When Elpenor's soul (*psukhē*) speaks to Odysseus he tells him explicitly:[29]

> Do not go and leave me behind unwept and unburied
> when you leave, for fear that I might become a gods' curse upon you

Elpenor asks for a burial appropriate to a hero, namely to be cremated along with all of his armor and then to have his ashes buried in a tomb on the seashore. Exactly how Elpenor's restless soul will become a curse by way of the gods is not stated. But this and other examples in Homer attest firmly to the belief that heroes who are not properly interred are already a serious cause for concern among the living. This concern continues through the classical period and later, and was in varied ways made the basis of more than one plot in Greek tragic drama.[30]

By the classical period, a number of named and unnamed divinities are invoked in the curse tablets in different but conventional ways. It is understood that they will intervene in the desired action, although their exact role as agents is still not fully understood. The most common divinities mentioned in the early Attic texts, for example, are Hermes, Persephone, and Hekate, but even in Attica other divinities like Gē, Erinyes, and Dikē are sporadically mentioned. More precisely to characterize the role of the divinities in accomplishing magic, attention has been paid to the formula 'in the presence of (named divinity)', as found for example in the following Attic text:[31]

Biaios, slave of Philonikos,
I bind and Agathon
in the presence of Hermes (*pros ton Hermēn*),
the one who binds (*katokhos*)

Here Hermes, like Persephone and Hekate in other tablets, is invoked in his role as 'binder'. The speaker of the curse binds his victim 'in the presence of (*pros*) Hermes', but there is some difference of opinion as to the exact meaning here. In commercial and legal transactions in the classical period, a transaction can take place 'in the presence of' someone charged with the authority to oversee it, such as a magistrate, witness, or jury.[32] Hence one proposal argues that the divinity presides over the curse, in the sense that they authorize it to proceed. Another proposal views the preposition *pros* as geographic in reference to its deposition in the precinct or cemetery in which the divinity lives.[33] But neither proposal is as straightforward as it seems. One problem is that the construction of *pros* with a noun in the accusative lends itself to several potentially relevant meanings, including 'with', in situations involving reciprocal action; 'towards', 'for', 'at the hands of' when one indicates toward whom one has a positive or negative emotion; and even 'in the mind of' in cases of slander when one wishes to indicate the persons who are aware of it.[34] Any or all of these meanings might be implied by an expression such as *pros ton Hermēn* in the context of a binding curse, in which Hermes' role may range from formally authorizing the curse to being the one simply to whose attention the curse is being called. If research could demonstrate that a formal, contractual basis underlay the *pros* expression already in the fifth and fourth centuries, this could be used as further evidence for the professionalization of curse tablet writing earlier than the Hellenistic and Roman periods. Moreover, it would lend support to the view that, along with the elegant handwriting on some tablets, many of the curse tablet writers are moonlighting from their day jobs as scribes or some other type of professional secretary or record-keeper.

The community of underworld divinities and the dead needs further investigation, if only to explain how their services came to be drawn upon with such regularity. The roles of Hermes, Persephone, and Hekate as leaders of and viators with the dead become more prominent in the fifth century BCE. This change is especially striking in the case of Hekate, who as early as the eighth century enjoyed an altogether different role as a goddess whose realms of influence included the earth, sea, and upper air.[35] The change in status for these divinities partly results from the fact that Hermes, and to some extent Hekate,[36] had traditionally been associated with movement between the underworld and upperworld, while Persephone, who was expressly associated with passage between the living and the dead, reigned among the dead as queen to Hades. Other divinities with a chthonic dimension, such as Demeter, are also addressed in the curse tablets.[37] Regional differences are evident here as well: in the tablets found in Roman Britain at the sanctuary of Sulis Minerva at Bath, this divinity as we might expect is the most frequently mentioned addressee.[38] Frequently unnamed *daimones* are addressed, although not necessarily the *daimōn* of the deceased in whose grave the tablet is placed, since we have many tablets that clearly indicate the speaker is unaware of and unconcerned with which *daimōn* is being addressed.[39] Along with the *aōroi* and *biaiothanatoi*, what is important is that curse tablets, unlike purifications that may be addressed to divinities as well as to the dead, primarily have currency among the dead. Thus they are addressed either to the deceased directly or to those underworld leaders who are in the best position to galvanize the dead into action.[40]

There is some evidence that the divinities addressed were meant to read the curses. One less common but significant feature of certain Attic tablets is that they are epistolary, meaning that the tablet itself is apparently construed as a letter to the dead. Some scholars have suggested an Egyptian precedent for this practice, since so-called "letters to the dead" survive from the period of about 2300–1200 BCE. But others have rightly cautioned that more attention will need to be paid to the differences between these Egyptian letters and Greek curse tablets before such an influence can be established with certainty.[41] We have, for example, one Attic tablet that announces itself as a letter (*epistolē*) being sent to *daimones* and to Persephone,[42] while in another the speaker claims that he is sending 'this letter' (*tēnde epistolēn*) to Hermes and Persephone.[43] In a third, from Rome and written in Greek, the speaker addresses himself to 'you *daimones* and the other gods written on this lead tablet . . .', implying that the divinities would recognize themselves as the appropriate recipients.[44] One also thinks here of the "illiterate" texts, or pseudo-inscriptions at Bath, with Tomlin's conjecture that Sulis Minerva required her petitioners despite their illiteracy to write their own letters because "after all, the goddess would be able to read it."[45] These few examples are not enough to establish a clear link with Egyptian practice, nor are they enough to establish that curse tablets were originally conceived as letters,[46] but they all suggest that the invisible divinities to whom the tablets are addressed were imagined as capable of reading.[47]

Other tablets are equally interesting, if somewhat contradictory, in this respect. For example, in a third- or second-century BCE Attic text that binds Kerkis,[48] his words and deeds, in the presence of 'those who died before marriage' (ἠΐθεοι), the speaker adds, 'and whenever they read this'.[49] This clause appears to suggest that the untimely dead will read the curse. In contrast, the parallel, so-called "Pasianax" tablets,[50] found in a tomb, written in Doric Greek, and possibly from Megara, read:

> Whenever you, Pasianax, read this letter, but neither will you, Pasianax, read this letter (*ta grammata tauta*), nor will Neophanes ever make a lawsuit against Aristandros. But just as you, Pasianax, lie here without sensation, so will Neophanes become insensate and nothing.

If, as is now commonly accepted, Pasianax is the dead person to whom the tablet is addressed,[51] then the speaker seems to suggest that Pasianax will not be able to read it.[52] Whether the dead Pasianax is altogether incapable of reading, however, is unclear.[53] It is, however, implied in the exchange that Pasianax understands the nature of a lawsuit. As unremarkable as that may be, it reminds us that the extended social community of the dead understands how to operate in the world of the living. And at least for this tablet, the effect of the curse depends on a parallelism between Pasianax not reading the letter and Neophanes failing to make a lawsuit against Aristandros. But it is difficult to determine whether it is a question of Pasianax's choice not to read the letter, or his inability to do so, that is at issue.

Imagining the divine addressees as reading is a more significant point than it may seem, since literacy rates in classical period Athens at least are notoriously difficult to specify. If it is true that only a small portion of the citizen population was able to read, we may have here a hint that literate tablet writers were professional scribes, or at least conversant in a world in which such formal communications were involved.[54] On the other hand, the noun *epistolē* in classical period Greek can also mean the 'order' or 'command' that is being sent, exclusive of whether that command is sent in the form of a letter. We have then to ask whether the features of formal communication and letter-writing are owed more to the authors of these tablets, or whether they derive more generally from a cultural understanding of the tablets as letters or commands. So few of these examples survive in Greece that I am doubtful much headway can be made without further discoveries.

'Characters'

One feature of some curse tablets that has puzzled scholars and relates to the parameters of communication between the practitioner and his invisible agents is the appearance of 'characters' (χαρακτῆρες, *kharaktēres*) or engraved images. The noun derives from the verb χαράσσω 'to cut, carve, stamp, engrave', and can refer to cutting stone or carving wood, engraving metal, and so forth. These images, which sometimes recall letters in the Greek alphabet, but which are often tipped with circles or nodes, appear on curse tablets, amulets, public inscriptions, and in Gnostic treatises beginning in the second century CE. They continue to appear in manuscripts throughout the Middle Ages and into the early modern period. Their exact origins are unknown, but the best current theory as to their origin is astrological,[55] and we have examples of *kharaktēres* that correspond to signs of the Zodiac.[56] To give some indication of their perennial interest to magical practitioners, they are found, for example, in the famous medieval Arabic manuscript on magic and astral power, the *Ghayat al-Hakim* or *The Aim of the Sage*, known in the West as the *Picatrix*.[57] This work was translated in the thirteenth century from Arabic into Spanish at the bidding of Alfonso the Wise (Alfonso X, King of Castile and Leon, 1252–84), and was then later translated into Latin. The anonymous author's outlook is dualist – in medieval cosmological terms, dualism privileges spirit over matter – and his exposition is dedicated to showing how spirit can be brought down from its pure realm among the stars and descend into matter. Among the many detailed and sometimes bewildering instructions given in the text, the power of spirit dwelling in the stars can be attracted through drawing the correct *kharaktēres*, on gems and sometimes on lead tablets, to which the astral spirits will descend.[58]

   Kharaktēres, not unlike the writing on ancient curse tablets themselves, arguably function as vehicles of communication between the visible and invisible world, between men and gods, but what they indicated exactly is not known. It is important to recognize, however, that the basic view that *kharaktēres* function as communication developed over time, especially between the second and fifth centuries CE. Different authors held different views about how they worked. For example, the view that magic in general is a form of communication between men and gods can be found in the work of that expert on ancient magic – himself a defendant in a trial for magic – Apuleius (ca. 125–d. after 170 CE). In his defense, Apuleius writes that a *magus* is properly one who accomplishes whatever he wants through a certain force of incantation and a shared dialogue with the immortal gods, which he refers to somewhat obscurely as a *communio loquendi* 'association of speaking'.[59] It seems that for Apuleius incantations (*cantamina*) are the primary mode of communication with the gods. The view that men communicated with the gods in a special language and through special signs, such as *kharaktēres* and foreign names (technically called *voces magicae* 'magical utterances'), was articulated by both Christian[60] and Neoplatonist authors. But Neoplatonist authors such as Iamblichus (fl. ca.

165–180 CE) interpreted *kharaktēres* within the framework of theurgy (literally 'divine work'), which was a practical magical and religious program dedicated to bringing a practitioner into communion not with lesser divinities but with the ultimate divinity – the One. According to this framework, about which we shall see more in chapter 4, *kharaktēres* functioned as vehicles (technically known to theurgists as *sumbola* 'symbols') to convey divine power directly to the practitioner.[61]

St. Augustine of Hippo (354–430 CE) authoritatively established the view, which was to remain influential among medieval Christian authors on magic, that *kharaktēres* were a form of secret communication between humans and demons.[62] It is entirely plausible that Augustine has the passage of Apuleius referenced earlier mainly in mind here, only that he has replaced Apuleius' 'immortal gods' with what to a Christian, because they were not the ultimate god, could only be *daemones*. For Augustine and many medieval theologians after him (notably Thomas Aquinas, 1224/5–1274), demons were the only "real" agents capable of actualizing magic. For magic to succeed, it was the view of Augustine that certain consultations or contracts (*pacta*) were arranged between the magical practitioner and demons, and it is this fundamental view that became the basis for the development of medieval demonology and witchcraft.[63] For Augustine the 'magical arts' (*magicae artes*) represent a dangerous superstition, under which the books of diviners (*haruspices*) and augurs ought to be included:[64]

> To this category belong all the amulets (*ligaturae*) and remedies which the medical profession also condemns, whether these consist of incantations (*praecantationes*), or certain marks which their exponents call 'characters' (*characteres*), or the business of hanging certain things up and tying things to other things, or even somehow making things dance. The purpose of these practices is not to heal the body, but to establish certain secret (*occultas*) or even overt meanings (*significationes*).

The term Augustine uses for 'amulet', *ligatura*, literally means a 'binding', but refers to the Greek magical practice of tying an amulet (περίαμμον or περίαπτον, both from the verb περιάπτειν 'to tie on') or cords onto the body.[65] The point should not be missed that, although he is here concerned with magic used in healing the body, Augustine is broadly familiar with Greek and Roman magical practices. Ligatures, incantations, and *kharaktēres* are all equivalent from a functional point of view insofar as they create meanings (*significationes*), of which some may be occult, for demons. It is not entirely clear along which lines Augustine draws the distinction between occult and overt meanings, but a fair guess would have it that articulate spells are overtly meaningful, while rituals such as ligatures and images such as *kharaktēres* are occult. The meanings associated with magic are dispositive for Augustine. Indeed, he writes elsewhere that it is not merely by virtue of the magical operation (such as hanging an amulet around a sick person's neck) that the magic is efficacious, but explicitly by virtue of additional features such as *kharaktēres*:[66]

> But in the absence of incantations or invocations or 'characters' it is often doubtful whether the thing tied on or attached in some way for healing the body works by nature – in which case it may be used freely – or succeeds by virtue of some meaningful association; in this case, the more effectively it appears to heal, the more a Christian should be on guard.

Together these passages reveal that while Augustine is at pains to caution his readers to avoid magic, since its powers do not derive from nature, nevertheless he regards magic as potentially efficacious. It is noteworthy that Augustine places less faith in the distinction Plato advanced in the *Laws* between one type of magic that harms by means of nature, to which he would assign for instance drinks and food, and a second type which, by means of wax figurines and other 'signs', reinforces in both practitioner and victim the belief that magic is real.[67] For Augustine, the sign systems such as incantations or *kharaktēres* that instruct demons as to what effect in the visible world they have been charged to create, in conjunction with an operation like an amulet or ligature, are the sources of magical power. Accordingly, all magic can have potentially real effects in the world, provided it is accompanied by the secret communication with demonic agents.[68]

This theory that *kharaktēres* are a form of communication between men and demons must be treated cautiously, because we have very little evidence apart from Iamblichus' Neoplatonist formulation of what purpose *kharaktēres* served from the mouths of magical practitioners themselves. When we look to examples of magical tablets and papyri with *kharaktēres*, it is often difficult to know precisely the purpose they served. Many curse tablets and spells written on papyri, for example, have *kharaktēres* pictured on them. In some cases, at the end of a written spell there are instructions for the practitioner to compose *kharaktēres*, often detailing exactly where to place them.[69] In others, the *kharaktēres* appear along with a spell with no explicit reference to them.[70] In contrast to these, other tablets make more animated use of *kharaktēres*. Consider the following late fifth- or early sixth-century CE 'athletic curse' tablet from Apamea, a Greek city in Syria, in which the speaker addresses the *kharaktēres* directly for the purpose of hobbling the Blue chariot team in favor of the Green. The Blues and Greens, known in later antiquity for their

fierce rivalry, raced in the hippodrome in Apamea and the client who commissioned this curse did so presumably on the eve of a major race. Above
the first line of text, 36 *kharaktēres* are inscribed and the text itself begins
with an invocation to them:[71]

> Most holy Lords, *Kharaktēres*, tie up, bind the feet, the hands, the sinews,
> the eyes, the knees, the courage, the leaps, the whip, the victory and the crown-
> ing of Porphyras and Hapsicratēs,[72] who are in the middle left, as well as his
> co-drivers of the Blue colors in the stable of Eugenius. . . .

The author of this text conceives of the *kharaktēres* as divine agents
capable of accomplishing the binding magic stated in the text. There has
been speculation as to whether the *kharaktēres* here named and the 36
kharaktēr images on this tablet have some association with the 36 divi-
sions of the heavens in Egyptian astrology.[73] Whatever the exact reference
may be, the point I wish to make is that the *kharaktēres* addressed in this
curse are not merely pictographic signs, which to Augustine would have
served the purpose of conveying secretive meanings. Rather, here they are
conceived as animate beings called upon to realize the curse. As others
have noted, the magical papyri suggest that all spiritual beings have
kharaktēres as their signatures, as it were, which are in some way empowered.[74] But empowered by what or whom?

A third- or fourth-century CE recipe for a short binding spell found
in the magical papyri raises the possibility that the *kharaktēres* have
names:[75]

> Binding spell (*Katokhos*). Write on a tin tablet with a bronze stylus before
> sunrise the names: Khrēmillon Moulokh Kampu Khrē Ōphthō Maskelli
> (formula) Erēkisiphthē Iabezebuth. Then throw it into a river, or [the] sea
> before sunrise. Also write on it these *kharaktēres*: '(6 pictographs) Powerful
> gods, restrain'. Add the usual, whatever you wish.

Again we see the *kharaktēres* directly addressed at the end of this spell
as the divine entities charged with accomplishing the restraining action.
We also have examples in this excerpt of *voces magicae*, which combine
Coptic, Hebrew, and Greek elements. A few of these names are at least semi-
intelligible.[76] Whether the first six names mentioned, for instance, correspond to the six *kharaktēres* drawn is unclear. But as yet there has been
no systematic attempt to elucidate the meaning, let alone the function, of
kharaktēres.

Even so, it is one thing to say with Augustine that *kharaktēres* function
as signs to convey meaning (*significatio*) to invisible powers. In some sense

the *kharaktēres* in this view are passive vehicles of meaning. But in our two spells above, the magical practitioner addresses the *kharaktēres* directly as independent divine agents who will carry out the desired operation. In the anthropological terms of Alfred Gell, the social agency of the *kharaktēres* is more fully realized – they can hear spells, for instance, know the technical language of binding spells, in addition to understanding the intricate dynamics of chariot-racing – and the magical practitioner interacts with them as with other divine beings whom he may call upon to effect his aims. Therefore we must be careful not to retroject Augustine's views of *kharaktēres* – informed as they are by the Neoplatonist underpinnings to his general views of magic – into earlier periods, when *kharaktēres* first appear. Equally important to note is that in Augustine's formulation *kharaktēres* are essentially representational – in the basic sense of the term 'sign' – but the *kharaktēres* that are addressed as animate beings in our spells above cannot merely be representations. Instead they are living beings, in the sense presented in chapter 1, and as such have to be treated differently than if they were symbolic forms. The situation is still more complicated than I have indicated up to this point. If the *kharaktēres* mentioned in the two spells above are asked to bind or restrain a designated victim, some of the same *kharaktēres* appear elsewhere in the magical papyri to thwart such binding spells. Several of the same *kharaktēres*, for example, in the two spells above also appear in a *PGM* recipe for a 'Spell breaker' (*Lusipharmakon*).[77] This kind of irregularity in the appearance of *kharaktēres* is partly to blame for why scholars have largely avoided a sustained treatment of them.

Body Parts and Health

One of the most interesting shifts in the curse tablets from the classical period forward involves the progressive 'fragmentation' of the victim to be bound. In many of the earliest Attic tablets, we find only a name (in the nominative or accusative), then a verb such as *katadein* or *katekhein* appears in the first person with the name, and then key intellectual and physical parts of the body appear along with the name or names of the victims as features to be bound. This progression does not hold across all geographic regions in which tablets have been found – the earliest tablets from Selinus being an important exception[78] – but the pattern is widespread enough to deserve further scrutiny. We have already seen some examples of the simpler tablets. Let us now look at those that show increasing complexity. A typical example of a late fifth- or early fourth-century Attic tablet that binds more than a name is the following:[79]

> Of Dēmētrios I bind
> his spirit (*psukhē*) and mind (*nous*), feeling (*thumos*)
> Of Telesarkhos: I bind
> his spirit and mind, feeling. . . .

Another simple Attic text adds the equally common features of the tongue, hands, and feet (abbreviated):[80]

> . . . Theodotē
> I bind
> both her
> and her tongue
> and hands
> and feet . . .

The common explanation that has been offered for why these features of the individual start to be singled out for mention in the tablets is that they capture the intellectual and physical faculties of the victim. We have already referred to the example of Gnaeus Sicinius, who in the 70s BCE suddenly forgot his entire case and blamed his lapse of memory on the spells and incantations of the defendant, Titinia.[81] This sudden loss of mental faculty seems to accord with the frequent mention in the tablets of binding the soul, tongue, and feeling, and with the occasional mention of the head, words, speech, and even memory, of the victims. In a more general sense the binding of the *psukhe*, here roughly translated as 'spirit', has been taken to refer to the victim's will, which is bound so as to motivate the victim either to do or not to do something. What has not been adequately explained, however, is the binding of hands and feet (or arms and legs), as well as in later tablets the veritable proliferation of other body parts that can be bound.[82] It is not clear whether, for instance, the command to bind hands and feet ought to be taken literally. In cases where the mental faculties of the victim are at issue, one wonders what restraining the victim's hands and feet – and essentially rooting the individual in place – accomplishes.

The misplacement is especially clear in curses having to do with staunching a victim's ability to speak, whether in a judicial or a more general social context. One of two Attic tablets about a fellow named Mikion, which was found in the nineteenth century in a grave in Peiraieus, can be taken as illustration:[83]

> Mikion
> I took
> and I bound

his tongue,
and soul,
and hands
and feet,
and if he is about
to say something wicked about Philon,
may his tongue become lead.
Pierce his tongue, and may his possessions
which he has or manages, become displaced and portionless.

For all intents and purposes this may be a judicial curse and Mikion may well be a prosecutor in an upcoming case against Philon, perhaps like that of Sicinius against Titinia. But even if we cannot establish the context of this curse with certainty, it is the intellectual faculties that are at issue, not Mikion's hands and feet. Therefore we can say with some certainty that the hands and feet, no less than the tongue and soul, comprise a basic anatomical formula. Hands and feet are part and parcel of a binding formula that requires the mention of intellectual and physical faculties.

There may be more than meets the eye, however, in the mention of hands and feet. I have already noted that in Greek mythology we have several accounts of mortal and divine attempts to bind divinities, often by their hands and feet, only to discover among immortals that such binding is at best temporary, and among mortals that such binding may jeopardize their lives (e.g., Dionysus, in the *Homeric Hymn to Dionysus* 12–14). These mythological parallels provide us with a quasi-historical context – *quasi* because Greek myth typically contains some distorted history – in which to view binding magic. But there may still be a broader cultural framework in which binding the faculties and limbs figures as such. One direction that has not been explored is that binding a victim's mental and physical faculties is a realization, through magic, of Greek notions of disability and impairment. The most famous disabled dramatic character on the Athenian stage was Oedipus, whose own ankles were pinned or pierced by his father when he was exposed, presumably to hobble his ghost after death and prevent it from seeking revenge.[84] As noted earlier, piercing a folded tablet with a nail gives visible expression to the metaphor of binding, and some tablets expressly call for piercing (*kentein*) the victim's body parts.[85] We may regard Oedipus, then, as having effectively undergone a binding of his limbs, even if magic *per se* is not mentioned in the context of his story.[86]

The culturally relevant understanding of disability as the inverse of binding extends further. We have a late passage from the physician Soranus of Ephesus (98–138 CE), whose *Gynaecology* is unique among Greek medical texts for its description of the main features of health in a newborn child.[87] Soranus writes that the child:[88]

should be perfect in all its parts, limbs and senses, and should have unblocked passages, namely of the ears, nose, throat, urethra, and anus. The natural movements of each limb should neither be heavy nor weak, the limbs should bend and stretch, its shape should be appropriate, and it should be very alert.

If we interpret binding magic in terms of a Greek definition of health, we can see that magic inverts the very markers of health identified by Soranus. A newborn's limbs and senses should be perfect and flexible in movement, and none of its passages should be blocked. Binding magic aims to accomplish just the reverse: limbs and senses are restrained and thereby impaired, with the intent of rendering the victim incapable of achieving his aims. In some cases, as in the judicial curses we have seen, the aim is actually to render the victim unalert or insensate, insofar as his memory, his speech, and his ability to present a lawsuit will fail. There has been some effort to situate binding magic into a broader cultural understanding of disability or deformity,[89] but this is still an area that needs further research. In any case, to the extent that Soranus' views can be taken as generally representative of earlier generations, we may have cause to argue that binding magic depends for its appeal on the inversion of cultural notions of health – not in general, but in the specific definition of health with regard to the freedom of the senses and limbs.

Later stories, on the other hand, for example those of Theophilus and Theodōros of Cyprus, make the relationship between binding magic and lameness explicit. In the case of Theophilus, whose hands and feet had been magically bound, thus rendering him painfully lame and paralyzed, a carved bronze image in human form was removed from the sea. When the four nails in the image driven into each hand and foot were extracted, Theophilus recovered and regained movement.[90] Theodōros of Cyprus was similarly lamed by magic, and when the unspecified 'instrument of the sorcerer' was discovered buried near the doorway to his bedroom he too, we are to infer, recovered from his disability.[91] Although late (sixth century CE), these stories both illustrate that in late antiquity binding magic was understood to have the literal effect of pinning the hands and feet of its victims. However, we must be cautious not to retroject that view to earlier eras in which binding spells served apparently to block their victims' will rather than literally to transfix them.

In various parts of Greece and Rome, the practice of abandoning congenitally deformed or disabled infants in the wilderness until death was sanctioned by law.[92] This may run counter to our modern sensibilities but, in Greece for instance, the birth of a deformed child (known as a *teras* 'monstrous birth'[93]) had religious implications, insofar as it was interpreted to mean that the parents or community members were being punished by the gods. Some but not all Greek city-states, like Sparta, had legislation that specifically enjoined the tribal elders of deformed children to expose them.[94] Rearing a child in Sparta was a state decision, and we are told that newborns were examined by the elders of the tribes to determine their fitness and health. Should the infants be found mentally or physically defective, the Spartan elders ordered the father to deposit the child at a predetermined location actually called Apothetai, or "Exposure Place," at the foot of a local mountain. In this way it was the state that determined whether its members were of advantage to it or to themselves.

On the same principle, Plutarch informs us, Spartan women bathed their newborns not in water but in wine to test their constitutions. He then reports the general view that bathing children in wine specifically throws epileptics and sickly infants into convulsions, whereas healthy children are tempered and strengthened in body by it.[95] Without knowing for certain, I suspect the Spartan mothers engaged in this practice because they understood the antiseptic properties of alcohol, and knew that the strong fumes would provoke some kind of physical reaction in the infants. But the rationale as reported by Plutarch has other implications for magic. We have already seen in the Hippocratic treatise *On the Sacred Disease* the connection between epilepsy and magic, and the narrower correspondence between the binding language of magic and the description of epileptics as 'held down' or 'restrained'. Although magic is not mentioned explicitly in the context of this Spartan practice, nevertheless it is suggestive that epilepsy is one kind of congenital ailment for which the mothers are specifically looking. The symptoms of epilepsy invert the free movement of the limbs and the alertness of the mind that mark a healthy infant. If these Spartan examples have wider currency, we may go so far as to say that binding magic aims, in effect, to engender the symptoms indicative of epilepsy. The larger point that needs to be made, however, is that conceptions of magic operate within cultural categories, such as Greek notions of health. Accordingly, the effects of binding magic – whether it restrains the limbs or dumbfounds the awareness – are not random, but are intelligible within prevailing cultural conceptions of health. Taken together, Soranus and Plutarch both suggest that mental and physical notions of Greek health are in some fundamental sense defined in opposition to epilepsy.

Situating binding magic within broader Greek or Roman notions of health does not preclude other explanations for how to interpret its peculiar features. As we move forward in time, later curse tablets proliferate the number of body parts that can be bound. There is no clear reason why this should be the case, although analogies have been proposed with the progressively more detailed language found in Greek and Roman legal documents and contracts. It turns out that this may be more than an incidental point of convergence. A cache of curse tablets found at the Stoa of Attalos in the Athenian Agora dated to the mid-third century CE are all written by the same hand.[96] The aims of these tablets differ – with some written to attack athletes and prostitutes, while the purpose of others is less clear – and at least one tablet employs a common formula but leaves blank spaces for the insertion of the victim's name.[97] The curse tablets in this find point clearly toward the professionalization of tablet-writing, as we have already noted, and it is not hard to imagine that a local scribe or cleric was moonlighting for extra pay. As another example, an analysis of the language on curse tablets found at the temple of Sulis Minerva at Bath, England, shows clear affinities with Roman legal and financial terminology.[98] Words commonly found in catalogues and summaries are also present, giving the impression that the authors of these texts were clerks. The petitionary formulae and language of the Bath tablets suggest that the appeal to otherworldly powers was not altogether different than what one might expect in an appeal to a local magistrate or military commander. Here again we see how magic unfolds one sphere of cultural interaction into another. But whether such a turn toward professionalism and legalism is adequate to explain the fragmentation, or dismemberment, of the body that we find in later tablets is an open question.

There are numerous examples of curses and curse tablets with extended lists of body parts. They begin to appear in the late classical period, but then increase during the Hellenistic and Roman periods. To take a Greek example first, consider a second-century CE Athenian tablet that targets its victim apparently for a theft.[99] After addressing 'underworld messengers', and underworld Hermes, Hekate, Pluto, Korē, Persephone, the Fates, all the gods, and Cerberus, the canine guardian of Hades, the speaker of this tablet 'enrolls . . . the hair, brains, mouth, teeth, lips, shoulders, arms, breast, stomach, back, lower belly, pubes, thighs, . . . toes, nails' of the victim.[100] We may compare this Athenian tablet above to a Roman tablet found in a tomb near the amphitheater at Minturnae, undated but almost certainly late.[101] This tablet was placed on the skull of the deceased in the tomb, and was found along with an unusually well-sculpted marble figurine of a woman with braided hair, 11 centimeters tall. The figurine was presumably identified as the woman, Tyche, who is the target of the curse. The curse itself aims at the general demise of Tyche and her property. After dedicating her to the infernal gods, the speaker enumerates for binding, from head to toe, Tyche's head, hair, shadow, skull, brow, eyebrows, mouth, nose, chin, jaws, lips, speech, face, neck, liver, shoulders, heart, lungs, intestines, stomach, arms, fingers, hands, navel, bladder, knees, legs, ankles, and the soles of her feet.

The usual explanation that individual features are singled out to capture the intellectual and physical faculties of the victim seems to fall short in these examples. Nor are professionalization and creeping legalism in themselves adequate explanations. The motif of cursing someone from head to toe may have a non-Greek origin,[102] and further research may help us to understand this pattern better. It has been suggested that these tablets ought to be viewed as part of a process of gradual accumulation, which perhaps culminates in a tablet that curses 'all the 365 muscles of the body'.[103] Two recent approaches have more appeal. The first draws upon the anthropological work of Annette Weiner[104] and focuses on the rhetorical value of listing as a weapon that strips its victim of protection.[105] The protection at issue in Weiner's model is a form of social shame that is maintained in normal social interaction and discourse through euphemism, discretion, and avoidance. Magical language employs what she calls 'hard words' that serve to destroy a victim's social autonomy and anatomy and that 'recreate perceived realities'.[106] This approach has the advantage of highlighting the rhetorical strategies that may be at work behind the detailed mention of body parts. Such strategies are harder to discern, however, than may be realized. The main proponent of the rhetorical approach, Richard Gordon, argues that:[107]

> the remorseless enumeration of parts of the body enables the practitioner imaginatively to dismember the victim so that the curse moment, the period of the practitioner's projective fixation upon the victim, can be extended as long as possible.

I am sympathetic to Gordon's approach, but fear that he has projected his own psychological understanding of magic onto the imagined practitioners and/or composers of these tablets. The evidence does not allow us to "get inside" the head of an ancient practitioner, despite our best efforts, nor are matters made easier when we confront the reality that curse tablets were often composed by others and commercially sold. We simply cannot trust that the first-person ("I") speaker of a curse tablet tells us anything personal, which in turn prevents us from making any claims about a practitioner's "imaginative fixation." There are certainly rhetorical dimensions to the tablets, but they are better understood within the broader context of a collective magical tradition, whose boundaries by definition are permeable with those of other cultural and social institutions.

A second approach focuses on how these later tablets reflect methods of torture derived from judicial punishment. The proponent of this approach, Henk Versnel, has shown that some Roman tablets make unequivocal mention of the rack as an instrument of torture.[108] He cites several parallel references to torture that single out particular body parts, especially in Hebrew texts, and suggests that curse tablets that betray Jewish and more generally Near Eastern influence tend to make more explicit references to torture. However, despite the fact that the Romans instituted increasingly crueler corporal punishments to slaves and, in later times, to *humiliores* ('persons of lower class'), there is little evidence that lists of body parts of the kind that we find in our tablets have any parallel in Greek or Roman penal codes or practices.[109] Moreover, the same phenomenon of enumerating body parts also appears in spells that serve purposes other than punishment, such as a fifth-century CE Coptic Christian spell, written on papyrus, to protect a woman in childbirth.[110] After invoking 12 archangels with 12 bowls filled with water, the speaker says, 'When I cast it into the fire, you must fill the 12 bowls with fire (and) cast them into her heart – her lung(s), her heart, her liver, her spleen, (into all) the hundred twenty-five body parts'.[111] Thus in the listing of body parts, we have again to do with a phenomenon that is independent of the aims to which it is put within particular magical formulae.

Note that in our sample of Athenian and Roman tablets, we observe a heightened interest in naming external physical features and limbs, and in the Roman tablet, in addition to external features, a mixture of internal and external organs was named. It might be argued that some of these internal organs have a role to play in other institutional practices, such as in the widespread practice of divination. For instance, organs that comprise the viscera, especially the liver, have an established history in Greek and Roman divination. The liver has a long history in Greek and Roman thought as the source of emotion and as the principal organ, both in animals and humans, through which the gods communicated their desires to men.[112] But body parts such as the stomach or navel, let alone the chin and knees, have no such traditional place. To the extent that internal organs become more prominent in curse tablets, it might on the other hand be argued that an increased understanding of human anatomy is responsible. Greek natural philosophers and medical writers, including the Presocratics, Hippocratics, and Aristotle, advocated the dissection of animals as a means to study the human body, since there were strong religious taboos until the Hellenistic period against dissecting or vivisecting human bodies. Both dissection and vivisection of human subjects, typically criminals, begin in the Hellenistic period in Alexandria by major figures in the history of medicine such as Herophilus and Erasistratus.[113] The connection between medical knowledge of anatomy and the more frequent mention of anatomical features on curse tablets may deserve further research. Even if one could demonstrate, however, that new anatomical knowledge was disseminated through academic learning to the populace, it would still not explain why naming individual body parts became more salient in magic.

There is one area of research in this regard that has not been given adequate consideration. Naming body parts in curse tablets shares similarities with the Greek and Roman religious practice of dedicating ex-votos modeled on human body parts. The term ex-voto refers to an offering made after the fulfillment of a vow, as when an individual prays to a divinity to heal an ailment. Should that ailment be healed, in Greece and Rome it was appropriate to offer a figurine, a sacrificial animal, and so forth, at the temple of the relevant deity as a thank-offering. There is, however, in both Greece and Rome a class of votive figurines that directly concerns the healing of diseases and these are terracotta models of human parts – including human heads, eyes, ears, noses, mouths, jaws, arms, breasts, hearts, lungs, bladders, hands, genitals, uteri, legs, and feet. These body part votives have been found at sanctuaries in classical period Greece – most prominently at the Asclepium in Epidaurus – and at Republican Roman sanctuaries as early as the fourth century BCE throughout central Italy and Sicily.[114] Most of the votives found to date are made of terracotta, but body part votives have also been found made of gold, silver, amber, and wood. In the opinion of one expert who has studied these votives, the Greeks had a preference for external human organs, whereas Romans modeled internal organs more often and generally made more ex-votos than Greeks.[115] There is as yet no explanation for the difference between the Greek and Roman sensibility toward what has been called 'sacred anatomy', but one avenue of research should seek to document whether, on the whole, Roman curse tablets actually refer more often than Greek ones to internal organs, and then explore what that might mean.

The entire phenomenon of body part votives offers a suggestive context in which to understand curse tablets. At the temple of Sulis Minerva at Bath, for example, both curse tablets that enumerate body parts and medical ex-votos have been found. This may not be surprising insofar as the goddess Sulis, like many Greek and Roman divinities generally, exercised multiple functions for her devotees. The votives are the body parts that have been healed by a divinity, whereas the anatomical curse tablets seek to disable individual body parts. The correspondence is not exact between the Bath tablets and ex-votos but may have generally to do with the health of a victim, as we suggested earlier. Nonetheless, consider tablet no. 97, which deals with the theft of a silver ring:[116]

> . . . so long as (someone), whether slave or free, keeps silent or knows anything about it, he may be accursed in (his) blood and eyes and every limb,

or even have all (his) intestines quite eaten away, if he has stolen the ring or been privy to (the theft).

In many respects this list resembles the examples we have already seen, which came from regions largely outside of Britain. The mention of 'blood' (*sanguis*) is common in the Bath tablets and may be peculiar to Britain,[117] but this formula seems generally to mean that the health of the accursed is at issue. Among the votive objects found at the Bath site is a tin mask of a man, with Celtic features, and with eye sockets cut out and each backed by a roundel of metal, which suggests that the sockets had at one time been filled with glass. After comparing this mask to numerous others, mostly of bronze, the editors write that the mask "is probably to be classed with medical ex-votos and represents a visitor to the shrine who came to be healed in body or mind rather than a deity."[118] A pair of ivory breasts cut from a tusk, as well as a bronze breast made from a sheet, was also found. They are compared by the editors, among other things, to the medical votives found for instance at Ponte di Nona, a sanctuary 15 kilometers east of Rome, in which a cache of votives the majority of which were feet and eyes was discovered.[119] Whether the breasts at Bath were originally worn by a lactating woman or were made specifically for dedication is unknown, but they demonstrate "that Sulis was invoked in her capacity as a healer (equivalent to Minerva Medica)."[120]

This comparison at Bath is not detailed enough for us to draw the conclusion that the body parts being healed were the same as those targeted in the curse tablets. Nor do I wish to imply a prediction that a given temple site that contains anatomical curse tablets will also contain medical votives. More research along these lines would certainly have to be done first. Rather, contrary to current scholarship, which at present does not bring these phenomena into relation with one another, I am suggesting that both project the body, although through different media, as fragmented or dismembered and invite a divinity to act upon its parts. Along with the possibility of increased anatomical knowledge coming from the centers of academic medicine (e.g., Alexandria, Ephesus, Rome), it is hard not to think that the users of medical ex-votos bolstered the recognition among magical practitioners – since as in the case of Bath they surely frequented the same sacred sites, if they were not occasionally the same persons – that individual body parts needed singling out to attract the attention of the relevant invisible agent. Surely curse tablets accumulate body parts while ex-votos single them out, but underlying both practices is a conception of the body as extensible and anatomically distributable in space and time.

The psychology behind medical votives and curse tablets is extraordinarily difficult to pinpoint. Certainly the ex-votos were dedicated to divinities in the aftermath of healing, and to that extent they advertise the power of the healing divinity, much as aretalogies do. But we do not know, for example, whether the votive dedication was meant to entrust that healed body part to the care of the divinity in the future as well, which would suggest that it was invested with contagious magical properties. As we shall explore below in more depth in the case of figurines, the balance of evidence for Greeks and Romans suggests that a given manufactured body part entrusted to a divinity's care was taken to be a real, not a symbolic, extension of a person. Accordingly, it would understate the significance of manufacturing and depositing ex-votos to say that they merely 'represent' a real body part – in some sense they are identified with that body part.[121] Similarly, we know that binding spells have occasionally been found folded around or containing human hair.[122] This is contagious magic and the hair is understood to be a physical extension of the victim's body – in fact, the hair may stand for the victim's entire body and mind, or self, *pars pro toto*. Along with the anatomical curses, these ritual practices all operate according to a distributed notion of the self which, in Lévy-Bruhl's terminology, participates through dedication in temples or gravesites in the sacred space of the relevant divinity.

Erotic Magic

Binding curses that involve erotic magic reflect an important development in the genre. These curses typically 'bind' a victim so as to incite uncontrollable passion, or *erōs*, in them. They are commonly called *agōgē* or *agōgimon* spells, which technically means 'a spell that leads', because the aim is to lead a victim to the spell's practitioner.[123] Erotic curses also mention body parts, often with a violent overtone, by which the speaker of the curse enjoins his invisible agents to retrieve his victim. But erotic curses also offer a transition into the fashioning of figurines, which represent the second major type of binding magic. As we are about to see, recipes for erotic curses can also contain instructions for the manufacture of clay or wax figurines to accompany them. Actual figurines made in accordance with known binding spells have been found.

In *PGM* IV, a magical handbook dated to the fourth century CE, which contains sections that date 200 years earlier[124] and was probably authored by Egyptian temple priests,[125] we find a 'Wondrous Erotic Binding Spell' (*Philtrokatadesmos thaumastos*, IV.296–469). It instructs its user to fashion two figurines, male and female, from wax or clay. The male is to be made in the form of Ares, with a sword in his left hand poised to plunge it into the neck of the second figure, a female with her arms behind her back and kneeling. Various *voces magicae* or magical words with Egyptian and Near Eastern referents are to be written on her head, eyes, ears, shoulders, arms, hands, breast, belly, genitals, buttocks, and the soles of her feet. Allowing for some variation, these are largely the same body parts mentioned in the Athenian and Minturnaean curse tablets cited earlier – key anatomical points of reference. After these body parts are inscribed, the female figurine is to be pierced with 13 copper needles – one in the brain, two in the ears and two in the eyes, one in the mouth, two in the midriff, one in the hands, two in the pudenda, and one in each sole of the foot – and while piercing each body part the user is supposed to say, 'I am piercing such and such a member of her, so and so, so that she may remember no one but me, so and so'. Then the user is told to take a lead tablet, write the same spell on it, and recite it. It is important to distinguish the piercing of this figurine, in the context of erotic binding magic, from any popular associations with Haitian voodoo (properly Vodou) dolls. The piercing of key points of the body, as revealed by the erotic spell that is supposed to accompany the piercing, serves to stimulate the memory of the victim and keep him or her mindful of the magical practitioner. Figurines used in binding magic that aim at permanent injury are comparable to Vodou dolls (such as the sixth-century CE examples of Theophilus and Theodōros of Cyprus considered earlier), but erotic magic demands that the will of the victim be bound to the practitioner's wishes, not that he or she be physically disabled or injured.

An earthenware pot was discovered in Middle Egypt containing a folded lead curse tablet that has been pierced, along with a single female clay figurine – kneeling, with her feet tied together and her arms bound behind her back, and pierced with 13 pins placed more or less exactly as *PGM* IV prescribed.[126] However, the figurine itself, unlike in *PGM* IV, is not inscribed. The tablet has been dated to the second or third century CE, and both the tablet and figurine are now housed in the Louvre museum. The curse on the tablet closely follows *PGM* IV.336–78, but it is not an exact parallel and does not include the last 88 lines or so of the recipe. This is important to note, since it suggests a certain freedom of variation and adaptability in composing actual curses from recipe books. Our tablet concerns a man named Sarapammon, who perhaps commissioned the curse and figurine, while Ptolemais is the woman whom he intends to attract. I quote the curse in full:[127]

> I deposit this binding charm with you, chthonic gods, Pluto and Korē
> Persephone Ereskhigal and Adonis, also called *Barbaritha*, and chthonic
> Hermes Thoth *Phōkensepseu erktathou misonktaik* and mighty Anoubis
> *Psēriphtha*, who holds the keys of the gates to Hades, and chthonic *daimones*,

gods, men and women who suffered an untimely death, youths and maidens, year after year, month after month, day after day, hour after hour, night
after night. I adjure all the *daimones* in this place to assist this *daimōn*
Antinous. Rouse yourself for me and go into every place, into every quarter,
into every house, and bind Ptolemais, whom Aias bore, the daughter of
Horigenes, so that she not be screwed, not be buggered, not do anything for
the pleasure of another man, except for me Sarapammon only, whom Area
bore, and do not allow her to eat, to drink, to resist or go out or to get sleep
apart from me, Sarapammon, whom Area bore. I adjure you, corpse-*daimōn*
Antinous, by the dreadful and frightful name of the one at the sound of whose
name the earth will open, at the sound of whose name the *daimones* trem-
ble fearfully, at the sound of whose name the rivers and the rocks break. I
adjure you, corpse-*daimōn* Antinous, by *Barbaratham cheloumbra barouch
Adōnai* and by *Abrasax* and by *Iaō pakeptōth pakebraōth sabarbaphaei* and
by *Marmaraouōth* and by *Marmarachtha mamazagar*. Do not disobey,
corpse-*daimōn* Antinous, but rouse yourself for me and go into every place,
into every quarter, into every house and bring me Ptolemais, whom Aias bore,
the daughter of Horigenes. Keep her from eating and drinking until she comes
to me, Sarapammon, whom Area bore, and do not allow her to have experience of another man except me Sarapammon only. Drag her by the hair,
by the inward parts until she does not stand aloof from me, Sarapammon,
whom Area bore, and I have her, Ptolemais, whom Aias bore, the daughter
of Horigenes, subject for me the entire time of my life, being fond of me,
loving me, telling me what she has in mind. If you do this, I will set you free.

Note first the addressees of this charm, with whom the charm is
deposited. The speaker is hereby requesting that his charm be formally
acknowledged by the underworld divinities. The typical Greek underworld divinities are named, along with Ereskhigal, the Babylonian goddess
of the underworld often identified with Hekate and Korē-Persephone,
and Adonis (to be identified with Adōnai), who is a Semitic angelic figure
important in Gnosticism and magic. Anoubis and Thoth are Egyptian
divinities: Anoubis is the jackal god who presides over mummification,
and Thoth is the god of wisdom, writing, magic, and underworld guide of
the souls of the dead, whom the Greeks identified with Hermes. Later,
the speaker adjures or 'exorcises' (*horkizein*), which means to bind to an
oath, a series of Jewish demons.[128] This mosaic of identities has suggested
to some scholars that the professional magicians or scribes in late Roman
Egypt who composed this text sought to appeal to a wide array of ethnic
interests,[129] as they almost certainly sought syncretically to coalesce the
power of different ethnic divinities. It also provides us further evidence of
a certain creative freedom in the composition of magical texts.

In addition to the major divinities, lesser *daimones*, gods, and the
untimely dead (*aōroi*), both male and female, are also addressed. It is likely

that the earthenware pot containing the tablet and figurine was placed in a grave, as the speaker not only refers to the *daimones* in 'this place', but addresses his request specifically to the *daimōn* Antinous, who was presumably the dead person to whom the grave belonged.[130] The speaker asks that all the divinities and *daimones* he has named assist Antinous in fulfilling his request, and Antinous is asked to spare no quarter in his search for Ptolemais. This is a common phrasing in later curse tablets, as is the contractual relationship the speaker sets up with the *daimōn* Antinous. Note that at the end of the curse, the speaker says he will set Antinous free (*apolusein*) should he do his bidding. Later curses frequently exhibit a complex relationship between the practitioner and the demonic or divine figures addressed. Here, we can observe that the *daimōn* Antinous is in fact interested in his freedom, which must be interpreted to mean that he will be relieved of wandering restlessly and, perhaps, of being exploited for further magical operations in the future[131] – but only if he agrees to undertake the practitioner's wishes.

When Ptolemais is found, the *daimōn* is to bind (*katadein*) her specifically to prevent other men except for Sarapammon from having sexual relations with her. This raises an interesting question with respect to the figurine found along with the curse and stuck with 13 pins. We know from the prescription offered in *PGM* IV that the genitals along with the bodily limbs and other features are to be stuck with needles. But we do not know how the piercing of the figurine in the genital region corresponds with the particular wish in the curse above that Ptolemais not have sexual relations with other men. For instance, is the piercing meant to represent some kind of blockage or restraint? If so, how does that correspond with the piercing of the eyes, head, and other limbs of the figurine? According to *PGM* IV, all of the piercing serves to keep the magical practitioner in the mind of the victim. But with a curse aimed at least partly at preventing a woman from sleeping with other men, it is hard to believe the piercing of the figurine is not also sexually suggestive.

Starvation, thirst, and sleep deprivation, which Sarapammon next asks Antinous to induce in Ptolemais, are common requests in erotic tablets, because they serve to distract the victim in such a way that relief can only be found in company with the practitioner. Moreover, such methods are meant to incite an uncontrollable passion (*erōs*) in the victim. The methods of torture that are called for in this spell correspond to a long-standing tradition in Greek culture that viewed erotic seizure as a pathological disease.[132] In many Greek poets, for example, *erōs* is explicitly called a disease (*nosos*). Whether depicted as a young, winged boy, as he commonly is in classical period vase paintings, or whether spoken of in abstract terms, Eros often 'melts', 'hammers', 'whips', or 'burns' his victims. Eros is not only spoken of as burning or melting his victims. In erotic magic, the burning and melting of wax figurines, sometimes called *kolossoi*, are important acts, which can also be found in non-erotic rituals. For instance, burning and melting of *kolossoi* can be found in public rituals that establish oaths. In terms that are explicitly analogical, the oath takers are bound and wax figurines are burned, and the oath takers agree that should any of them transgress the oath, they will melt and dissolve like the figurines.[133] The literary representation of erotic magic highlights the melting of images. The most well-known example is in *Idyll* 2 by the Hellenistic poet Theocritus (fl. 270s BCE). There a lovelorn woman, Simaetha, burns a wax image of her beloved, Delphis, in the hope that he will once again passionately burn for her.[134] Apart from the metaphorical connotation of burning and melting in love, which has an established history in the Greek poetic tradition, the act of burning is torture and is meant to induce temporary pain and anguish in the victim to prevent him or her from forgetting the beloved. Thus the common accouterments of Eros – the whip, the torch, and the bow and arrow, coupled with the emblematic ritual burning in erotic magic – strongly suggest that he "began his career as a frighteningly demonic figure."[135] It is in this vein that we are to understand Sarapammon's further requests of the *daimōn* Antinous that when he finds Ptolemais, he is to drag her by her hair and innards until she is subject to Sarapammon for the remainder of his life. We may note, finally, that Theocritus' representation of burning a wax figurine of a beloved does not actually correspond, at least in this instance, with either Sarapammon's spell above or the instructions for the spell given in *PGM* IV. Had they done so, there would have been no figurine of Ptolemais to unearth.

Figurines

Magical figurines used in the context of a binding curse have been discovered throughout the Mediterranean basin. Figurines made of wax, clay, wool, lead, bronze, and marble have been found both on the Greek mainland and on the islands (Attica, Arcadia, Cephalonia, Delos, Crete, Euboea), in Sicily and Italy, North Africa, Egypt, Palestine, Asia Minor, and in areas near the Black Sea.[136] Some of the figurines have been found inside tightly closed "coffins" made of lead, with workable lids.[137] There are some typical features of these figurines that have been conveniently summarized by others.[138] The figurines often have their limbs and legs bound or twisted, sometimes grotesquely, behind their backs to enact a binding. Some figurines have been pierced by nails. The head and feet, as well as occasionally the upper torso, have been twisted around, again as a form of binding. The figurines, and occasionally the coffins, have been inscribed with the victim's name and with longer curses. The figurines were discovered in graves, sanctuaries, or bodies of water – all places associated in the Greek and Roman imagination with entrances to the underworld. There is a good deal of variation in the craftsmanship and realism of the figurines, from refined examples such as the female Louvre doll to others that are intentionally ugly and ill-formed. Finally, although some of the figurines were used for erotic magic, as we saw earlier in the context of the instructions in *PGM* IV, and hence to attract a victim, others were used to bind or restrain a practitioner's enemies.

Three lead figurines, for instance, recovered along with their lead coffins from the graves of two young boys (*aōroi*) in the Ceramicus in Athens and dated to around 400 BCE all show enlarged male genitalia.[139] It is unclear whether the exaggerated parts serve an apotropaic or magically defensive function,[140] but the curses written on the inside of the coffins are judicial in nature – in other words, they are aimed at restraining an opponent in the law court. In one case, as is common, the coffin is inscribed with the names of the intended victims: 'Theochares son-in-law (?) of Theochares, Sosistratos, Philochares, Diokles, and the other opponents at law.'[141] Then on the back of the figurine's right shoulder is the letter *theta* (θ), and on the left arm, the name Theochares. So much is straightforward insofar as Theochares is the main target of the figurine, while his fellow opponents, so as not to be excluded, are named in the coffin. But an interesting variation on this pattern occurs with another figurine and its coffin. On the inner surface of this coffin's lid are the names Theozotides, Diophanes, Diodoros, and Kephisophos, misspelled for Kephisophon. The figurine occupying the coffin, however, is also inscribed with the same names – Kephisophon (the correct spelling) runs down the back and left leg, Diophanes on the left leg, Diodoros down the right arm and down from the back of the head, and Theozotides down the left arm and the outer side of the right leg.[142] David Jordan has argued that Theozotides is the target of the figurine, since because of the rarity of the name, he can be identified with the father of Nikostratos, a member of Socrates' circle,[143] and as having proposed controversial legislation concerning state stipends in 403/2.[144] From the point of view of the magical operation of the figurine, it serves to target not only Theozotides, but also all of his fellow opponents. Of course our inscriber might have taken it upon himself merely as added insurance, or out of convenience, to copy his victim's names on the coffin as well as the figurine. But this also suggests that different users understood figurines to work differently, and at least in some cases generalized a figurine's magical power across individuals.

This should not be taken to mean, however – as is commonplace in the available scholarship – that magical figurines were viewed by their users as symbolic. Simply put, a common view is that the figurines were fashioned, then twisted, bound, pierced, or whatever, to "represent" the intended victim. One approach along these lines has sought to compare the binding of figurines to the binding of cult statues, for example that of Ares, as a restraint against the onslaught of hostile armies or pirates.[145] While there are some important parallels in these kinds of examples, they lead inevitably to the conclusion that the operative magical force is sympathetic, understood in light of Stanley Tambiah's view that magic is sympathetic in a persuasive, analogical sense.[146] But within that explanation resides a nest of other assumptions that does not square with the broader Greek and Roman treatment of statuary generally, of which figurines can be considered a subset. I can illustrate the complexity of this treatment by relating the story of the fifth-century BCE athlete Theagenes of Thasos.[147] Theagenes was renowned in his day for his relationship to bronze statues, which began in his youth when he carried an extraordinarily heavy statue from the marketplace to his house and back again.[148] According to Pausanias, after Theagenes died a bronze statue in his image was erected. One of Theagenes' enemies, unable to wreak vengeance on him during life, undertook to do so in death and repeatedly flogged his statue at night as if it were Theagenes himself. 'But the statue stopped the outrage by falling on him, and the sons of the man who had died prosecuted the statue for murder.'[149]

Prosecuting a statue for murder may at first glance seem absurd to the modern reader, but as we noted in chapter 2 the Athenians actually reserved a special court, the Prytaneum, for the trial of inanimate objects.[150] They did this because what we would consider to be inanimate objects – e.g., statues, wood, rocks, iron – were not as clearly so for the Greeks, hence such objects were held legally and morally responsible for their actions, just like humans.[151] In the context of this story, Theagenes' statue fell on its abuser because it was outraged – no differently than a human being – and it sought retribution. But there is more to the story. At trial, the statue was found guilty of murder and was sentenced, as was customary in verdicts of homicide, to exile. It was thrown into the sea, which satisfied the basic demand of exile that the offending entity be removed from the boundaries of the, in this case Thasian, community. But then the Thasians were hit with famine and, upon inquiring of the Delphic oracle for a solution, were told to retrieve their exiles. The famine did not dissipate and, by way of a second Delphic oracle, the Thasians realized that not only their former community members had to be retrieved, but also the statue of Theagenes, since it too was technically an exile. Fishermen recovered the statue in their nets, and the Thasians set it up in its original place and sacrificed to it as to a god for appeasement, and the famine disappeared.[152] Again we can see that abuse of the statue, this time in the form of exile, was met with retribution, in the form of famine, except that the statue is elevated in the end to divine status. This is because in the context of Greek religion it is divinities who typically cause widespread catastrophe like famine.

In anthropological terms, the statue of Theagenes is a *social agent* – it is effectively a human being and is therefore, from the functional viewpoint of the relevant community, treated like one.[153] As Alfred Gell has argued, any object, whether animate or inanimate from our perspective, which is treated in significant respects like a person can be considered a social agent.[154] This approach to objects has wide applicability in the Greek and Roman worlds, especially with regard to cult statues, because both Greeks and Romans at various times considered them capable of physical movement and expression.[155] Even where that attitude is not explicit, the range of effigies that were treated in significant respects like humans is almost too numerous to catalogue. For example, in the classical period monthly food offerings were set out before statuettes of Hekate because the goddess needed to eat.[156] The Greeks regularly cleaned *xoana*, or carved wooden images, and dressed them in new robes – a practice that was preserved in the quadrennial public festival of the Panathenaia, in which a new robe was presented to the statue of Athena in the Parthenon. Prayer was addressed to cult statues since, as some authors expressly stated, communication with the gods took place through them.[157] In later antiquity, there are not only many examples of Greek statues that exhibited human behavior like talking, moving, bleeding, and crying,[158] but also examples of statues that were treated as sexual objects. Herakles' return of Alcestis' mute, statue-like corpse to her husband Admetus, with its necromantic and necrophiliac overtones, is one example.[159] The most famous literary adaptation of treating a statue as a living sexual object is the story of the artisan Pygmalion and his carved ivory statue, which was animated by Venus and became the mother of Pygmalion's child.[160] However, there are several historical accounts of men actually sleeping with marble cult statues, which – whatever else one might think "really" happened – nevertheless indicate the profound effect that statues could exercise over people.[161]

A complete account of the treatment of effigies cannot omit dolls and puppets, which were described in Greek and Latin by a variety of names (e.g., *korē, koros; nymphē, puppa, mania, bulla, effigies, imago*). Ancient dolls have been found made of wood, bone, wax, fabric, clay, precious metal, and other materials. Although we have little evidence for how Greek and Roman children played, the care that is often given to the hair, clothing, lips, and adornment of these dolls is further evidence for social agency and its acculturation in children. Now the link between children's dolls and statuary may not be immediately evident but, from an anthropological point of view, cult statues are big dolls.[162] The ancient treatment of dolls in fact has directly to do with the ritual treatment of cult statuary, insofar as boys and girls dedicated their dolls to certain divinities, which were themselves embodied in statuary form. In Greece girls dedicated *korai* to Artemis in preparation for marriage, while in Rome unwed girls dedicated *puppae* to Venus.[163] Roman boys, for different reasons, dedicated *bullae* to the Lares,[164] which are numinous entities that probably had their origin as *daimones* or ghosts, but were later associated with crossroads. In a rather striking instance of the role of dolls in ritual appeasement, on the eve of the Compitalia, which was a celebration at the crossroads in Rome and in the countryside, male and female puppets – each representing a free member of the household – and balls representing each slave member, were hung so that the Lares might spare the living and accept the effigies as surrogates. The puppets are replacements for human beings, and as such they function as agents within a social network that includes both the living, who are visible, and divinities and spirits of the dead, who are not.

It is within this broad network of ancient social agents, which is defined by interaction with statues and effigies generally as living presences, that we should situate the manufacture and deposition of magical figurines. In 1915 in an important, but today rarely cited, study of the Greek treatment of statuary in late antiquity, Charly Clerc argued along lines similar to the ones I am proposing here.[165] Clerc's survey remains one of the most comprehensive to date, and he clearly saw connections between, for instance, wooden images (*xoana*) and children's dolls,[166] and between *xoana* and magical figurines.[167] His theoretical approach to magical figurines, which was common at the time in classical scholarship, relied almost entirely upon James Frazer's theory of sympathetic (homeopathic) magic. But his overarching view that the humanlike treatment by Greeks of images – understood to include the range of effigies we have discussed, from oversized statues to tiny dolls – ought to be interpreted within the same continuum is in line with my own. This continuum in the Greek and Roman treatment of statues and effigies should again caution us from assuming that magical figurines merely represented, symbolically or otherwise, an intended victim. As one type of social agent, it is entirely within reason to regard magical figurines, in view of the story of Theagenes' statue, as capable of injury and retribution, if not of movement. If this line of reasoning is correct, magical figurines were abused through twisting and binding, not as symbolic acts, but literally to arouse their anger. In turn, it was expected that they would somehow discharge their anger on the intended victim or victims, hence the need to write their names and the desired curse on the figurine or on its coffin. After all, the figurines needed to know whom to attack.

Erōtes

We can extend the model of social agency to include one final group of figurines not yet discussed that are used in erotic magic. In the following examples, we will see clearly that figurines could operate as agents of a magical practitioner, complete with a premeditated mission. I refer to the wooden or waxen images of Eros (*erōs*), from whom they take their technical name 'Eroses' (*erōtes*). In two fourth-century CE magical papyri, *PGM* IV.1840–70 and XII.14–95, we find procedures described for acquiring Eros as a magical assistant. The procedures involve fashioning either wooden or waxen images of Eros (*erōtes*), consecrating them with fruit offerings, sacrifices, and spells to animate them, then sending them to accomplish erotic magic – literally sending them out by flight to attract whichever man or woman the practitioner desires to retrieve. In addition to the actual Greco-Egyptian spells, we are fortunate to possess a text by the second-century CE author Lucian of Samosata (*Philopseudes* 34.14) that describes how *erōtes* work and offers some indication that animating Eros figurines was a distinctive and well-known procedure.[168]

In Lucian's *Philopseudes* we find numerous miraculous stories of foreign magicians, notably that of an unnamed Hyperborean who can fly, walk on water, and walk through fire barefoot (34.13). These are his great feats. Among his trivial feats, he can, much like a typical itinerant religious specialist or witch in the classical period, call forth *daimones*, the dead, make the goddess Hekate appear, draw down the moon – and send *erōtes* to people. As Lucian relates it, the Hyperborean once offered his services to a young man named Glaucias, who had just inherited his deceased father's estate and fallen in love with a married woman named Chrysis. The young man paid four *minas* in advance to sleep with Chrysis, and promised sixteen if he should succeed. The Hyperborean did several things in preparation, including waiting for a waxing moon, digging a pit in the courtyard of the house to summon Glaucias' dead father, Alexicles, for his approval, and then he summoned Hekate. Alexicles at first disapproves of the union and becomes angered, but eventually consents. Finally, the Hyperborean fashioned a little Eros (*erōtion*) from clay, and ordered it to go and fetch Chrysis. Next we read that 'the clay flew away and soon [Chrysis] stood on the threshold knocking on the door, came in and embraced Glaucias as if she were madly in love with him, and slept with him until we heard the cocks crowing' (34.14).

Although Lucian does not describe in any detail how the Hyperborean fashioned the Eros figurine, two such spells survive in the Greco-Egyptian magical papyri. First, in *PGM* IV.1716–1870, we have an erotic spell that begins by consecrating a magnet inscribed with images of Aphrodite sitting astride Psyche and holding her hair, while Eros stands beneath Psyche holding a torch and burning her. We saw earlier how torches and burning are among the standard means that Eros employs to inflame his victims with desire. But this is also a reference to the famous love story of Amor (Cupid/Eros) and Psyche, as told by Apuleius.[169] The magnet is to be placed in the mouth, and a longer spell is said, with the aim of turning the soul of the victim toward the practitioner 'so that she may love me and feel passion for me, so that she may give me what is in her power' (1807–10). A burnt offering is also required, which is said to 'ensoul' (ἐμψυχοῦν) Eros and the entire rite – in other words, to animate him. Finally, there is the rite for acquiring Eros as an assistant (*PGM* IV.1842–71):

> There is also a rite for acquiring an assistant, which is made from mulberry wood. A winged Eros is made, having a cloak, his right foot put forward and having a hollow back. Into the hollow put a gold leaf after writing so and so's name with a cold-forged, copper stylus [and]: "MARSABOUTARTHE – be my assistant and helper and sender of dreams." Go late at night to the house of the woman you want, knock on her door with the Eros and say: "Behold, so and so dwells here; stand beside her and, after assuming the likeness of the god or *daimōn* she worships, say what I propose." And go to your home, set the table, spread a pure linen cloth and seasonal flowers, and set the figurine upon it. Then make a burnt offering to it and continuously say the invocation. And send him and he will act without fail. Whenever you turn [her to your will] with the magnet, on that night he sends dreams; for on a different night he is busy with other things.

The second example comes from *PGM* XII.14–95 and offers the most extensive rite for fashioning an Eros. Among the operations this rite of Eros can complete, we are told that he can send dreams or cause sleeplessness and, if used in a proper and holy manner, he can also free one from an angry spirit. The practitioner is to mix wax with every kind of aromatic plant, then fashion a torch-bearing Eros about 5 inches high with a large base to support it. A bow and arrow is to be placed in his left hand and, as in the previous spell, a figurine of Psyche much like that of Eros is to be made. At this point, the practitioner is to conduct a three-day consecration: he is to present Eros with fresh fruits of every kind, seven cakes, seven

pinecones, sweetmeats, and seven lamps. In addition there are to be dag-
gers, votive tablets, a bow and arrow, dates, and a bowl of honeyed wine.
Next the Eros is to be placed on a table with the fruit and he is to hold the
seven lamps as they blaze with clear olive oil. Specifically, we are told that
all of this is to be done 'so as to persuade the wondrous Eros' (XII.26); however, this is not quite the same thing as the persuasive, analogical magic
as formulated by Tambiah.

One detail in the description of the first day of consecration of this
Eros that we do not find elsewhere is the mention of strangling seven birds.
This is necessary in order to animate the figurine, understood in literal
not analogical terms. A pure altar is to be built for the Eros, and unbaked
bricks are to be fashioned into little trees on which fruit-bearing branches
are laid. Then a cock, partridge, wren, pigeon, turtledove, and any two
nestlings are to be captured but not made into a burnt offering (*PGM*
XII.32–35):

> Do not make a burnt offering of all these, but taking them in hand you will
> choke them while holding them up to Eros, until each of the animals suffo-
> cates and their breath enters him. And then place the strangled creatures on
> the altar with aromatic plants of every variety.

These actions may seem ghastly to a modern reader, but the practice of
strangling animals so as to transfer their breath to an image of a divinity
does occur elsewhere in late antique magic. In another spell in the magical papyri, for instance, we hear that one ought to 'sacrifice a rooster, so
the god may ungrudgingly take the breath (*pneuma*)'.[170] In this respect,
the transfer of breath from an image to a divinity is not enacted symbolically but literally, and the final exhalation of the victim becomes the first
inhalation of the newly animated divinity. In addition, on the second day
of consecration in *PGM* XII.14–95, a male chick is to be strangled and then
burnt for Eros as a whole offering, while on the third day another chick is
to be placed on Eros' altar, then consumed by the practitioner. If these
actions are performed in a holy and pure manner, the practitioner will have
complete success.

As E. R. Dodds recognized in 1951, there is undeniably a theurgic ele-
ment to the process of animating statues as it is attested in *PGM*.[171] The
theurgists, including the Neoplatonist Proclus, advocated the ritual animation of statues that culminated with the placing of the *sumbolon* or token
(a piece of stone, metal, a gem, or an herb) into the mouth of a figurine.[172]
This practice should immediately recall the inscribed gold leaf that
was to be placed inside the hollow back of the winged Eros in *PGM*
IV.1848–54, mentioned above. The theurgist would thereby invoke the

presence of a divinity, which responded to the invocation not out of compulsion but out of overflowing benevolence. A common goal for animating statues among the theurgists, which is very unlike what we have with the *erōtes*, was for the statues to foretell the future.[173] Moreover, in all of these Greco-Egyptian spells, the animation of figurines for whatever purpose must be set against the generalized Egyptian belief that the images of their gods were ensouled.[174]

The animation of *erōtes* in the magical papyri is also different from the practice of the theurgists in other respects. When we compare the Eros rites to other rites in *PGM* for animating statues (*PGM* III.282–409, Apollo for prophecy; IV.2359–72, Hermes for business; IV.3125–71, three-headed animal for prosperity; V.370–446, Hermes for prophecy) the Eros rites appear different because of how the figurines are treated by the practitioner. First, the offering of flowers and use of aromatic plants in *PGM* IV and XII, which is not common to these other rites, suggests the long-standing poetic and visual association of Eros with flowers and springtime.[175] The preponderance of birds in the Eros consecrations (esp. in *PGM* XII) does suggest that an analogy has been drawn between the classical depiction of Eros as a winged divinity and the need to offer the figurine winged sacrifices as the source from which he takes his breath. The Eros figurines are made with wings (as stated at *PGM* IV.1845), and we have already seen that in Lucian's *Philopseudes* the clay Eros flies away (34.14.9).

Recall that in *PGM* XII we are told that the three-day consecration is performed 'so as to persuade the wondrous Eros' (XII.26). I take this to mean that simply animating a figurine of Eros and telling him what to do, as the Hyperborean does in Lucian, is not enough. Rather, he must be enticed with offerings to do the practitioner's bidding. We might compare, for instance, *PGM* V.395–97, the animation of a Hermes figurine for prophecy, which only requires burning incense, a little earth, rock salt, and an invocation for him to accomplish what you ask. The range of offerings of seasonal flowers, fruit, cakes, pinecones, sweetmeats, and burnt victims to Eros suggest that he needs quite a bit more in return for accomplishing the practitioner's bidding. In fact, compared to the rites for animating other statues, the amount of offerings to Eros is extraordinary. Note also that in *PGM* IV.1842–71, after the offerings are made, significantly the practitioner is to take the figurine to the house of the beloved and actually knock on the door with the Eros.

To varying degrees all of these examples can be better understood with reference to social agency. In the context of *erōtes*, we can appropriately ask how the practitioners of the rites socialize the figurines. My conjecture here is that Eros is conceived in the spells, not unlike the visual depictions of him in vase paintings and sculpture throughout antiquity, as a young boy or a child. Indirect evidence for this view comes from the second-century CE physician Galen, who refutes the claim that those who experience erotic frenzy do so as a result of 'some small and newborn god holding burning torches'.[176] Although this remark does not mention figurines, it confirms that in Galen's time the conception of Eros as an agent of erotic suffering was as a newborn, or in any case a very young child. From our perspective, such a view helps to explain why the rites for animation in *PGM* IV and XII relative to the others emphasize appeasement and persuasion, and perhaps why in the case of *PGM* XII.1842–71 so much "food" is offered to the figurine – including nestlings and chickens. It also may explain why the user of this Eros figurine has to take it to the door of the erotic victim – the figurine literally has to be shown the way, which suggests that it is not socialized here as an adult that would be expected to know such things. At the same time, the rite of offering flowers and food to the Eros figurine is exactly what one might expect a real person to offer his beloved. Moreover, by taking the figurine to the door of the beloved and knocking on it as part of the spell, not only does the practitioner enable the figurine to find its way, the spell also enables the practitioner to go some way toward accomplishing what he has set out to do in the first place. The rite ensures that he may at least have an opportunity to establish contact with his beloved.

Unlike previous approaches to Eros figurines that are preoccupied with whether they "actually" move,[177] the model of social agency used here is ultimately concerned with how the users of magical objects deploy them into available social categories. Late antiquity is rife with stories about animated statues and figurines of many kinds, as authors such as Pausanias, Plutarch, Iamblichus, Apuleius, Lucian, and others attest. But they are not all treated equally. Showering an Eros figurine with gifts of flowers and sweets is to treat it like a beloved, but it is also to entice a young and perhaps characteristically independent "child" into cooperating. Abusing a figurine in the context of a binding curse that identifies its victim angers the figurine and leads it, as we might expect from an injured person, to ventilate its outrage on the intended victim. The terms of each case have to be examined separately, because not all effigies behave equally. In turn the rationale for the ritual treatment they receive can only be understood once the nature of a figurine's "personality" and behavior has been determined.

There are no simple ways to summarize the evidence for binding magic and, as an outflow of it, erotic magic. We have seen, for example, that the underlying notion of binding in earlier tablets is often metaphorical, whatever the specific genre of curse, while in later antiquity the metaphor tends to become literalized. Some attempts are made to restrain the relevant body parts as they relate to specific realms of activity – so tongues and minds are restrained in judicial curses, since these are the relevant features of one's judicial adversaries, while in competitive chariot race curses (which we have not discussed here in any depth) the running, power, soul, onrush, speed, and legs of individually named horses are bound since these are the most salient features to disable.[178] There is also the curious, and perhaps non-Greek,[179] feature that binding curses which enumerate body parts typically flow from head to toe. In some sense, then, we can say that the curse formulae envisage or project its target person – standing – as its language unfolds, body part by body part, but the reasons for this pattern as yet are unclear. Nor is it clear why body parts accumulate in curses over time, as if a developing sense of "completeness" were at issue.

Erotic magic extends the metaphor of binding into the realm of Mediterranean passion. Despite recent research in this area,[180] some important unanswered questions remain about Greco-Egyptian erotic spells. For example, the binding of external body parts is consistent with curse tablets in other genres. However, in the second- to third-century CE Sarapammon and Ptolemais spell from Middle Egypt we considered,[181] the speaker also makes reference to dragging Ptolemais by her 'inward parts' (τὰ σπλάγχνα, l. 23) until she comes to Sarapammon. This formula is also found in other Greco-Egyptian curses,[182] but does not appear to be common in Attic or other curse tablets.[183] There are other references to the inner body parts of people in the Greek magical papyri – some of which are quite shocking, as in the slander spell to Selene that claims as part of its slander of the goddess that she has made a headband from a man's 'intestines' (τὰ ἔντερα).[184] If it is true, as we have noted, that spells in the Greek magical papyri and those adapted from it were composed by Egyptian temple priests, it may be worth investigating whether their typical practice of mummification of the dead, with its elaborate preservation of internal organs, contributed this kind of local color. Interestingly, the Middle Egypt spell for Sarapammon does, after all, address itself to numerous divinities including Anoubis, the underworld jackal god who presides over mummification.

Figurines used in binding curses and especially the *erōtes* used in erotic spells dramatically illustrate the need to contextualize the use of figurines within the broader attitudes toward Greek and Roman statuary generally. I have offered Alfred Gell's model of social agency as an approach to inanimate objects that avoids the trap of "symbolism." But this is a complicated issue and approaches to it have never fully divorced themselves from Emile Durkheim's formulation of symbolic forms, or 'collective representations', which separate a literal and symbolic meaning in ritual action.[185] One effect of viewing magical figurines of any kind within the broader context of Greek and Roman social agency is that it subsumes magical behavior into ritual behavior generally toward objects, in this case statuary.[186] I have not dwelt at any length here on the scholarly use of the term 'magic' and its underlying conceptions, apart from the brief considerations in chapter 2, partly because good treatments are available elsewhere, but mainly because I think the discussion is largely misleading to the extent that it focuses on terminology rather than on specific ritual practices.[187] It is not, ultimately, a question of whether the Greeks or Romans called a given practice 'magic', let alone whether we call it that. Rather, the task at hand is to show which social – understanding social to include visible and invisible agents – constructions of communication, emotion, health, disability, the fragmented body, or integrated personhood underlie the rituals of binding and erotic magic that we find in the ancient world.

CHAPTER 4

Homeric Incantations

ᄆᄆᄆᄆ

Homer presents the earliest examples of magic in Greek literature, including the episodes we have seen with Circe, the drugs of Helen (on which see below), the healing of Odysseus' thigh with an incantation,[1] and Aphrodite's magical strap (*kestos himas*) used to incite erotic passion.[2] Curses were attributed to him[3] and there is some evidence that late authors, such as Philostratus, conceived of Homer as a necromancer.[4] This chapter focuses neither on Homer's representations of magic in the *Iliad* or *Odyssey per se*, nor on later biographical conceptions of him as a magician. Rather, we shall here be concerned with the ways in which Homer's verses were excised from his poems and used as incantations to solve practical problems. Although the practice of using Homeric verses in magic is originally a Greek phenomenon, the practice itself extends from the late archaic period to the Middle Ages, with earlier Greek examples eventually forming the basis for both Byzantine and medieval Latin healing charms. Some of these later examples are quite useful in helping us to understand why verses from Homeric poetry remained the authoritative source for incantations.

The incantatory use of Homeric verses for healing ailments, disease, general misfortune, and, more rarely, cursing one's enemies is a type of magic that is distinctive to the Greek and Roman worlds. On the face of it, verse magic is straightforward: extract a verse or verses from an epic to write or speak, accompany them with some sympathetic ritual, and *voilà*, one's ailment is healed. But which verses does one take for a particular problem? Moreover, why take verses from Homer's *Iliad* and *Odyssey* as opposed to the works of some other poet? The reasons for this are complex but they owe much to the cultural and intellectual place held by Homer as the first divinely inspired poet. Although there were many great Greek and Roman epic poets, from the point of view of magical practitioners in later antiquity neither a Hesiod, Vergil, nor the Silver Age Latin epic poets held the same authority and pride of place as Homer – the famously blind poet who called upon the Muses to sing his *Iliad* and *Odyssey*.

Our sources for the use of Homeric verses as incantations are quite diverse. They include Egyptian papyri, Second Sophistic literary sources, medical, veterinary, and agricultural handbooks, inscriptions on potsherds, stone amulets, and a gold tablet or *lamella*.[5] These sources are generally concentrated within the first four centuries CE. However, the use of Homeric verses for magic actually does not stop then but continues well into the Middle Ages both in the Byzantine East and in the Roman West.[6] The Homeric verses were selected from many different books of the *Iliad* and *Odyssey*, both from books that were considered genuine and from those, like book 10 of the *Iliad*, that were considered spurious by critics in antiquity. Interestingly, preparers of spells involving Homer were well aware of ancient Homeric criticism. For example, in a spell attributed to Julius Africanus, a third-century CE Christian author, we find extended passages from book 11 of the *Odyssey* (*PGM* XXIII.1–70), and it is explicitly stated that verses were incorporated which the Athenian tyrants known as the Peisistratids left out.[7] Of the verses in Africanus' spell, some of them (e.g., *Odyssey* 11.38–43) were criticized in antiquity by the great Alexandrian literary critics Zenodotus, Aristophanes of Byzantium, and Aristarchus.

There is some evidence outside of literature and the biographical tradition, which attributes the practice to early figures such as Pythagoras and Empedocles, for the efficacy of incantations derived from Homer. According to Alexander of Tralles and Rufus of Ephesus, the second-century CE Roman physician Galen was said to have experimented with Homeric incantations himself, and to have found them effective in the treatment of a scorpion sting and for the dislodging of bones stuck in the throat.[8] Other second-century CE Roman physicians, such as Marcellus, corroborate the efficacy of employing written Homeric verses to dislodge bones from the throat.[9] In this chapter we shall set forth the main principles on which the use of Homeric verses as incantations was based. Once these have been outlined, we will be in a position to apply them both to Homeric verses whose rationale in magic has not yet been explained, and to occurrences of Homeric verses in contexts not immediately associated with magic.

Pythagoras and Empedocles

By and large the majority of Homeric verses used in magic were employed either to protect or to heal, but the exact origin of their usage is not known.[10] However, the authors who first comment on it, such as Iamblichus (second half of third century CE), attribute it to earlier figures such as Pythagoras and the seer/purifier Empedocles, who were said to have used Homeric verses as well as music to heal.[11] The mechanism by which the healing took place, according to the evidence in Iamblichus, was largely purificatory. Unfortunately, we do not have direct evidence to support Iamblichus' claims, nor do we know why early Pythagoreanism placed more emphasis on the verses of Homer, and to a lesser extent Hesiod, than on the verses of poets like Orpheus and Musaeus, who were both cathartic poets *par excellence*. About Orpheus and Musaeus it was well known in the classical period, for example, that their verses or books, in addition to being employed as oracles, could also be used to heal diseases or offer release and purification from unjust deeds.[12] In the biographical tradition, Pythagoras was said to have had close associations with Homeric poetry. He was, for one, entrusted by his father for a time to Creophylus, the famous Samian rhapsode whose school of Creophylei rivaled that of the Homeridae from Chios.[13] Hermodamas, a descendant of Creophylus, was said to have been the teacher of Pythagoras.[14] Pythagoras' favorite Homeric verses, which served as his epitaph, were said to be *Iliad* 17.51–60. These lines detail the death of the Trojan Euphorbus, the slayer of Achilles' closest friend, Patroclus, at the hands of Menelaus. Pythagoras was said to have demonstrated to his disciples that in a former life he had actually been Euphorbus.[15] Perhaps we need look no further than this evidence to explain Pythagoras' perceived preference for Homeric verses in his healing. What this evidence does not explain, on the other hand, is why only Homeric – and not Hesiodic, Orphic, or Musaeic – verses are actually attested in the documented history of this magical tradition.

With regard to Pythagoras' and Empedocles' use of Homeric verses for healing specific ailments, Iamblichus tells two related stories in support of his claim that the practice originated with them. In the account of Pythagoras, we are told that he believed generally that music contributed greatly to health.[16] In the springtime, he used to seat a circle of patients around a lyre player, who played while the patients chanted paeans in unison. The paean is of course the form of hymn especially reserved for Apollo, the god of healing. Through their chanting, we are told, the patients expected to become joyful, graceful, and rhythmical. At other times Pythagoras used music in the treatment of specific ailments. After digressing to note that different melodies correspond to different emotions and states of the soul (despondency, rages and angers, desires, and so forth), Iamblichus says that Pythagoras preferred the music of the lyre and that (25.111):

He used selected verses of both Homer and Hesiod for the
improvement of the soul.

Of Pythagoras' famous deeds, one is especially interesting: according
to Iamblichus, he is said to have quelled the anger of a drunken youth
who after a revel one night assaulted his mistress at the gate of a rival,
with the intention of burning the rival's house down. The youth was
inflamed by an *aulos* – a flutelike instrument that was especially disliked
by Pythagoreans[17] – that was being played by someone in the fast and excited
Phrygian mode.[18] So Pythagoras encouraged the reed player to stop and
switch to a spondaic mode, which is slow and solemn, and this immediately restrained the youth and caused him to return home in an orderly
manner (25.112). This story was repeated numerous times in antiquity in
slightly different form, both by Greek and Roman authors, usually in the
context of discussions of the emotions and the effect of music on the soul.

The second story Iamblichus tells is about Empedocles and it involves
both music and a Homeric verse. Empedocles is, like Pythagoras, also said
to have quelled the anger of a youth, but on this occasion the youth had
drawn a sword against Empedocles' host, a man named Anchitus.
Anchitus was a judge who had sentenced the youth's father to death, and
in a rage the youth rushed forward with a sword to strike him. According
to the account, Empedocles was already engaged in playing the lyre for
Anchitus when he saw that the youth was about to attack him, so he
suddenly changed the musical mode to one that was sedate and soothing,
and straightaway recited *Odyssey* 4.221:[19]

soothing sorrow and angerless, causing forgetfulness of all ills

Once he recited this line the youth calmed down and Anchitus was saved
from death. And we are told that as a result of this deed later on the youth
became the most famous pupil of Empedocles. Now the verse itself is of
some interest because it illustrates a pattern that we will work out in some
detail in what follows. The line is taken from the scene in the *Odyssey* when
Telemachus and his companion Pisistratus are visiting King Menelaus and
Helen in Sparta, to obtain information about Odysseus' whereabouts
after the Trojan War. After some conversation about Odysseus that leads
to lamentation, Helen decides to slip a *pharmakon* into the wine, which
she serves them to put them at ease before she recounts how she met
Odysseus at Troy. Our verse above describes the *pharmakon* and its
effects. What is important for our purposes is that in the story of
Empedocles this verse was chosen because it occurs in a narrative context in which similar effects of soothing and easing are at issue.

Iamblichus' story of Empedocles is probably apocryphal and it would merely be amusing if not for the fact that the use of Homeric verses in magic is attested in many other sources and, at least early on, follows this pattern. Even if the story of Empedocles is unreliable, to a reader of Iamblichus in the late third or fourth century familiarity with this practice from contemporary sources or experience would at least have made the account of Empedocles', and before him Pythagoras', actions plausible. As we shall see, the first secure literary depiction of the magical use of a Homeric verse is attested by Lucian of Samosata (b. ca. 120 CE) in his dialogue *Charon* (7.12–13), and there the aim of using the verse is specifically to heal. This witness at least supports Iamblichus' implicit assumption in *De Vita Pythagorica* that the magical use of Homeric verses for healing needed explanation, though of course it does not prove a Pythagorean or Empedoclean origin for the practice.

The Mechanics of Homeric Incantations

The basic principle behind the usage of Homeric verses in magical contexts is analogical. Richard Heim, who compiled the first important collection of Greek and Roman literary verses used in magic, expressed this well when he wrote that "some verses as it were agree with the magical action or the disease to be healed" (*nonnulli tamen versus cum actione magica vel cum morbo sanando quasi cohaerent*).[20] This means that the choice of a given verse is determined by how well the action within it coheres with the desired magical action. More recently, scholars have emphasized the narrative context from which a given verse is taken, as in the example of Empedocles above, as a determining factor in the magical analogy that underlies its use.[21] Others have related the selection of Homeric verses to the use of verses from sacred books for healing, in which a broader, "mythic" underpinning is tapped for its power to transform present circumstances.[22] It has also been argued, for example by invoking notions of 'traditional referentiality', that the selection of a Homeric verse evokes a larger and more 'echoic' narrative context than the verse itself.[23] But this observation applies most strictly only to the earliest examples that we find, as for instance in Lucian. In Lucian's *Charon* (7.12–13) the god Hermes says that he can heal Charon's short-sightedness quite easily by taking a charm from the *Iliad*, and he recites *Iliad* 5.127–28, where the goddess Athena is aiding the hero Diomedes in his *aristeia* or moment of valor against the Trojans. The verses that describe how she invests him with courage and the divine ability to distinguish gods from mortals form the charm Hermes takes for Charon (*Iliad* 5.127–28):

take away the mist (*akhlus*) from your eyes, which was there before,
so that you may well recognize who is a god or a man

In the context of the *Iliad*, Athena's aid will help Diomedes eventually to
see and wound Aphrodite as she is helping Aeneas (*Iliad* 5.330–33). When
Lucian's Hermes speaks the same lines, they allow Charon to see more
clearly. In this example the narrative context of the verses structures the
meaning of the chosen verses themselves, although a further analogy
must still be drawn between the 'mist' (*akhlus*) of the verse and Charon's
poor vision.

As we move forward in time after Lucian, especially between the
second and fourth centuries CE, the importance of narrative context
diminishes or is forgotten, and the action within a given verse or verse
segment becomes predominant. At the same time, the verse or the action
within it becomes more broadly evocative, not of narrative context but
of attributes or qualities generally thought to be related to the action of
healing, protection, or, occasionally, harm that is desired. The approach
that we shall follow, which was in some ways anticipated by scholars almost
70 years ago,[24] offers a vantage point from which to understand the rationality of this kind of magic. It will also offer important clues as to the type
of Homeric readers with which we are dealing.

Obstetrics and Gynecology

Three examples of verses selected indifferently to their narrative context
come from the Greek magical papyri, as in *PGM* XXIIa.9–10 (fourth or fifth
century CE). In the first, we find that for breast and uterine pain in new
mothers they are to write *Iliad* 2.548:

the daughter of Zeus <u>nourished</u>, and the fruitful land <u>bore</u>.

This verse comes from the description of Athens in the Catalogue of
Ships. The people of Erectheus, the Athenians, are the direct objects of both
verbs in this verse, which are not in the verse itself. Now it is possible that
a verse such as this, taken from a description of the rich Athenian land,
informs the background of meaning behind why it was chosen to relieve
breast and uterine pain, but this background will hardly have had the same
resonance in late imperial Egypt. Instead, what is salient is that the verse
mentions a daughter of Zeus who nourished (*trephein*) and mentions that
the earth gave birth (*tiktein*). We can surmise that the verse was thought
to indicate success in birth and nourishment, and that the magical

action, unlike in the previous examples, does not depend on narrative context but inheres largely in the verbs themselves.

From the same papyrus we find another verse, *Iliad* 3.40, used to prevent pregnancy. A woman is either to wear this verse inscribed on a magnet or to say it aloud (*PGM* XXIIa.11–12):

Would that you were <u>unborn</u> (*agonos*) and had died <u>unmarried</u> (*agamos*)

Significantly, the context of these verses has nothing to do with pregnancy. They occur in the beginning of book 3, when Paris has just seen Menelaus on the battlefield and in fear retreats behind his fellow Trojan soldiers. Paris' brother Hector then scolds him for his cowardice and after calling him a string of epithets, like ill-omened, woman-maddened, and a cheat, he says the verse above. To a woman desiring to prevent pregnancy, however, none of that could be directly relevant. Indeed, the magical interpretation of this verse actually shifts the meaning of the original Homeric Greek. In its Homeric context, the adjective *agonos* is used passively in this verse to mean 'unborn', whereas the magical practitioner needs to give it an active meaning, 'without offspring/sterile', which is the more common later meaning,[25] lest she wish herself out of existence. Although we cannot be exactly sure whether the verse is to be addressed to the fetus, the most likely audience is the woman herself at risk of becoming pregnant. Hence what is relevant is her desire for childlessness. The adjective *agamos* in the verse above is not used in its Homeric sense either. As Matthew Dickie has recently argued, the noun *gamos* in the Greek magical papyri often does not mean 'marriage' but 'sexual union'.[26] Similarly, I submit that *agamos* in our verse (*Iliad* 3.40) was interpreted to refer, not to a desire to be unmarried, but to avoid sexual union, which is more consistent with the verse's overall aim of preventing pregnancy. Thus we have two levels of meaning at work in this verse, as if the situation of the woman seeking help were conceived in two stages: desiring to avoid sexual union (*agamos*) and desiring, should that first condition not hold, to avoid conception (*agonos*).

This interpretation of the adjectives *agonos* and *agamos* finds further confirmation in the additional ritual procedures recommended in conjunction with the writing or speaking of the verse. If written, the verse should be inscribed on a magnet (*PGM* XXIIa.10), which is traditionally associated with contraception. In the context of ancient medical treatises on obstetrics and gynecology, there was much lore that surrounded the magnet or "lodestone," not the least being its ability to forestall uterine hemorrhage and to assimilate blood. Several ancient authors of medical and pharmacological treatises record the use of magnets in these kinds of charms, including major authorities like Dioscorides (first CE), Soranus of Ephesus (early second CE), and Galen (second CE), which attests to the widespread understanding of this charm as well as to its fixed place in the repertoire of women's medicine. Assuming the magnet's ability to stop bleeding was understood by the Greco-Egyptian magical practitioners whose spells are the *PGM*, it has been suggested that it was not a far step to extend the magnet's effects to contraception.[27] Indeed, the basic principle involved appears to be sympathetic, but further research is needed to clarify the exact relationship between the magnet and bleeding. For instance, if was it desired that a woman stop bleeding by using the magnet to assimilate blood (presumably it is the iron in the blood that causes the attraction), does this accord with how the cessation of menses was understood after contraception? If so, then we may have a typical *similia similibus* 'like to like' magical framework, based on the simple analogy that the magnet stops bleeding, and contraception results in loss of bleeding, hence the magnet is useful in contraception. The problem is that in real medical terms the loss of menstrual bleeding signifies pregnancy, not its prevention. So it is still not altogether clear why the magnet's ability to stop bleeding was thought useful in contraception.

Be that as it may, in *PGM* XXIIa, after writing the verse on a fresh piece of papyrus, it is further advised that some hairs of a mule – a notoriously sterile animal – are to be wrapped around it. This procedure is more transparently sympathetic because it is desired that the sterility of the mule be transferred through its hairs to the papyrus and the spell written on it. However, the verse employed (*Iliad* 3.40) is one of the clearest examples we have that the Greco-Egyptian consumers of this type of magic, whether temple priests or their non-professional clients, were not always reading Homer in its original semantic context.[28] Verses like *Iliad* 3.40 were extracted from their narrative context and "misread" – not as a result of illiteracy but as a way of semantically tailoring them to very specific and practical needs. Such a procedure also suggests that the verses of Homer used in incantations had achieved a measure of autonomy and independent agency by the fourth or fifth centuries CE.

A different kind of example comes from the same papyrus, *PGM* XXIIa, which involves both speaking and writing a Homeric verse, and is employed to cure bloody flux (*haimar<r>roikon*), which is possibly a reference to hemorrhoids.[29] The instruction for the person doing the healing is to speak *Iliad* 1.75 to the patient's blood (*PGM* XXIIa.2–7):

the wrath (*mēnis*) of Apollo, far-shooting lord

However, the instruction continues, if after the patient is healed he is not grateful, the healer is to throw coals into a fire, place amulets in the smoke, add a root, and write *Iliad* 1.96:

> for this reason the far-shooter gave pains and he will still give them

Both of these verses come from the speeches of Calchas, the famous prophet who accompanied the Achaeans to Troy, and the lines refer to the plague Apollo sent among the Achaeans that sets off the events of the *Iliad*. Because Apollo is a god of both healing and harm, we can see how each side of him is articulated through these verses.

The first, spoken verse (*Iliad* 1.75) seems to derive its efficacy from naming Apollo's wrath with no further action specified, while the second, written verse (*Iliad* 1.96) less ambiguously highlights Apollo's power to give pain. In the first verse, one commentator has suggested that it operates by chilling hemorrhoidal blood,[30] except that it is not at all clear whether this would be desirable, at least not immediately so. The reason is that in the medical treatises associated with the Hippocratic physicians as well as in the works of Galen, whose writings are still central to academic medical practice in the fourth and fifth centuries CE, we find a standard assumption that hemorrhoids are indicative of nature's own cure. In terms of humour theory, nature is purging the body of excess blood, and periodic purgings were thought to be indicative of health.[31] We have a story from the Hippocratics that when a man suffering from hemorrhoids was treated for them, he actually went mad.[32] Another Hippocratic author relates that when hemorrhoids are treated too soon, patients can suffer from inflammation of the lungs, swellings, sores, boils, and other diseases.[33] And Galen connects the premature suppression of hemorrhoids with dropsy, or an excess accumulation of water in other parts of the body.[34] In each case, by suppressing the flow of blood in hemorrhoids, other fluids build up elsewhere. Although one must be cautious in generalizing from professional physicians to a practitioner of magic,[35] this evidence raises the strong possibility that *Iliad* 1.75 is not aimed at curing hemorrhoids at all, but some other kind of bloody flux. Further support for this view comes from the fact that *PGM* XXIIa.5 states that by speaking *Iliad* 1.75 to the blood the verse 'cures' (*iātai*) the 'blood flow', which is now termed *haima<r>roia*.[36] In the Hippocratic authors the equivalent term (*haimorroia*) can refer to other kinds of blood flow, such as the nosebleeds that young men under thirty who live in cooler climates are said to experience in summertime.[37] So while it is not necessary for us to settle on one meaning of *haimorroia* to make sense of *Iliad* 1.75, the aim of the charm is clearly to stop the blood flow rather than let it take its course, giving us good grounds to exclude hemorrhoids.

A context that better fits both the rationale of preventing blood flow and possibly the diction of *Iliad* 1.75 is menstruation. The complexities of menstruation in the Hippocratic treatises have been dealt with by others and a full treatment here is not in order.[38] However, a few relevant points can be made. The humoural basis to Hippocratic menstruation theory holds that because women absorb more fluid from their diet than men, the surplus in fluid needs to be regularly purged.[39] Heavy blood flow was expected, lest the excess fluid build up and thereby disturb the other organs, leading to disease or death.[40] The regularity of menstrual blood flow was based on monthly cycles, which is apparent in the Hippocratic terminology used to refer to it: *katamēnia*, *epimēnia*, and *emmēnia* (all compounds from Greek 'month' *mēn*).[41] In a pattern that we will examine further in due course, in which key nouns and verbs in a given verse relate or are made to relate to the ailment to be healed, the mention of Apollo's wrath (*mēnis*) in *Iliad* 1.75 could have suggested a connection with the Greek word for 'month' *mēn*, which in turn made this verse appear relevant for stopping menstruation. Although heavy blood loss was considered to be healthy, a passage in the *Diseases of Women* expected the period to last two to three days; more or less time than that was indicative of disease.[42] Moreover, checking excess menstrual flow was a concern in the Hippocratic texts, and procedures such as cupping the breasts (so as to withdraw the menses from the lower to the upper regions of the body) were offered as remedies.[43] In this context, it becomes possible that the *haimorroia* at issue in *PGM* XXIIa.5 is excessive menstrual blood flow. And for the thankless patient who is healed through *Iliad* 1.75, the regular recurrence of menstruation makes further sense of using *Iliad* 1.96, along with the other ritual procedures, for retribution: 'for this reason the far-shooter gave pains and he will still give them'.

Such an interpretation of *Iliad* 1.75 and 1.96 in the context of menstruation[44] adds to the impression that all of the verses offered in *PGM* XXIIa may refer to the medical issues of women. The remaining two verses not considered here are *PGM* XXIIa.1 (= *Iliad* 17.714), which is also used to cure bloody flux, and *PGM* XXIIa.15–16, which is used to heal elephantiasis and utilizes *Iliad* 4.141, a verse that specifically mentions a 'woman' (*gunē*) as well as 'ivory' (*elephas*, later used in post-Homeric Greek to mean 'elephant'). But we may be able to take this impression a step further. At the end of these prescribed verses, we find an invocation to Helios 'Sun' and a reference to the 'seventh heaven' (*hebdomos ouranos*), from which at least one scholar has detected a reference to the goddess Isis *heptastolos* (*PGM* XXIIa.17–20).[45] Thus the entire collection of verses in *PGM* XXIIa may refer not only to women's medicine, but also to women who participated in cults of Isis. Furthermore, Isis was the most popular divinity in the Egyptian Fayūm and delta regions, and was specifically associated with women and marriage, maternity and newborns, as well as being the guarantor generally of fertility in the fields and harvest. If this line of interpretation is correct, it would represent the best example that we have of a collection of Homeric verses with a clearly defined group of patients whose specific medical needs – pregnancy, childbirth, menstruation – are being served. Finally, *PGM* XXII also illustrates how the more clearly a given constituency for the incantations can be defined, the more readily the interpretation and relevance of a specific Homeric verse – stripped of its narrative context – can be elucidated.

Verse Combinations and the Power of Metaphor

We have other examples of Homeric verses that were selected indifferently to the narrative context from which they were drawn, which show a cumulative magical effect when used together. Three of them are from book 10 of the *Iliad* (10.521, 564, and 572) and are found together in three different places in the 'great Parisian magical papyrus', *PGM* IV (fourth century CE), which suggests they were treated as a coherent set. They appear first in *PGM* IV.468–74 (a spell for quelling anger and gaining friends) before the 'Mithras Liturgy', clustered with other verses.[46] Next they appear at the end of the 'Mithras Liturgy' in *PGM* IV.821–24, together with one other verse (*Iliad* 8.424). It does not appear that the Homeric verses, although they deliberately frame the 'Mithras Liturgy', have anything directly to do with it.[47] Most strikingly the verses reappear at *PGM* IV.2146–50, in the broader context of 2145–240, where they are written in larger letters than the rest of the text. This incantation has a wide range of uses and will serve as our point of departure.

The incantation is simply designated 'Assistance from three Homeric verses' (*PGM* IV.2145) and the verses appear as follows:

(a) Thus speaking he drove the single-hooved horses through the trench (*taphros*) [*Iliad* 10.564]
(b) and men gasping (*aspairein*) in the harsh bloodshed [*Iliad* 10.521]
(c) and they washed off much sweat (*hidrōs*) in the sea [*Iliad* 10.572]

It is possible that the narrative context, book 10 which in antiquity was known as the *Doloneia*, of these verses has some relevance here, especially for verses (a) and (c), coming as they do after the successful night mission of Odysseus and Diomedes to the Trojan camp, while (b) could certainly be seen as having to do with conquest. But each verse actually has a more broadly metaphorical meaning, which depends not on narrative context but on the action within each verse or within a verse segment.

What has not been fully appreciated is that the lines immediately following these verses, *PGM* IV.2150–60, correlate respectively with each verse and give clues as to the basic action in each verse on which the magical analogy is built. So for example, verse (a) above can be paired with lines 2151–55, where we are told that if a runaway carries these verses on an iron tablet he will never be found. What does driving single-hooved horses through a trench have to do with runaways? In my view the analogy resides in both the notion of the horses and the trench. With regard to the horses, what is significant is not so much that these are the famous Thracian single-hooved horses (*mōnukhes hippoi*) in *Iliad* 10, commandeered by Diomedes, but the notion of *mōnukhes hippoi* generally. The phrase already has an independent existence in archaic Greek poetry and can be found frequently in the *Iliad* (5.236, etc.), once in the *Odyssey* (15.46), as well as in elegy (Theognis 997, 1253 [= Solon fr. 23.1 W], and 1255). It is their speed in particular that is highlighted. Moreover, we have external confirmation of their usefulness in healing magic because the same noun phrase already appears in the first-century BCE "Philinna Papyrus." The pertinent lines are (*PGM* XX.15–16 = *Supplementum Hellenisticum* 900.19–20):

> Flee headache, flee . . . under a rock;
> As wolves flee, as single-hooved horses (*mōnukhes hippoi*) flee

The comparison between the headache's swift flight and that of *mōnukhes hippoi* connotes speed. In turn this comparison suggests that the phrase *mōnukhes hippoi* itself and not the action in the entire Iliadic verse (a) already indicates speed. When applied to the runaway, according to the magical analogy in (a), he will be too fast to be caught.

The notion of *taphros* 'trench' in verse (a) is also important. In the *Iliad* the trench that is at issue is the one the Achaeans have dug around the encampment of their ships on the shore. In Sophocles this same trench signals the boundary between an as yet protected Achaean encampment and the disaster that Hector creates by leaping it (*taphrōn huper*) and setting the Achaean ships on fire (*Ajax* 1279). When extracted from its Homeric context, the idea of 'trench', I submit, represents a boundary more generally.[48] We may recall that the verse is meant to help prevent a runaway slave from being caught, and boundaries, in a more abstract sense, are crucial here. Runaway slaves were common in Rome as elsewhere and often headed for harbors, secluded rural areas, or larger cities where they could disappear into a crowd.[49] In the *Digest* of Justinian (533 CE) we find detailed definitions of what constitutes flight on the part of slaves. The most important consideration, of course, is their intention, but we also find some interesting spatial dimensions to flight that involve boundaries. The jurist Caelius writes that a slave should be considered a fugitive if 'he takes himself somewhere whence his master cannot recover him and still more one who takes himself someplace whence he cannot be removed' (*Digest* 21.1.17.13). And Caelius further records a case in which a freedman was living with his patron in an establishment whose premises could be locked with one key. One of the freedman's slaves concealed himself for a night outside the freedman's quarters, but still within the patron's establishment, except that because the slave had the intention of running away and not returning, he was nevertheless deemed a fugitive (*Digest* 21.1.17.15). Thus the boundary between servitude and freedom can be both literal and metaphorical, as long as it marks the limit of an owner's ability to recover a slave. On this view, the *taphros* 'trench' in verse (a) represents a metaphorical boundary to a runaway slave, on the other side of which is freedom, while the single-hooved horses represent the speed that the slave will need to cross that boundary successfully.

In a similar way, as scholars have recognized, verse (b) above corresponds with lines 2155–56 of *PGM* IV, where it is said that by hanging an iron tablet with the verses inscribed on it around a man on the verge of death an answer will be given for any question asked. The analogy inheres in the perception that the moribund are prophetic, and we have literary examples of this from Greek epic and tragedy, as well as from the Roman literary tradition of necromancy, although I have not found an exact parallel for the actions prescribed in this spell.[50] The general action of men breathing out their last breath in battle (or maybe the particular verb *aspairein* 'to pant/gasp', used only of the dying in Homer) coheres with a dying man; nevertheless, it is not the specific narrative context of the verse that is determinative.

Finally, verse (c) corresponds to what is said at 2159–60 of *PGM* IV. There we read that if anyone believes themselves to be magically bound (*katadedesthai*), they should speak the verses while sprinkling (themselves with?) seawater. The action within the verse itself mimics purification ritual, and we know from sources like *On the Sacred Disease* that the offscourings from such rituals were often deposited in the sea.[51] Once again it is the metaphor of purificatory action in this verse, and not the particular narrative context – which involves Diomedes and Odysseus washing, but not actually religiously purifying themselves after returning to camp – that is effective in ridding one of binding magic.[52] And this is altogether more striking because elsewhere in the *Iliad* there are verses such as 1.314, 'and they purified themselves and threw the offscourings into the sea', which does derive from a narrative context that involves purification, but is not used here or anywhere else so far as I know as a magical verse. This suggests even more strongly that metaphor and analogy, rather than narrative context, are governing the choice of verses used.

There are many more uses for the three verses in *PGM* IV.2146–241 than I can treat in detail here. The spell has general protective properties, for example, allowing contestants of several kinds – charioteer, gladiator, defendants in court – to remain undefeated. Further, wearing the tablet with the verses inscribed will also keep away demons and wild animals; it will make one invulnerable in war and inspire fear in one's enemies; it will create favor and desire in others to render anything that is asked; it will make one irresistibly beloved, and so forth. All of these uses can be explained in terms of analogy, as we have seen, or in terms of what we might call secondary elaborations that depend upon metaphors and similes that are created from the verbs, nouns, and noun phrases within the verses.

It is important, however, to be careful when using the notion of analogy in this context, because some verses may give rise to more than one analogy. Let us look more closely at verse (a). In addition to being told how this verse will prevent a runaway from being found, we are also told that if this verse along with the other two are written on a tin tablet, and garlic along with snakeskin are burned, the tablet will be useful for overturning a chariot in the games (2211–12). Since *Iliad* 10.564 of the three is the only one having to do with horses and chariots, this must be our key verse. But note that the action of driving single-hooved horses through a ditch is now highlighted for the damage an opponent's chariot may suffer as a result rather than for the speed of a victor's horses. We thus have two asymmetrically sympathetic actions that are metaphorically generalized from this same verse – the first for speed and propagation, and the second for hindrance. This example, more than any other that we have seen, strongly suggests that caution is in order when analyzing the underlying metaphor of a magical verse, because the interpretive process exercised by its users can be expansive rather than narrowly fixed. Such a view, moreover, accords with Tambiah's observation, which was drawn from an entirely different set of cultural evidence, that in magic "words excel in expressive enlargement."[53] The challenge is to disentangle the metaphors and analogies at issue and to understand how they work together.

Besides verse (a), the other two verses presumably connote conquest (b) and protection or cleansing (c), which simultaneously allows the charioteer to be victorious just as verse (a) will prevent his opponents from achieving success. The impulse to combine more than one verse to produce an effect supplies further evidence that narrative context is no longer controlling by the fourth century CE. New combinations of magical action are being sought by using different verses together, as well as by enlarging the metaphorical range of the action that is derivable from each verse.

We can take this same approach to another benefit said to accrue to one who has written the same three verses on a tablet, and then inserted it into the fatal wound of a criminal: he will enjoy a generally excellent reputation and will be loved by any man or woman with whom the bearer of the tablet has contact (*PGM* IV.2165–79). In other words, these verses can also produce amorous attachments. On the face of it, there does not appear to be any connection between the action within the verses and amorous sentiment, except in verse (c). If we look elsewhere within the magical papyri, we find that *hidrōs* 'sweat' does at least have sexually procreative associations. For example, in *PGM* V.96–172 (fourth century CE?), a text attributed to the scribe Ieu, we hear of the headless *daimōn* whose sweat falls upon the earth as rain so that it may be inseminated (152), and in *PGM* LXI.1–38 (third century CE), a love charm, olive oil, and some other ingredients are to be placed in a jar, and the liquid contents are to be addressed as the sweat (*hidrōs*) of the *Agathos Daimōn*, the utterance of Helios, the mucus of Isis, the power of Osiris, and the pleasure of the gods (5–8). Moreover, the sea was a common place into which charms of various kinds (*PGM* VII.420 and 437 [third/fourth century CE], both spells of restraint), including erotic spells (e.g., *PGM* VII.464), were to be thrown – probably because seawater was long understood to have purifying effects. Therefore we can surmise that our Homeric verse (c), with its reference to washing sweat off into the sea, could have generated sexual associations in another example of a secondary metaphorical elaboration, after the more apparent ones of cleansing and purification.

Intoxication, Choking, and Gout

If the rationale for the use of these Homeric verses as I have outlined it so far is at least plausible, it does not minimize the fact that the reasoning behind the usage of other verses remains less clear. Whether such verses were as opaque to their users as they are to us is a different, although equally important, question, but this is sometimes difficult to judge. Nevertheless, given the model of interpretation for these verses that I have outlined, I think we can make some headway in understanding them. As one example, consider a recommendation from the tenth-century CE agricultural handbook, the *Geoponica*, which although medieval preserves much late antique and earlier material. At one point it describes a series of remedies for alleviating drunkenness. We learn that one can eat a cooked goat lung, for example, or before drinking one can eat almonds or raw cabbage, but if none of this works, one can say *Iliad* 8.170 before taking the first drink (*Geoponica* 7.31.1–2 Beckh):

> Then thrice from the Idaean mountains thundered Zeus of the counsels.

Why was this verse thought to be effective against drunkenness? In the context of the *Iliad*, it describes Zeus thundering at the Trojans as a warning that the tide of battle is about to turn against them. But according to the chronological model for which I have been arguing, I would expect that when this verse became associated with alleviating drunkenness its narrative context did not matter at all. Although the metaphor of being 'thunderstruck by wine' is as early as the seventh-century BCE lyric poet Archilochus (fr. 120), we can surmise that Zeus' thundering in our verse was meant to keep the imbiber alert. Elsewhere in the *Geoponica* lightning and thunderbolts are negatively associated with bad weather, because they can herald too much rain that will harm the crops – and of the crops mentioned the grape harvest is specifically noted.[54] But this seems too general a field of association. A more decisive explanation may come from the role thunder plays in dream interpretation, as reported by the famous dream-interpreter Artemidorus of Ephesus (second century CE). Amid the free-ranging dream interpretations he offers, two basic principles underlie them: the first is that the thunderbolt is fire and it is the nature of fire to destroy all matter;[55] and the second is that whatever is struck by a thunderbolt loses its characteristic properties.[56] Although Artemidorus does not mention intoxication specifically, his account suggests that thunder was perceived, literally and metaphorically, to reverse a current state of affairs. I submit, then, that it is along lines of reasoning such as these that *Iliad* 8.170 was thought to negate the effects of intoxication.

Another example comes from the second-century CE Roman physician Marcellus' work *On Remedies* (*De Medicamentis*),[57] where we read about several spells for removing fish bones or other objects stuck in the throat. Two of these involve pseudo-Greek charms transliterated into Latin, and are accompanied by practical and magical procedures: one charm is to be spoken three times by the patient and then he is to spit; another involves a second person, who is to massage the patient's throat while saying a verse, preferably after secretly placing the backbone of the offending fish on top of the patient's head. It is in this context, however, that Marcellus relates a third possibility: one can speak *Odyssey* 11.634–35, from the underworld scene or *Nekuia*, into the ear of the patient, or write them on a piece of papyrus and attach it to the patient's neck with a string (Marcellus, *De Med.* 15.108):

> Lest dread Persephone send out the Gorgonian head
> of a terrible monster to me from Hades

There are some syntactical problems that seem to have gone unaddressed when these verses were taken from their narrative context. In the *Odyssey* the verses are spoken by Odysseus, who reports that after seeing a horde of dead souls approach him, he was seized with green fear, then follow our verses, which are thus part of a fear clause. We should properly translate them: 'Lest dread Persephone send out the Gorgonian head of a terrible monster to me from Hades'. However, in Marcellus the verses are out of context and instead function as a wish clause, technically an optative of wish: 'If only dread Persephone may not send out the Gorgonian head of a terrible monster to me from Hades'. It was Roeper who first suggested that these verses ought to be understood similarly to a Christian charm found in the medical handbook compiled by Aëtius of Amida, the sixth-century CE physician in Alexandria and Constantinople.[58] In this passage Aëtius recommends that for a bone stuck in the throat, the physician should seat his patient opposite him, and then say the following (Aëtius 8.54.18–20 Olivieri):

> Come up, bone, whether bone or stalk or whatever else, as Jesus Christ brought back Lazarus from his tomb and Jonah from the whale.

The comparison of this passage with the verses in Marcellus suggests that in our Odyssean lines we are to identify the Gorgon's head with the bone to be dislodged. Gorgons can be conceptualized as the ailment – for example, gout – to be healed in some magical texts.[59] In other magical contexts, the image of the Gorgon's head appears submissively to that of a stronger animal, such as a cat that grasps at it with its paw.[60] But I do not think the simile in the Aëtius passage above applies to our Odyssean verses, since that would suggest they were aimed at drawing the bone out. Instead, the grammar of the extracted Odyssean verses clearly implies that the Gorgon's head is *not* to be sent out from Hades. And while it may be the case that the grammar was overlooked, we do have several examples of Homeric verses that were consciously syntactically modified for their magical contexts.[61] So we must have to do with a request to prevent the bone/Gorgon from harming the patient by requesting that it remain in the stomach, or in any case below the throat – regions that, in the verses, are conceptualized as

Hades. In the context of Marcellus' three recommendations for a bone stuck in the throat we have three possible outcomes: in the first, the patient speaks verses and spits, which may cast out the bone; in the second, the patient's throat is massaged, which could cause the bone to move out or further back into the throat; and in the third, verse-only procedure, the above *Odyssey* 11.634–35 verses are recited as a request that the offending bone simply move down into the stomach and stay there.

One of the most obscure uses of a Homeric verse is for the treatment of gout. Alexander of Tralles (vol. 2, p. 581 Puschmann) recommends wearing a gold *lamella* inscribed with *Iliad* 2.95:

> The assembly was in confusion (*tetrēkhei*), and the earth groaned underneath.
> *tetrēkhei d' agorē, hupo de stenakhizeto gaia*

What is remarkable about this particular recommendation is that a gold tablet or *lamella* dated to the third century CE or later was acquired by Dumbarton Oaks in Washington, DC, in 1953 with this verse actually inscribed on it.[62] The *lamella* was rolled up, possibly for insertion into a tubular case, which probably would have been worn around the ankle of one of the gout-ridden feet. The verse occurs in book 2 of the *Iliad*, called in antiquity the *Diapeira* or 'Trial', on the morning after the messenger of Zeus, Ossa, has misleadingly informed Agamemnon of Zeus' intention to grant the Achaeans victory. It describes the turmoil caused by Ossa as she stirs up the Achaeans as they prepare to arm. But in view of what we have seen up to this point, we have good evidence to believe that narrative context is not at all relevant here. One scholar has suggested that one source of confusion, which might have made this verse seem relevant for gout, was that the verb *tarassein* 'to stir up/trouble', which gives us the perfect form *tetrēkhei* in the verse, was misunderstood by Alexandrian and later poets to derive from the adjective *trakhus* 'rough'.[63] The perfect infinitive *tetrēkhenai* would then mean 'to be rough', but I do not think this explanation is satisfactory.[64] In the context of contemporary medical theory, a different explanation is also possible. Numerous forms of gout from mild to severe are discussed by second- to third-century CE medical and literary authors. As one example, the Roman physician Marcellus divides the ailment into two classes: he calls gout that is not severe 'cold' (*frigida*), while he describes the more serious form as 'hot' (*calida*). He notes that the latter type would involve inflamed, red protuberances on the feet.[65] Lucian, in a play entitled 'Gout' *Podagra*, has the chorus refer to the more serious form of 'hot' gout when it describes the condition thus (69.123–24):

[gout] eats, devours, inflames (φλέγειν), overpowers, burns (πυροῦν) and softens, until the goddess commands the pain to flee.

Thus the Homeric meaning of *tetrēkhei* 'stirred up/troubled' could stand, and it would then refer to the agitated nature of the condition.

There may also be word-play with the Greek term for gout in the Homeric verse itself. In Greek, 'gout' is ποδάγρα (Latin *podagra*, a transliteration of the Greek), and should properly be derived from *pous* 'foot' and *agra* 'trap', in other words, 'gout' is a 'trap for the feet'.[66] While the term *podagra* is post-Homeric, the appearance (see the Greek transliteration of the verse above) in our verse of the particle and noun δ' ἀγορή (*d' agorē*, which is an Ionic dialect form for *d' agora*) followed by the preposition ὑπό (*hupo*) is extremely suggestive. If one were searching for a Homeric verse that contained the letters of *podagra* rearranged in an anagram, then our verse might have been selected and "misread" as if the words *d' agorē*, *hupo* contained a scrambled reference to *po-dagra*. As we noted earlier, in magical texts of the Roman period (first–sixth centuries CE), we observe a heightening in the sophistication of word games in spells, including palindromes, acrostics, and anagrams. The verse could then be interpreted to mean in effect that the gout was 'hot' and the earth, Gaia, was groaning as a result. This accords too with the way in which Lucian describes gout, when he says that it is, after all, 'the goddess' (ἡ θεός) who is responsible for it.[67] And among the many pharmacological remedies for gout that Lucian records, it is striking that among them are also 'incantations' (*epaoidais*), perhaps of the type we are examining here.[68] Although this interpretation is obviously speculative, such a reading gives the desired sense between the verse and the problem to be solved, based on the model that I have outlined for how Homeric verses were chosen.

Incantations and Divination

One important practical consequence of thinking about Homeric verses according to such a model, especially after the second century CE, is that it prepares us to entertain the possibility of magical intentions behind verses that appear in contexts not otherwise associated with magic. Certainly we must exercise caution here, because there is second-century CE evidence that knowledge of Homeric poetry outside of magical contexts, for instance in the symposium, could be extensive and detailed.[69] But the following two examples, since they have nothing to do with symposia and have parallels with the material described earlier, demand a different explanation.

The first is an inscribed graffito first published in 1939, then republished in 1950 by Jeanne and Louis Robert,[70] found on a wall in Rome dated to the second or third century CE. It features five verses, *Iliad* 24.171–75. There are some textual problems and metrical irregularities, especially in verse 172:

> Take courage, Priam son of Dardanos, she says, and do not fear anything.
> For I do not come here foreboding evil,
> but intending good things; I am, I assure you, messenger of Zeus,
> who although far away from you cares for and pities you.
> The Olympian commanded you to ransom glorious Hector.

These verses are an exhortation by Iris to Priam to undertake the journey to Achilles to retrieve the body of Hector. The Roberts suggest that since these verses are in effect a message from Zeus announcing his support for a difficult mission, they are apotropaic – a term that literally means to 'turn away', for instance, evils, which I think is probably correct.

The Roberts further suggest that the inscription was made following a reading from a 'Homer oracle' (*Homēromanteion*), in which presumably one of these verses appeared. This view deserves further consideration because it challenges the distinction between the divinatory and magical use of Homeric verses, but such a distinction is not always so clear. The use of Homeric verses for divination and incantations in principle should be distinguishable: in divination, the verse or verses are thought to contain a prediction; in incantations, the speaking or writing of a given verse or verses produces a change of condition, along the lines of the analogical and metaphorical processes that we have outlined. In practice, however, we know that at least one Homeric verse used as an incantation also appeared in the famous 'Homer oracle' (third to fourth century CE), *PGM* VII.1–148.[71] Furthermore, consider the story in Lucian about the false prophet, Alexander, who is said to have disseminated the following pseudo-Homeric oracle to all the Roman nations during the plague of 165 CE (Lucian, *Alexander* 36):

> Unshorn Phoebus (*Phoibos akeirekomēs*), keep away the cloud of plague.

The pseudo-Homeric quality of this verse is detectable in the phrase *Phoibos akeirekomēs*, as compared with the properly Homeric *Phoibos akersekomēs* 'unshorn Phoebus' (*Iliad* 20.39 and *Homeric Hymn to Apollo* 134), while the remainder of the verse is also not Homeric. According to Lucian, this 'oracle, delivered by the god himself' (*Alexander* 36.30) was then said to have been written over doorways as a 'charm against the plague'

(36.4–5). Thus a Homeric verse delivered as an oracle could also serve apotropaic purposes against evils like the plague when written down in publicly visible places. From the remainder of the story we can surmise that Lucian is not parodying the practice of writing such verses down for apotropaic ends, so much as the belief in their efficacy: the point of his parody is that those who wrote this verse actually *attracted* the plague to their homes rather than fended it off (36.5–12). Of course this outcome is funny. But the practice of using the same Homeric verses in divination and in magical contexts reminds us that inscribed Homeric verses, when encountered outside a strictly literary context, can have a specific ritual purpose.

The second example of an unusual citation of Homeric verses occurs in a Florentine papyrus from the Heroninus archive, which is located in the Fayūm area of Egypt and dated to the third century CE (*P. Flor.* II 259).[72] The cache was found in Theadelphia on the estate of Appianus, a prominent citizen and counselor of Alexandria who owned the estate until his death in 260 CE. One letter in particular is of interest, and it involves an exchange between two of the estate administrators, Timaeus and Heroninus:

> Timaeus to Heroninus his
> most beloved, greetings.
> It is now time for you to
> send up either the bags of grain
> or the price (for them); and let
> Kiot' know that if he does not
> give the other *sakkos* (= 3 art.) or
> come up and pay his dues,
> a soldier is coming down
> to get him. But all the same
> send them up. I pray for your health.

So far we have here a fairly mundane situation in which Timaeus is requesting Heroninus to make good on a purchase of grain and to remind a second fellow in Heroninus' employ, Kiot', that he too should pay Timaeus or he will be arrested. But Timaeus also appears to have had literary pretensions, or so that is what the editors of this papyrus have claimed.[73] In the left-hand margin of this letter, in the same hand,[74] Timaeus has written *Iliad* 2.1–2:

The other gods and chariot-fighting men
slept all night long (*heudon pannukhi*), but sweet sleep did not hold Zeus
They slept all night long (*heudon pannukhi*)

The literary jibe, as one commentator calls it, seems obvious: Heroninus has neglected his responsibilities and while he and his minions may sleep, others are keeping watch. To emphasize the point Timaeus has even repeated the phrase *heudon pannukhi* 'they slept all night long'. Granted, perhaps Timaeus was a close reader of Homer and knew that Heroninus would appreciate his wit. But in a day and age when Homeric verses were used so prominently as incantations and oracles, a strong case can be made that Timaeus sent a different sort of message to Heroninus. In effect, Timaeus put the Homeric verses there as a little magical insurance to ensure that in the larger scheme of things, his goods would be protected no matter what Heroninus did. We do not have to believe that Timaeus himself was actually practicing magic or reporting an oracle on this papyrus. What was significant was that by quoting Homer in this way Timaeus drew upon the Greek and Greco-Egyptian tradition of using Homeric verses in magic or divination. Thus both the Roman graffito and Timaeus' epistolary Homeric citation, when viewed in light of the magical and divinatory use of Homeric verses in the second or third century CE, are best understood not as literary but as ritualized gestures.

Neoplatonic Theurgy and Homer

We may be able to appreciate the broader context into which the magical use of Homeric verses fits if we look to certain Neoplatonic interpretations of Homer. The Neoplatonists may be summarized loosely as a philo-sophical tradition that took Plato's writings as their main source of inspiration, dating from the first century BCE down to the sixth century CE. Several of the later Neoplatonists, including Porphyry (234–ca. 305 CE) and Proclus (410/412–485 CE), in addition to the writings of Plato also exten-sively analyzed the Homeric poems for clues to the structure of the universe and the divine nature of the soul. The long and complicated tradition that led to Homer's divine status among the Neoplatonists has been illuminated in detail by others and need not detain us here.[75] What is important is that the Neoplatonic tradition credited Homer with being a sage with knowledge of the underworld and the fate of the soul after death. However, the writings of Proclus are particularly relevant for our purposes. In chapter 3, in the context of discussing how statues and *erōs* figurines were animated in the Greek magical papyri, we have already noted that Proclus described the theurgic process as culminating with the placement of the *sumbolon* or token (a piece of stone, metal, a gem, or an herb) into the mouth of a figurine.[76] Proclus is also knowledgeable about the incan-tatory use of Homeric verses, however, and he alludes to the same two verses discussed earlier that appear in Lucian (*Iliad* 5.127–28 in Lucian, *Charon* 7.12–13). By examining the theurgic ends to which Proclus puts these verses, as well as his understanding of what Homeric poetry was, we can better clarify how the efficacy of Homeric verses was thought to operate in the fifth century CE. We may also gain some insight into why Homer, above all other early poets, stood in the forefront of this particular magical tradition.

Let us take the issue of what Homeric poetry was for Proclus first. For Proclus the highest kind of poetry possible was divinely inspired, and thus Homer, Hesiod, and the Chaldean oracles, to name only some, fell within that purview. Over the course of nearly a thousand years, through a complex series of allegorical readings, commentaries, defenses, and critiques, extending from Theagenes of Rhegium (fl. ca. 525 BCE), the Pythagoreans, Plato, and the Middle Platonists, Homer finally emerged for the later Neoplatonists like Proclus as the most prominent sage who had articulated in his poetry a profound model of the universe. The Neoplatonists generally and Proclus in particular attempted to reconcile their respect for Homer with Plato's contempt for the mimetic dimension of poetry which he castigated in book 10 of his *Republic*.[77] To circumvent the scandalous depiction of the divinities in Homer, such as the tryst of Aphrodite and Ares in *Odyssey* book 8, Proclus undertook detailed allegorical readings of his myths to show that Homer was presenting symbolic images that referenced the cosmic order, but which were encoded in language that by definition corrupted the highest truths. Now much of this goes beyond our immediate concerns, but a passage from Proclus' *Commentary on the Republic* is revealing for its magical implications (I 86.15–19 Kroll):

> For in all such fictions found in the makers of myths, one thing is generally hinted at by another. In all that the poets indicate by these means, it is not a relationship of models to copies, but of symbols (*sumbola*) to something else which has sympathy (*sumpatheia*) with it by virtue of analogy (*analogia*).

Because Homer's poetry was divinely inspired, it reflected the divine world rather than the mortal one, which is why the model–copy relationship for Proclus was not appropriate. Instead, Homeric myths are *sumbola* (or, in other contexts, *sunthēmata*) that have to be interpreted, and do not have to be analogous in a strict sense to the truths that they express. Proclus draws further on the notion of analogy (*analogia*), which does not hold the modern sense that I have used elsewhere in this book. For the Neoplatonists *analogia* originally expressed a mathematical relationship, but in allegorical contexts it referred to a correspondence between the surface meaning of a text and whatever metaphysical truths the text expressed.[78] More specifically, *sumbola* to the Neoplatonists were certain animals, stones, plants, and names (i.e., linguistic symbols) that were believed, when used in theurgic rituals, to attract given deities from the heavenly and invisible spheres into the material and visible world – the ultimate purpose of which was to unify the theurgist with the One, the source of all godhead.[79] Theurgy (literally in Greek *theourgia* means 'divine work' or 'sacramental rite') was at once an intellectual, philosophical, and religio-magical program that various authors explain as the practice of bringing a practitioner into communion with ultimate divinity, the One. This unification was accomplished through *sumpatheia*, which for the Neoplatonists and Stoics generally was an ontological connection between the visible, articulated world on the one hand, and the unified, cosmic world on the other.

With this as background, we can now turn to Proclus' use of *Iliad* 5.127–28. The Homeric verses are:

> take away the mist (*akhlus*) from your eyes, which was there before,
> so that you may well recognize who is a god or a man

We recall that these verses were uttered by Hermes to heal the short-sightedness of Charon in Lucian, *Charon* (7.12–13), and in the *Iliad* they referred to how Athena helped Diomedes to distinguish god and man during his fight against the Trojans. Proclus alludes to these verses in two places in his *Hymns* which, as Van den Berg has recently argued, must be understood as "theurgy in practice," and as purificatory instruments themselves for attracting the divine powers.[80] Purification in this context is still magical, although it is subordinated to the salvific aims of approaching divinity. In *Hymn* 4, Proclus addresses the gods to whom the *Hymn* is dedicated (4.5–7):

> Hear, great saviors, and grant me from holy books
> pure light, after scattering the mist (*homikhlē*),
> in order that I might well recognize an immortal god from a man.

For Proclus and other Neoplatonists before him, the pure light that replaces the scattered mist allegorically refers to souls descended into bodies that can no longer directly contemplate true reality. The dispersion of the mist returns a noeric light to the soul, which in turn allows the contemplation of the (Platonic) Forms and living in accordance with Mind.[81]

This same idea is reinforced in Proclus' second allusion to *Iliad* 5.127–28, which occurs in his first *Hymn* to the god Helios 'Sun'. Helios was an important divinity for the Neoplatonists and Proclus as part of his daily ritual actually worshipped the sun at dusk, noon, and dawn.[82] Here we read (*Hymn* 1.39–41):

> may you always grant through your evil-averting aid
> pure, much-blessed light to my soul
> after scattering the man-destroying, venomous mist (*akhlus*)

The specific mention here of *akhlus*, which takes on a life of its own in Neoplatonic thought, links this passage quite clearly to *Iliad* 5.127 and has the same connotation here as the word for mist (*homikhlē*) in *Hymn* 4. Taken together, however, these allusions to *Iliad* 5.127–28 are not merely literary but magical – and, specifically, theurgic. The magical connotation of the passage above is also brought out by the reference to 'evil-averting aid', which is a magical reference to the apotropaic defense that Helios can grant. In both passages Proclus has allegorized *Iliad* 5.127–28 to refer to the purification of the soul from the body's dross. Whether Proclus learned of the magical use of these verses from Lucian or from some other source is not clear,[83] but he was generally aware of the Pythagorean use of Homeric verses for healing. In any case, the Iliadic verses and the myth to which they refer function for him as a theurgical *sumbolon*.[84]

We must be careful, however, not to confuse the theurgical use of Homeric verses in Proclus with what we find in the other Homeric verses that we have examined. As we have just seen, the ultimate aim of theurgic ritual is to unite the practitioner to the One, to the ultimate source of divinity. Hence the need for verses that signify the dispersion of the body's 'mist' or material veil that blocks access to true reality. Our other examples of Homeric verses are quite different. No higher or salvific motive is implied in selecting verses to prevent pregnancy, bleeding, or gout, or to ensure the safety of one's person or goods, other than to resolve those particular problems. Arguably, the emphasis in these examples on solving problems in the material world itself disqualifies them from consideration as theurgic. Nevertheless, a conceptual framework as that provided by the Neoplatonists or Proclus offers the best explanation for why Homeric verses in particular developed this kind of magical function.

This impression is reinforced when we contrast the magical and divinatory use of Homeric verses with the ritualized use of biblical and especially Vergilian verses. We are fortunate to possess one example of a veterinary text that recommends a biblical verse in one instance, a Homeric verse in another. And the comparison between them is telling. In the largely anonymous writings of the *Corpus hippiatricorum graecorum* (fourth

century CE) we find a remedy for a mare having trouble giving birth
(10.3.5): one should place a papyrus on it with Psalm 48.1–6, up until
the mention of the woman in labor. In these lines the mountain of
Zion and the city of the great king are mentioned, and are revealed to the
astonishment and panic of the Korahite kings. However, when a horse is
infertile, one should write *Iliad* 5.749 (= 8.393):

> moving on their own groaned the gates (*pulai*) of heaven (*ouranos*) which
> the Hours held

This is the only example to my knowledge of a Homeric verse used in the
treatment of animals, but it operates according to the same general principles that I have outlined. We may only guess at the extent to which the
'gates' and 'heaven' are generalized metaphorically to represent equine
anatomy. But if we can regard infertility as a relatively more serious problem than difficulties during birth, then it appears that the Homeric verse
is the more powerful one.[85]

Verses taken from the great epic of Vergil, the *Aeneid*, in contrast to
Homeric ones, were rarely employed for expressly magical aims. They
were employed, however, in divination by way of the so-called *sortes
Vergilianae* 'Vergilian lots', although our evidence for this tradition is
largely fabricated.[86] This practice was apparently similar to Homer oracles
but actually had more in common with the *sortes Biblicae* 'Biblical lots',
which involved opening the Bible and selecting a verse or verses in
answer to a question.[87] We may also mention in this context the different
but related practice of accessing selected verses through dice throws, as
in the *sortes Sanctorum* 'Saints' lots' and the *sortes Sangallenses* 'St. Gaul
lots' which then provided the answer to a question.[88] We first hear about
the sortitional use of Vergil in the fourth century CE, but the practice
is speciously attributed to emperors of an earlier time, beginning with
Hadrian (emperor 117–38 CE). Outside of these sources, it is difficult to
gauge the actual extent of popular usage of the *sortes Vergilianae*. But
throughout the fourth century CE (319–409), Christian emperors beginning with Constantine issued twelve edicts banning all forms of divination
by any means.[89]

As in the use of Homeric verses as incantations for healing, the underlying intellectual framework that reinforced the efficacy of sortitional
verses was also fundamentally Neoplatonic. We have striking testimony
to this view in a conversation between St. Augustine, whose entire life
famously turned on an oracular verse,[90] and Vindicianus, the former
astrologer turned court physician to Valentinian II sometime in 379/82 CE.
The topic is horoscopes and Augustine reports:[91]

> When I asked [Vindicianus] why many true things were foretold by astrology, he replied, ably enough, that the force of the lot, diffused everywhere in nature, brought this about. For if someone by chance consults the pages of some poet, who sang and intended something very different, a verse often turns out to be wonderfully in accord with some present business. He used to say that it was not to be wondered at if from the human soul, by means of some higher instinct unaware of what was happening in itself, some utterance occurs not by art but by chance (*sors*), which is in harmony with the affairs and actions of the inquirer.

The Neoplatonic crux of this passage emerges not so much from the attribution to chance (*sors*) of a correspondence between a verse and a given circumstance as it does from the recognition that the human soul exists in some sympathetic relationship to the universe.[92] Although Vindicianus is a former astrologer now, as he says, schooled in the Hippocratic writings and devoted to scientific medicine, his view suggests that sortitional verses – and by extrapolation magical verses – were perceived to operate according to this general principle. This passage also gives us a rare glimpse into the mindset of an acknowledged specialist on the ground, so to speak, whose views offer a nice counterpart to the intellectualized, theurgical interpretation of magical Homeric verses adopted by Proclus.

In contrast to the numerous sources for incantatory Homeric verses that we have seen, we have only one confirmed use of a Vergilian verse for magic, and its cultural context is unclear. In a tenth-century CE manuscript containing Pliny the Elder's *Medicina* (St. Galler codex 751), a remedy is offered for quartan fever that involves writing *Aeneid* 4.129 (= 11.1):

> Meanwhile Dawn rising left the sea.

This instruction only appears here, in an epitome to the third book of the *Medicina*, and its authenticity was suspected by the text's editor.[93] But it appears to parallel the use of Homeric verses that we have examined above and may therefore point to a medieval (southern Gaul?), if not earlier, tradition of employing Vergilian verses to cure certain ailments. Presumably the fever is to be identified with dawn in this verse, so that as dawn leaves so should the fever. In any case, although the Latin evidence is scant, we can say with some certainty that Homeric and not Vergilian poetry remained the authoritative source for incantations in later antiquity into the Middle Ages. And as we might expect, it did so more in the eastern than in the western part of the Roman empire.[94]

Conclusion

In summary, the model presented here for the incantatory use of Homeric verses builds on earlier approaches, but also modifies them in several important ways. First, although there are analogies between the action within a verse and the intended effect, as we have seen, we cannot depend too rigidly on a static view of what a given verse means in its Homeric context to predict its use as an incantation. Verses are interpreted metaphorically, and then can undergo secondary elaborations of meaning to derive sometimes contradictory effects from the same verse. This process expands the interpretive possibilities of the verses as it does the range of ailments and issues that can be addressed through them. Moreover, we know that Greek and Greco-Egyptian readers of Homer did not always retain the Homeric meaning of the verses themselves. Narrative context appears to have structured the earliest Pythagorean and Empedoclean use of verses according to the biographical tradition, and when verses are first independently attested apart from that tradition in the second century CE. But narrative context largely loses its significance by the fourth century CE, as individual verses are invested with different meanings relevant to the changing social, cultural, and medical circumstances of their users.

The Neoplatonist framework, which I have argued is important for situating especially the later use of Homeric verses in magic, allows us to draw some further conclusions. If, according to Neoplatonists like Proclus, Homeric poetry preeminently embodied the divinity which also inspired its expression, then select verses taken from Homer, irrespective of narrative context, still contained divine power. On that account, the verses also retained a sympathy between the cosmic and material world order. We are now in a better position to understand why verses were chosen that appeared to cohere with the ailment or problem to be fixed: the sympathetic nature of each verse, along with the proper ritual procedures, was restorative precisely because it renewed the link between the cosmic and material worlds. Homeric verses healed because they originated prior to the diminished state of the material world – hence they originated prior to all human debilitation and ailment.

CHAPTER 5

Magic in Greek and Roman Law

ᒻᒻᒻᒻ

This chapter moves out of the realm of understanding particular Greek magical practices and into that of its legislation. In order to put the legislation of Greek magic into a broader context that reaches into late antiquity, where as we have seen many practices including the animation of figurines and the use of Homeric incantations were alive and well, we shall also have to concern ourselves with Roman laws on magic. There will be numerous occasions to revisit particular magical practices – both Greek practices that we have seen and some Roman practices that we have not – except that our guiding framework will be to understand how such practices violated, or were perceived to violate, ancient laws put in place to protect the integrity of citizens and the state. Our discussion at the end of this chapter looks forward to the early medieval Christian interpretations of Roman laws against magic. As we have alluded to in chapter 1, some understanding of this is important because the legal basis for the prosecution of late medieval and early modern witchcraft has its origin in Roman law. And it was not by coincidence, but rather by the authority of an earlier tradition, that Roman jurists sought Greek precedents for their own understanding of magic and its effects.

There are several further reasons for extending our study of the legislation against magic into the high imperial Roman period. First, Rome has very few truly indigenous magical practices – most of the Greek magic we have reviewed up to this point, including incantations, drugs, binding curses, and figurines, find such close parallels in Rome and throughout its empire that they can only be explained by appealing to absorption and adaptation. In some cases, as with curse tablets, the vast majority are written in Greek including those found in predominantly Latin-speaking provinces, while the Latin tablets we do have clearly derive from Greek models. Second, Greek, in addition to Roman, practitioners of magic were prosecuted under Roman law, and in late antiquity we find evidence for a stereotype among upper-class Romans that Greeks, in particular, were adept at magic.[1] Third, from the point of view of later antiquity (especially the third–sixth centuries) attitudes among Roman emperors, jurists, and, after the Christianization of Rome, Church Fathers hardened considerably toward magic, and it did not occur to them to draw sharp distinctions between 'Greek' and 'Roman' magic. Because many of the activities they sought to legislate were given their fundamental shape in Greece, instead we often find Roman writers seeking the precise Greek terminology to explain Latin concepts. On the other hand, Roman authors did advance their own interpretations to explain and justify legislation against magical practices, and it is here where we find several distinctively Roman innovations.

Magic in Greek Law and Legal Imagination

There is surprisingly little evidence for a concern in Greek law of the classical period with magic.[2] For some city-states, like Athens, no legislation survives that directly concerns magic of any kind, while in others like Teos, on the coast north of Ephesus in Asia Minor, there is at least one narrow prohibition against the manufacture of harmful drugs, which may or may not have to do with magic. About the broader range of magical activities that we have seen, including purifications, incantations, the multiple families of curse tablets, binding spells, and figurines, Greek law is inexplicably silent. It is important, however, not to assume that the absence of legislation denotes the absence of concern with magic, nor do we have a full corpus of Athenian law on which to base our judgments. Nevertheless, there is a good deal of indirect evidence that some types of magic were considered more harmful than others, and that harmful magic could lead to damage to person or property. We have several legal cases, both real and hypothetical, that indicate a serious legal concern with the effects of magic, especially where it results in injury or death.

The legislative concerns that we do find in Athens and elsewhere, however, tend to converge primarily around the use of *pharmaka* (sg. *pharmakon*), a term that as we have seen basically means plant-based 'drugs'. The term *pharmakon* is notoriously ambiguous, and is employed regularly by medical writers to mean 'medicines', while in other contexts it can mean 'poisons'.[3] However, in magical contexts of all kinds *pharmaka* can refer to drugs and, in some instances, spells more generally, as does its abstract noun *pharmakeia* 'magic' and derivative verb *pharmattein* 'to bewitch'. The ambiguity of *pharmakon* persists well into the Roman period. The equivalent Latin term for 'poison/medicine/magical drug' is *venenum* and it exhibits the same indeterminacy. In erotic magical contexts, *pharmaka* specifically refers to 'philtres', or love potions, for instance those given to men so as to revive their affection for a lover or concubine. Technically, 'philtres' translates Greek *philtra*, but *philtra* and *pharmaka* overlap in contexts of erotic magic.[4] In its earliest magical attestations in the *Iliad* and *Odyssey* of Homer, *pharmaka* are usually qualified by adjectives that signal whether they are beneficial or harmful.[5] This provides further evidence that even in magical contexts Greeks distinguished between the *pharmakon* as 'drug' and the positive or negative uses to which it could be put. In matters of ancient law, it is thus not the *pharmaka* as such that dictate what interpretation to give them, but rather the context and intent of those who employed them. In a given legal case, whether to interpret a *pharmakon* as a harmful magical drug or as a helpful medical remedy sometimes hinged entirely on the nature of the damage observed and on the testimony of the parties involved.

Cases dealing with *pharmaka* that resulted in injury or death attracted the most legal attention in Athens, and they are of interest to us because they forced the parties involved to clarify the exact nature of the *pharmaka*.[6] Capital cases, in other words those involving intentional homicide or injury, were tried in Athens' most ancient and revered court, the Areopagus, as we learn from Demosthenes and Aristotle.[7] Several types of deliberate (*ek pronoias*) homicide or injury fell under the Areopagus' jurisdiction, including murder, bodily harm, arson, and cases 'of poisons (*pharmaka*), if anyone kills by giving them'.[8] But one man's poison was another man's love potion, and therein lay the rub. The penalty for intentional homicide was execution or permanent exile, provided the exile was taken before the court issued its final judgment.

We can compare this Athenian law against poisoning to a fifth-century BCE inscription from Teos, the so-called 'Teian Curses', which were to be recited every year by public officials.[9] It forbids the manufacture of 'harmful drugs' (*pharmaka dēlētēria*) – which significantly refers to those *pharmaka* that harm or kill, not to all *pharmaka* – on pain of execution for the perpetrator and his or her entire family. Whether the *pharmaka* here refer specifically to magical drugs is unclear, but as we have already seen the term lends itself to multiple meanings, including magical ones. Nor are physicians singled out as the manufacturers, which rather suggests that anyone was capable of making them. The Teian edict above all is concerned with protecting state interests, and this is further confirmed by the proscription that follows the one about *pharmaka*. At this time the Teians were regularly importing grain from Attica, and the next edict also punishes through execution of perpetrator and his entire family anyone who disrupts the importation of grain.[10] In conjunction with several other Teian edicts of the same character, it becomes clear that manufacture of harmful drugs was considered a threat to order in the city. We shall see this same concern revived in the proscriptions against poisoning in late Republican Roman law. Thus in the cases of both Athens and Teos, interests of state and body politic are at stake in the prosecution of individuals who manufacture and administer *pharmaka*, understood here as 'poisons' or 'harmful magical drugs'. In both examples, the outlook is empirical – first there must be damage to person or property, then a determination of a defendant's intent. In the few cases to survive from the classical period, the ambiguous status of *pharmaka* allowed both prosecutors and defendants to advance competing and diametrically opposed claims about what actually occurred.

Trials for Erotic Magic

A commonly cited case takes place in the orator Antiphon's (ca. 480–411 BCE) speech written for the prosecution, called *Against the Stepmother*. This case involves the death of two male friends, one of whom is the father of the prosecutor and husband to the stepmother named in the title, while the other is named Philoneus. Philoneus had a mistress, who was probably a slave, whom Philoneus was planning to set up as a prostitute. Upon learning this, the stepmother befriends the mistress, shares in her grief, and then encourages her to give both Philoneus and her husband a *philtron* 'love charm', to which the prosecutor refers by the more ambiguous term *pharmakon*. This would renew Philoneus' affection for his mistress and the husband's for the stepmother, provided everything went according to plan. Sometime later both Philoneus and the husband traveled to Peiraieus to celebrate the sacrificial rites of Zeus Ctesius, and after dinner the mistress slipped the *philtron* into their wine. She put more of it into Philoneus' drink, however, thinking that more of the love charm would induce him to love her more. Each man drank his last drink – Philoneus died immediately and the husband became ill and died twenty days later.[11]

The penalty for the mistress, not only because she administered the drug but also because she was in all likelihood a slave, was swift: she was tortured on the wheel and executed. The stepmother on the other hand has been spared, and it is the nature of her involvement in the death of both men that is the cause for her trial. We do not know the outcome of this case, but the prosecutor alleges that the stepmother killed his father with the *pharmakon* willingly and with premeditation, despite the fact that it was the mistress who actually administered it. For our purposes, the important point is that this case turns on the determination of the defendant's intent, not the nature of the *pharmakon*. Intent is the key factor in Athenian homicide law, as cited by Demosthenes. But note how intent also shapes the understanding of the *pharmakon* as the instrument of death: if the prosecutor succeeds in showing that the stepmother intended to kill his father, then the *pharmakon* is effectively a 'poison', yet if he fails and she is acquitted, then the *pharmakon* is merely a magical 'love charm' or *philtron*.

Aristotle (384–322 BCE) or a member of his school tells of a similar case in the *Magna Moralia*. In an account that resembles the one we have just seen, the author refers to a case of a woman who gave her husband a *philtron* to drink, from which he died, but she was acquitted on the grounds that she had not intentionally sought to kill him.[12] Her defense was that she gave the *philtron* to him to increase his affection for her. It turns out that there is a good deal of evidence from the classical period through late antiquity that wives, mistresses, and prostitutes used love potions and other aphrodisiacs to retain or strengthen the affection of their male companions and clients.[13] Such a practice, for instance, is at issue in the widely known case of the mythical Deianeira, wife of Herakles, who mistakenly and lethally uses the centaur Nessus' *philtron* to woo back her husband, after he takes a keen interest in another woman, Iole.[14] Although Herakles dies from the *philtron*, which had been made from the centaur's poisonous blood, Deianeira's attempt to increase his affection for her in this way appears to have been among the normal modes of recourse for disaffected women. Moreover, as these cases illustrate, the argument that a drug was a love charm and not a poison evidently was defensible in court. Similar cases and charges can be found well into the second century CE, often involving wives or partners of powerful men at court.[15]

Theoris, the Lemnian Witch

Apart from cases having to do with erotic magic, the only classical period case about which we have any detail that involves a criminal charge of magic has to do with Theoris of Lemnos.[16] This case has attracted a good deal of scholarly attention in recent years, with widely divergent opinions about the exact nature of her crime, as well as about the exact statutes under which she was charged.[17] The diversity of opinion is wholly due to the nature of our sources, which themselves conflict. According to our earliest account, Theoris was a 'witch' or *pharmakis* from the island of Lemnos who lived in Athens. She was prosecuted sometime before 338 BCE allegedly for trafficking in incantations (*epōidai*) and drugs (*pharmaka*). On the testimony of her servant girl, who obtained the incantations and drugs from Theoris, she was executed along with her entire family.[18]

The execution of Theoris along with her entire family resembles the punishment prescribed in the Tean edict, mentioned above, for the manufacture of harmful drugs, except that Theoris was executed in Athens. This discrepancy has led to some debate about whether Athenian law was more lenient than that of other city-states with regard to the prosecution of magic. An anecdote from Plato's *Meno* is often cited to prove Athenian leniency. In this dialogue, Meno has reached a point of bafflement with Socrates' dialectic, and says that he has been bewitched (*goēteuein*), drugged or put under a spell (*pharmattein*), and enchanted (*katepaidein*) by him – all terms that are here used metaphorically but in other contexts can refer to actual magical practice. Meno then says that if Socrates had done these things in any other city besides Athens, he would surely have been led away as a 'magician' (*goēs*).[19] The problem with this anecdote is that Athenian law nowhere addresses magic or magicians in clear and certain terms. As we have seen, the only relevant provision addresses intentional poisoning, but this provision could, depending on the context, include magical drugs. Meno's bafflement and benumbing, moreover, suggests the kind of effects that result from a curse tablet deposited to strike silent an opponent at law. Yet *defixiones*, binding spells, figurines, incantations, and the like are all excluded from any mention in what survives of Athenian law codes.

The two remaining later accounts of Theoris introduce new details that cannot be independently verified. One claims that she was a 'seer' (*mantis*) and was put to death after being convicted of 'impiety' (*asebeia*).[20] Many scholars assume that impiety was the formal charge against Theoris. Impiety was a serious and actionable charge in classical period Athens, as the example of Socrates' famous trial attests, but the charge itself was usually centered on claims of introducing unorthodox views about the gods that were formally recognized by the state or of innovating in divine matters. No such evidence exists for Theoris unless we assume that, like the Hippocratic author of *On the Sacred Disease*, the itinerant religious specialists who laid claim to magical expertise also implicitly claimed to manipulate divinity. Some such reasoning would have to apply to Theoris in order to develop the basis for a formal charge of impiety.

The final and latest account surfaces in Plutarch, who confuses the original unnamed prosecutor of Theoris with Demosthenes, in whose text (*Against Aristogeiton*) her account is first mentioned. Plutarch then calls

Theoris a 'priestess' (*hiereia*) and says that she was prosecuted 'for committing many misdeeds and for teaching the slaves to deceive'.[21] There is a strong possibility that Plutarch has confused the case of Theoris with that of another famous priestess, Nino, who is mentioned elsewhere by Demosthenes and was executed in Athens in the 350s or 340s BCE for participating in Bacchic rites.[22] In what appears to be an independent confirmation of that explanation, one commentator reports that Nino was executed because her Bacchic rites mocked the true mysteries, and a later authority, the historian Josephus, adds that she conducted initiations into the mysteries of foreign gods.[23] Nino was also accused of manufacturing love charms (called both *philtra* and *pharmaka*) and giving them to young men, but no further details of her magical activities in this regard are known. Thus it is entirely possible that Nino's main transgression was to have conducted initiations for her patrons into the cults of unknown or foreign gods, onto which the additional charge of dispensing love charms to young men was later grafted. But if such magical charges were not wholly invented, they suggest that the range of activities for a priestess such as Nino or Theoris was understood to include the manufacture and dispensation of philtres and drugs.

This bewildering state of affairs in the evidence for Theoris only serves to remind modern readers how carefully ancient sources have to be scrutinized. It is probably correct to assume that the trials of Theoris and Nino were not typical and might well have had political ramifications that escape us.[24] On the other hand, the fact that both women were executed on charges that, in one way or another, attracted the mention of magical activity gives us some ground to suppose that adding magic to an otherwise actionable offense could only help to sully the reputation of the defendant. Attention is sometimes called to an account of an anonymous, wealthy 'woman magician' (*gunē magos*) in the fables of Aesop,[25] which were first collected by Demetrius of Phalerum in the fourth century BCE. According to the fable, the woman magician made her living dispensing spells (*epōidai*) to quell the anger of the gods. She was sentenced to death for 'innovating in divine matters', which falls under a charge of impiety (*asebeia*). Assuming the framework of this case is real and not merely a fable, it has been argued that in the fourth century BCE using spells specifically to placate the anger of the gods was liable to a charge of impiety.[26] But we should be cautious here. We have already seen in chapter 2 that several other texts, including the Hippocratic *On the Sacred Disease*[27] and Plato in his *Republic*,[28] refer to purifications and magical practices specifically aimed at quelling the anger of divine spirits, which suggests that this was a common activity for itinerant religious specialists. It is hard to accept that, granted such common and frequent activity, our only surviving "case" that turns on this issue serves as the background to a fable, which may or may not actually date to the fourth century BCE. Surely, more references to such charges of impiety should survive given how well known itinerant specialists were in Athenian society and how flexibly the charge of impiety could be invoked. Moreover, the upshot of the fable points in an entirely different direction: upon leaving the courtroom, a bystander asks the woman magician how was it that she could profess control over the gods and yet have been unable to convince the jury of her innocence. The fable points as much to the absurdity of such claims to divine control, and to their inherent illogicality, as it does to the credibility of her magical ability. In this it resembles the arguments of the author of *On the Sacred Disease*. But we cannot use it to suggest a criminal charge for magic which, in the period in question, is otherwise wholly unattested.

Plato's Laws Against Magic

Some support for the view that magical practice did not automatically entail impiety comes in the context of Plato's discussion of the ideal punishments for the impious men and women who practice magic. In his discussion in the *Laws* about impiety (*asebeia*), Plato seems to accept that impiety and magic are two different things. Impiety is the more serious charge, and magic – charming the souls of the dead, promising to persuade the gods by bewitching them through sacrifices, prayers, and incantations – because it implies that the gods are negligent or open to bribes is an exacerbating factor. But in Plato's view magical practice is incidental to impiety, which may thereby be enhanced and spread more effectively throughout the city-state and the individuals and families who comprise it, the more the impious magical practitioners are led in their efforts by avarice.[29] If convicted of impiety, such individuals are to be imprisoned in the worst of three proposed prisons, namely the one located in the middle of the country in the wildest and loneliest spot possible outside the boundaries of the city-state. They are to be prohibited from contact with free men and, upon death, cast outside the city's boundaries without burial – which is rather glaringly odd, because this is a recipe for the creation of more 'restless dead', the very agents upon whom a practitioner calls in depositing a curse tablet. To my mind, at least, this leaves an open question as to whether Plato fully understands the dynamics of binding magic. Curiously, Plato also regards neither impiety nor magical practice as hereditary: the children of the convicted, provided they are fit for citizenship, are to be taken into the care of the guardians of orphans no differently than the typical orphan.[30] Such a provision is in stark contrast, for example, to the Teian law mentioned earlier that regards the extermination of both the convicted manufacturer of 'harmful drugs' (*pharmaka dēlētēria*) and his or her entire family as fitting punishment. In any case, although Plato's imaginary laws cannot be taken directly to confirm the legal atmosphere in Athens, they do suggest that at least in his mind magic did not inevitably entail the more serious charge of impiety.[31]

As to the punishments ideally meted out to magical practitioners *per se*, Plato draws a distinction along two different axes: the magic (*pharmakeia*) either results in death or in injury that falls short of death, and the practitioner is either an expert or not. At issue is the harm (*blabē*) that is done to a person, his employees, flocks, or beehives, and where death of the defendant is not required, the court will assess a penalty commensurate with the damage. What determines a capital punishment is the professional status of the defendant. In a case of 'poisoning' (*pharmakeia*) that does not result in death, a lay person pays damages while a medical expert is sentenced to death. In a case of magic involving binding curses (*katadeseis*), incantations (*epagōgai*), or spells (*epōidai*), again a lay person is assessed according to the cost of the damage, while a prophet (*mantis*) or diviner (*teratoskopos*) is sentenced to death.[32] Athenian law did make provisions for private suits for damage, whereby an individual brought suit against his offender. If Plato has this form of legal procedure in mind in the cases where damages are to be paid, it suggests that wherever *pharmakeia* involves lay persons and death does not result, he regards these cases as private matters to be settled by the individuals involved. But wherever death results or professionals are involved, the resolution of these cases bears on the health of the city-state as a whole and hence those responsible must be purged.[33]

It is difficult to know exactly why Plato establishes equal punishment for the professional who peddles magic, regardless of the outcome, as well as for anyone whose magic results in death. He does, however, give some indication of his thinking on this point. Earlier in the discussion, he has occasion to reflect on atheists, which to his mind fall into two categories. Both harbor pernicious beliefs about the gods, but it is only those who are intemperate in their pursuit of pleasure and pain, and who possess powerful memories and sharp wits, that one need worry about. He regards this group in particular as specially gifted by nature, full of guile and craft, and out of whom come many diviners (*manteis*) and experts in 'deception' (*manganeia*, a term that also means 'magic'). From this class too come tyrants, demagogues, generals, and those who plot by their own mystic rites – which means rites that are not public and open to view – and the devices of sophists.[34] In other words, Plato regards professionals with what we might describe as a charismatic influence over others as especially dangerous, and his laws are justifiably aimed at containing their influence. But to execute a professional whose magical activities have not resulted in death suggests that Plato regards magic in this instance as a pretext for the removal of men whom he assumes to have unworthy political or social ambitions. Above all in this respect, it appears that Plato holds the professional seer who practices magic in the lowest regard.[35]

One is left to wonder whether Plato's imagined provisions speak to some deficiency in the Athenian law of his day with regard to magic – exclusive of *pharmakeia* or poisoning, about which as we have seen there was an applicable law in the case of serious injury or death. On one hand, Plato holds lay persons and professionals to sharply different standards when death is not involved, which may point to a view that in his day professionals, such as seers, were held to no further account for magic than their lay counterparts. On the other and more important hand, Plato clearly allows that binding curses (*katadeseis*), incantations (*epagōgai*), and spells (*epōidai*) can cause damage, which ought to be provable in court and for which a victorious plaintiff would thereby be entitled to recompense. We observed in chapter 2 that with regard to these types of non-pharmacological magic, Plato hesitated to concede that they exerted physical effects in the world.[36] But, paradoxically, here he establishes a court in which charges for such magic can be heard. My speculation is that the gravity for Plato of suspect professionals was such that, where they could be reached through charges of magic, a court needed to exist – even if the rest of its time were consumed in the resolution of relatively less important private disputes.

Magic in Roman Law and Legal History

Unlike the sporadic concern with magic in classical period Greek law, we have evidence beginning in Republican Rome down to the late imperial period of a sustained interest in the regulation of magical activities. An understanding of key statutes in the Roman juridical tradition as they pertain to magic – and especially the *Cornelian law on assassins and poisoners* of 81 BCE – is important not only for its own sake, but because such statutes give direct witness to how earlier Roman laws were expanded over time as the definition itself of what could be considered magical expanded. As earlier statutes were interpreted by later jurists, their writings gave the appearance that Rome had always condemned magical practice. Recent research, however, has drawn that conclusion strongly into question, because already by the second century CE the definition of *magia* (Greek *mageia*) had become merged with that of *maleficium*, which originally meant 'an evil deed/crime', with no connotation of magic. Thus by late antiquity an explicitly criminal coloring was given to all activities that could be squeezed into a definition of 'magic'. Yet earlier legislation was surprisingly narrow in its enumeration of what qualified as magic – if it even concerned magic at all. This legislation was so narrow, in fact, that one can almost see the manipulation of judicial precedent at work so as to create the appearance of a seamless legal tradition.

The Twelve Tables

The earliest Roman legislation concerning magic is found in the Twelve Tables, which were traditionally composed between 451 and 450 BCE to give a legislative basis to customary law. Much controversy surrounds the order of the Tables and the exact meaning of their provisions, largely because the Tables are known to us through writers of the late Republic, starting in the first century BCE. It is worth stressing that although we depend on later writers for our knowledge of the Tables, they have not transmitted the statutes in the tablets that pertain to magic in an unambiguous form. As a result, in an important recent assessment of the tradition of the Twelve Tables, James Rives has shown that these writers often imputed a later and broader conception of magic to the earlier statutes.[37] This has the effect of making it seem as if Roman legal commentators were always talking about the same thing with regard to magic, when in fact the Tables appear to have been extremely narrow in their outlook.

Two examples of how later viewpoints were retrojected onto the Twelve Tables will serve as illustration. In the first, we learn from Pliny the Elder (ca. 23–79 CE), who is our most important source for the two relevant magical provisions in the Twelve Tables, that one law restricted 'whoever has incanted an evil charm (*malum carmen*)'.[38] This provision has been taken almost universally by scholars to refer to magic in the form of an incantation or spell, as it was by Pliny. However, it has recently been demonstrated that a *malum carmen* can also refer to slander or even to cursing in the sense of using abusive language.[39] While this interpretation does not rule out the magical one, the evidence as we have it does not permit us to say without a doubt that the law in the Twelve Tables refers exclusively to a magical charm, even if later authors such as Pliny thought it did.

The second and more detailed example comes to us in a remark made by the late fourth-century CE grammarian Servius, in his commentary on Vergil's eighth *Eclogue*. Vergil modeled this poem on Theocritus' second

Idyll, and it concerns a lovelorn woman who uses magical means to draw her lover, Daphnis, back from town. The speaker says that she uses herbs (*herbae*) and drugs (*venena*), culled from Pontus in Asia Minor, which she has witnessed turn men into wolves, call spirits from their graves, and 'draw sown corn to the field of another' (*Eclogue* 8.99). In his commentary on this line, Servius remarks that drawing sown corn to the field of another takes place through 'certain magical arts (*magicae artes*); whence in the Twelve Tables [it says:] nor lure away (*pellicere*) another's crops'. Servius was not the only author who made this connection: Augustine and Cicero also linked this provision of the Twelve Tables to the same line in Vergil's eighth *Eclogue*, which gives evidence that this view might have been common.[40] The problem, however, for us as outside observers is that by the fourth and fifth centuries CE, the term 'magical arts' had very specific, negative legal ramifications that were not in place in the mid-fifth century BCE, while the Twelve Tables themselves nowhere mention herbs (*herbae*) and drugs (*venena*) as the means used to accomplish the transfer of another person's crops.[41]

According to Pliny, the second law from the Tables that relates to incantations is 'whoever has enchanted out (*excantare*) the harvest'.[42] This law is the closest to Servius' reference above to luring away sown corn, but it is important to note that the terms used by Servius and the Tables as Pliny reports them are not identical. The verb used in Pliny's version, *excantare*, is not common but does seem to denote drawing or attracting one thing from one place to another by invisible means.[43] The uncompounded verb *cantare* certainly denotes recitation of a poem, performance of a song, if not of a magical incantation. So it appears that a harvest could be magically – which is to say invisibly and imperceptibly – transferred from one place to another by means of a charm. Beyond the charm, the means by which such a transfer was accomplished are less than clear.

We have only one recorded case that was prosecuted under this provision of the Twelve Tables, and it involved a Greek freedman named C. Furius Chresimus.[44] Toward the beginning of the second century BCE, Chresimus was summoned to court by his neighbors, who were envious that he had reaped from his small fields a harvest more abundant than theirs, and they accused him of having attracted their harvests through 'magic' (*veneficium*). Fearing that the vote might go against him, on the day of trial Chresimus brought his workers and farm equipment to the forum and proclaimed to all of his tribe members present that these were his 'magic' (*veneficium*), nor could he show or bring to the forum his late night labors, his vigils, and his sweat.[45] The reaction was immediate and positive, and Chresimus was unanimously acquitted. This trial illustrates that the provision in the Twelve Tables concerning the attraction of another's harvest is fundamentally about the violation of property and the destabilizing effects this could have on an agrarian community.[46] But the fact that 'magic' (*veneficium*) is mentioned both in the charge and the defense raises the possibility that it is by this means specifically that a harvest was magically transferred.

The term *veneficium* (pl. *veneficia*) has two distinct meanings in Latin. The first is concerned with 'drugs/poisons' *venena* (sg. *venenum*[47]) and means 'the act of poisoning/poison'. The second more generally refers to 'magic' and, in addition to that, can mean a 'philtre' or 'magical substance'. One who uses *venena* is called a *veneficus*, and the same bifurcated meanings apply: the *veneficus* is either a poisoner or a magician. Now it is important to stress that the ambivalence observed in the use of *venenum* 'poison/magical drug' in Latin is roughly equivalent to that found in the Greek term *pharmakon* – roughly, because the Latin term does not include the meaning 'purification' as *pharmakon* does in Greek medical texts.[48] Roman legal scholars or jurists were acutely aware of the ambivalence of the term *venenum* and drew parallels with Greek terminology. As one example, the famous second-century law professor and jurist Gaius, who wrote a treatise on the Twelve Tables, once remarked:[49]

> Someone who says 'drugs' (*venena*) must add whether it is bad or good; for medicaments (*medicamenta*) are also drugs (*venena*) since under that name everything is contained which when applied to something changes the nature of that to which it is applied. Given that that which we call drug (*venenum*) is called by the Greeks *pharmakon*, among them also medicaments (*medicamenta*) as well as harmful drugs are included in this category.

To illustrate his point Gaius next quotes a verse from Homer's *Odyssey* (4.230), 'drugs (*pharmaka*) mixed together, many good and many harmful', which describes the drugs Helen places into the wine she offers Telemachus, Odysseus' son, and her husband Menelaus. Interestingly, this is an appeal, which is rare enough in the law codes, to Homer's authority on magic, and it gives clear evidence of the extent to which even later Roman jurists sought Greek precedents to define Latin magical terms.

In any case, Gaius' remarks thus give us some reason to conclude that the *veneficium* mentioned in the case of Chresimus specifically refers to the use of 'drugs' (*venena*), and some scholars have taken this view.[50] However, the abstract noun *veneficium* has the same ambiguity as Greek *pharmakeia*, and can mean both 'poisoning' and 'magic', and the 'magic' here does not always imply the use of drugs. Both *pharmakeia* and *veneficia* can refer to spells or to a generalized notion of magic.[51] This is the crucial point: it appears that when Chresimus points to his farm equipment and workers and refers to them as his 'magic' (*veneficia*), he means magic in the general Roman sense of the term, inclusive of but not specific to having used drugs. Even if we could imagine the use of drugs to destroy a neighbor's crops, the provision of the Twelve Tables refers only to the charming or luring away (*excantare*) of another's crops, which is not the same thing. On the other hand, the application of drugs to crops somehow to attract them to the field of another is unprecedented. A parallel for such attraction does exist, however, as we have seen more than once, in the realm of charming and spells, as in the famous Greek example of using 'spells' (*epōidai*) to draw down the moon. Closer to Rome, the Marsi, a central Italic people, were famous for using charms to attract serpents, even while they slept,[52] while erotic attraction spells were the very *raisons d'être* of Theocritus' second *Idyll* and its Roman counterpart, Vergil's eighth *Eclogue*. It would thus be toward the more general sense of *veneficium*, rather than a narrow reference to drugs, that the case of Chresimus seems to point.

The Lex Cornelia

As to why Vergil has the speaker say in his eighth *Eclogue* (published in 37 BCE) that she uses herbs (*herbae*) and drugs (*venena*) which she has witnessed 'draw sown corn to the field of another' (8.99) – a statement that in effect marries two different magical ideas – there is one significant explanation. Vergil does this because after 81 BCE the entire Roman definition of 'magic' (*veneficia*) had become bound up with 'drugs' (*venena*) with the passage of the most important piece of legislation against poisoners (*veneficus*) – and later, magicians – the *Lex Cornelia de sicariis et veneficiis* or the *Cornelian law on assassins and poisoners*. This law was henceforth the main statute under which all subsequent cases of magic were prosecuted, partly because the very name 'poisoner' (*veneficus*) was the same as that for 'magician'. The law's original intent could thus be flexibly interpreted as later generations of jurists, magistrates, and prosecutors applied it in specific cases.

In 81 BCE the Roman dictator L. Cornelius Sulla passed a legislative programme largely aimed at strengthening the power of the Senate. In addition to minor changes, he reorganized the system of standing courts (*quaestiones*) and increased their number, commensurate with his enlargement of the Senate to 600, which was more than double its previous count. Cases dealing with 'poisoners' (*veneficus*) and 'assassins' (*sicarius*) had existed on an ad hoc basis at least since the fourth century

BCE,[53] and a standing *quaestio inter sicarios* had existed prior to Sulla.[54] But after 81 poisoning and homicide cases were subject to Sulla's new, expanded *quaestio* and were tried under the *Cornelian law on assassins and poisoners*. The importance of this law for the future of Roman jurisprudence on magic cannot be underestimated, because it was to this law that all subsequent legislation against magic, in one way or another, related. Owing both to the ambiguity of its original terms and to the creativity of later Roman jurists, the scope of the Cornelian law was gradually extended by the third century CE to include a variety of suspicious behaviors that were not originally within its purview.

The original intent of the Cornelian law, as best we can reconstruct it, was aimed at trying individuals accused of murder by stealth. The term 'assassin' (*sicarius*) covered not only 'murderer' but especially murderers who accomplished their killing through concealment and planning.[55] The term 'poisoner' (*veneficus*), as we have mentioned, referred generally to one who used 'poison' (*venenum*) to murder, but the fundamental ambiguity of the term *venenum* left open to question whether such drugs were simply poisons or magical substances. As in the examples from Greek law that we have seen dealing with *pharmaka*, the definition of *venenum* was open to interpretation depending on the circumstances. But if the most recent construction of the *Lex Cornelia* is correct, intent to kill with *venena*, as well as the nature of the *venena* themselves, were part of the law's original scope.[56]

Already in the fourth century BCE, centuries before the passage of the Cornelian law, a spectacular and memorable case for poisoning had been held that hinged on the correct interpretation of *venenum*. According to Livy (59 BCE–17 CE), the first case for poisoning was tried in 331 BCE, and it involved a conspiracy by noble Roman matrons to murder their husbands.[57] That year, numerous prominent noblemen found themselves suffering from an unknown malady. A maidservant, promised immunity by the Senate, revealed the identity of the conspiring matrons, who were discovered at their homes in the act of manufacturing *venena*. Twenty matrons were allegedly involved and two of them, Cornelia and Sergia, contended that they were making *medicamenta* 'medicaments' or beneficial drugs, not poisons. The maidservant then challenged the matrons to drink their 'medicaments' to prove her suspicions wrong. After some deliberation, all twenty matrons consented to drink the drugs, and all twenty died. Livy reports that in all some 170 matrons were found guilty of poisoning – a number that almost defies belief – and the whole event was hailed as a prodigy.[58] As this case illustrates, it was crucial to determine whether the drugs at issue were beneficial or harmful, and we can still see this concern echoed in the comments of the second-century CE jurist Gaius (quoted earlier), whose distinction between *medicamenta* and harmful drugs neatly parallels the case of the Roman matrons.[59] Thus the logic of pairing the poisoner together with the assassin in the Cornelian law was clear enough: in both cases the means by which someone was murdered was clandestine or in any case not obvious, and the threat of such crimes to the state in 81 BCE was serious enough for Sulla to warrant expanding the reach of the permanent court.

There are many more cases involving poisoning attested in Roman history after 81 BCE, which give a reasonably, although not exactly, clear picture of how the Cornelian law was broadened over time to incorporate magical activity. It is important to remember, however, that Roman law was regularly subject to revision and expansion as new trials occurred, as earlier laws were modified by later statutes, and ultimately as jurists, both pagan and Christian, weighed in to update and elucidate a given statute's meaning.[60] Nevertheless, what we witness in the subsequent revisions to the Cornelian law and to cases prosecuted under it is an attempt by Roman authorities to rein in behaviors that threatened the tranquility of the state. The devil was in the details, however, and what Roman authorities considered to be threats to that tranquility were increasingly defined in terms of a normative notion of religious behavior (*religio*). The concept of *religio* (not quite translatable as our modern term 'religion') referred to the proper, state-sanctioned honors traditionally paid to the gods.[61] In contrast, what the Romans referred to as *superstitio* (not quite translatable as 'superstition') was conceptually opposed to *religio*, and meant excessive or otherwise improper honors and rituals paid to the gods.[62] Of course the definition of what constituted *superstitio* was flawed from the beginning, since it was a term routinely used by those who considered themselves *religiosi* – or the properly observant – to slander others. Now here is the crux: among the various so-called deviant behaviors covered by the term *superstitio*, especially after the first century CE, magical activity emerged at the forefront. To Romans of the first century CE, magic was the "ultimate *superstitio*."[63]

The reasons for this shift in perspective are complex, but they certainly received support from the infamous and very public death in 19 CE of Germanicus, adoptive nephew of his uncle, the emperor Tiberius (emperor 14–37 CE). As Tiberius had been adopted by Augustus (emperor 31 BCE–14 CE), Germanicus was in a direct line of succession to the throne and had been favored by some to supplant Augustus at his death in 14 CE. In 17 CE, Tiberius appointed Cn. Calpurnius Piso, with whom he had served as consul in 7 BCE, as governor of Syria, in part as a check on Germanicus, who had been given command of the eastern provinces. In 19 CE Germanicus entered the imperial province of Egypt without permission

– a law that Augustus himself had imposed on senators to protect the vital supply of grain to Rome – and offended Tiberius. On his return to Syria, Germanicus found that Piso had tried to thwart some of his arrangements, and so ordered him to leave the province. No sooner had Piso left Syria than Germanicus fell ill, and he maintained to his death that Piso had poisoned him. The horror of Germanicus' death, however, was augmented by what was found in his room. As the Roman historian Tacitus (56–ca. 118 CE) explains:[64]

> In the floor and walls were brought to light remains of human bodies, spells (*carmina*), curses (*devotiones*), lead tablets engraved with the name 'Germanicus', half-burnt ashes smeared with blood, and other magic (*malefica*) by which it is believed that living souls are dedicated to the infernal powers.

The human remains and ashes had no doubt been taken from funeral pyres, while the spells, curses, and lead tablets all point toward binding magic of the kind we examined in chapter 3.[65] Indeed, the Latin term *devotio* can mean the same thing as Greek *katadesmos* 'binding curse'.[66] It is almost certainly the case that Germanicus was poisoned, as the accusers of Piso maintained later at his trial in Rome before the Senate, but it appears that Piso was plausibly able to deny the charge of poisoning (*veneni crimen*).[67] We see from Tacitus' account, however, that even if poisoning was the effective means from our point of view of killing Germanicus, it was nevertheless coupled in a dramatic way with magic. We have, therefore, a very clear association in this case between magic and drugs, making it plausible that by 19 CE magic could be prosecuted under the Cornelian law since it prohibited the use of *venena* 'poisons/magical substances'.[68] But to the Roman imagination, no matter how you translated it, the *venenum* was a dangerous thing, especially when shrouded in magic. As Pliny once said generally of Roman attitudes toward magic, 'there is no one who does not fear being bound (*defigere*) by frightful imprecations'.[69] Thus the dual fate of Germanicus. In spite of Piso's having refuted the charge of poisoning, the senatorial and popular opposition to him was too great, nor was Tiberius sympathetic to his plight, and shortly thereafter Piso ended his life by suicide.

Magia *and* Maleficium: *Magic and Witchcraft*

When Tacitus describes the other magic (*malefica*) found in Germanicus' room, he introduces an explicitly Roman concept that will over the next century add to the coloring of magic as criminal behavior. The term *magus*, borrowed in Latin from the Greek *magos*, had been in use since the 50s BCE and retained its primarily neutral reference to Persian magi down to the first century CE. However, as we saw in chapter 2, both *magus* and its associated complex of terms, including *magia*, *magicus/a*, and so forth, also bore the weight of meaning 'magic', 'magical', in terms more closely associated with the abominable devices found in Germanicus' room. By the second century CE, alongside *magus* and the ever-ambivalent *veneficus* 'poisoner/magician', we find another family of terms built around the native Roman concept of *maleficium*, which originally meant 'evil deed/crime'. *Maleficium* is a noun built from *male* 'evilly/wrongly' and *facere* 'to do', and the perpetrator of *maleficium* is a *maleficus/a* 'evil-doer/criminal'.

In describing the other things found with the dead Germanicus, Tacitus uses the plural adjective *malefica* – uniquely, it might be said, in his writings – in a manner that soon became commonplace to characterize magic and its practitioners. Less than half a century after Tacitus' death, *maleficium* was used as commonly as *magia* and *veneficia* to mean 'magic', except that now it carried the taint of intentional harm; the noun *malefica* (note the feminine form) was explicitly a 'sorceress' or 'witch',[70] and by the third century CE the *maleficus* 'magician' begins to supplant the *magus* in the most important Roman law codes.[71] As medieval and early modern authors returned to Roman literary, historical, and legal sources to define their own concepts of magic and its increasingly distinct counterpart, witchcraft, it was to *maleficium* and its cognates that they primarily looked. *Maleficium* became the dominant term for medieval 'witchcraft' and *maleficus/a* (pl. *malefici/ae*) the term of choice for 'witch'.

By the seventh century CE, authors such as Isidore of Seville (560–636, bishop 600–636 CE), who like Pliny the Elder before him wrote on the history of the magi, and following Augustine[72] understood magic to operate through the intercession of demons, explained that in his day the magi were:[73]

> usually called *malefici* because of the greatness of their crimes. They throw the elements into commotion, disturb men's minds, and without any drink of poison (*venenum*) they kill merely by the violence of a charm (*carmen*).

Note that to Isidore, the more important crime is now incantatory magic, exclusive of poisoning, which diverges from what we have seen in the comments of the second-century CE jurist Gaius. Next Isidore quotes Lucan's (39–65 CE) poem *Pharsalia* (6.457) to the same effect, from its famous necromantic scene.[74] He then writes that the *malefici*:

summon demons, and dare to brandish such juggleries that each one kills his enemies by means of evil arts (*malae artes*). They also use blood and victims, and often touch the bodies of the dead.

In terms of a Christian theological explanation for magic, now commonly referred to as 'magic arts' (*magicae artes*) or 'evil arts' (*malae artes*), Isidore is naturally quite removed from the explanations current in pagan Rome. But it is not hard to see how an author such as Isidore easily found the rudiments of magic and the outlines of magicians (*malefici*) – the precursors to medieval witches – readily available in Roman literature and history. By the fifteenth century, *malefica* was enshrined as the preeminent theological and legal term for 'witch', as evidenced in the publication by the Dominicans Heinrich Krämer (Institoris) and Jakob Sprenger of the most important witch-hunting manual of the age, the *Malleus Maleficarum* 'Witches' Hammer' in 1486.

A detailed history of the Christian theological development of magic into witchcraft is beyond the scope of this study.[75] Yet, as we have briefly sketched, much of the groundwork had been laid for this transformation between the first and fourth centuries CE. Two important developments in this period of late antiquity have yet to be highlighted, and each in its own way confirmed to medieval and early modern authors that magic was a legitimate source of concern for the state. The first development concerned the most famous trial for magic in the second century CE involving Apuleius of Madaura. Not only was this case notorious in its own day, but the evidentiary basis for Apuleius' prosecution, and its implicit confirmation of the existence of magic, was still being discussed among educated magistrates preoccupied with witchcraft well into the sixteenth century. The second development was more extended than a single case, and it concerned the third-century CE Roman jurists, especially Paulus, whose commentary and updating of the Cornelian law fortified the legal framework for the prosecution of magic in a manner that lasted for centuries, long after the fall of the Roman Empire.

Apuleius the Magus

Apuleius of Madaura (which is in modern Algeria) was a flamboyant figure, educated, handsome, and eloquent, with many accomplishments to his name: Platonist philosopher, orator, poet, naturalist, and – most troubling – *magus*.[76] His trial is only known to us from his *Apology*, which is almost certainly a revised version of the defense speech he gave before the proconsul of Africa, Claudius Maximus, in 158/9 CE.[77] The trial itself took place at the law court in Sabratha, situated about 45 miles west of Oea, which is modern Tripoli, the capital of Libya. The basis for the charges against Apuleius stems from a journey he made to Alexandria, cut short by illness, as a result of which he made a visit to Oea. In Oea Apuleius stayed with an old friend, Sicinius Pontianus, who helped him recover and whose mother was the wealthy widow, Aemilia Pudentilla. After recovering from his illness, and initially with the encouragement of Pontianus, Apuleius married the widow Pudentilla in order to protect her inheritance for Pontianus, her eldest son, and her younger one, Sicinius Pudens. The marriage caused tensions among Pudentilla's relatives, however, especially Sicinius Aemilianus, the brother of Pudentilla's first husband, and Herennius Rufinus, who was father-in-law to Pontianus.

The details of the family members and their previous legal maneuverings are more complex than I have indicated, but the key point is that Aemilianus and Rufinus claimed at trial that Pudentilla had vowed never to remarry – indeed, she had remained single for almost 14 years. Moreover, at approximately 40 Pudentilla was roughly a decade older than Apuleius at the time, which defied the expectation of Aemilianus that she would marry a man her senior. Thus Aemilianus and his cronies charged Apuleius with being a *magus* who had used erotic magic to win her affections and, as an opening gambit, they produced a letter to prove the point. Pudentilla had written a letter in Greek in which she claimed that 'Apuleius is a *magos*, and I am bewitched by him and in love'.[78]

In response to this and other charges, Apuleius' defense speech is masterful and triumphant – the hallmarks of a man who was ultimately acquitted.[79] His oratorical skills are on dazzling display as he cleverly reverses the arguments of his accusers, challenges their interpretation of facts, mocks their inability to supply witnesses, and generally satirizes their ignorance and ill intentions. Every charge against him he explains away, but it is how he does this that raised the eyebrows of later authors. Rather than deny the charges against him, Apuleius instead admits the charges as if they were facts and then offers a non-magical explanation for them.[80] As he proceeds, however, addressing his accusers charge by charge, it becomes clear that Apuleius knows a great deal about magic – so much, in fact, that to a modern reader the conclusion is virtually inescapable that he was capable of practicing it. The question before his audience at trial was whether he used erotic magic to woo Pudentilla, and obviously this was not proven. But his *Apology* leaves the distinct impression that buried beneath the clever rhetoric and skillful lawyering, we are dealing with a man whose innocence lay more in the strength of his arguments than in the moral clarity of his deeds.

The main charge against Apuleius was a charge of magic (*crimen magiae*),[81] but because of Aemilianus' efforts prior to the trial to discredit him, the grounds for the charge as Apuleius says several times are largely based on the calumny or slander that he practiced magic (*calumnia magiae*).[82] Not only has Aemilianus charged that Apuleius practiced magic, he has also characterized that magic as explicitly maleficent. This is brought out in a reading before the court of the document containing the formal charge toward the end of the work, in which the term *maleficia* (pl. for *maleficium*) 'wicked deeds' is used.[83] It is also brought out in another phrase Apuleius frequently employs to name the charge against him, *magica maleficia* 'maleficent magic'.[84] This phrase is significant because for the first time in Roman literature *maleficia* and its cognates, used in an expressly magical sense, are strongly identified with *magus/magia* and their cognates both here and in other writings of Apuleius.[85] For all intents and purposes, the long history of *maleficium* as 'maleficent magic' and, later, 'witchcraft' begins with Apuleius.

Most commentators agree that Apuleius was charged under the *Cornelian law on assassins and poisoners*, and in a clever allusion Apuleius himself refers to the law. In rebutting the claim that he is a maleficent *magus*, Apuleius argues that magi were originally Persian holy men, descendants of Zoroaster and Oromazes,[86] whom one should be inclined to emulate. If, on the other hand, his accusers claim that he is a common *magus* who has the power to communicate directly with the gods to achieve whatever he wants, then why, he asks, have his accusers entered court without defending themselves? Shouldn't they be afraid?[87] His allusion to the Cornelian law comes when he adds that anyone summoning an assassin (*sicarius*) would have come with an escort, while anyone accusing a poisoner (*venenarius* – like *veneficus* this form is also built from *venenum*) would dine with more scrupulous care – both types being unlike his accusers who have taken no pains to protect themselves.[88] It might seem an excessively bold gesture for Apuleius ironically to apply to his accusers the very terms of the statute under which he is being prosecuted, but he can do this because he has not actually been charged with 'poisoning' *veneficium*. In more than one place Apuleius states clearly that he has not been indicted for *veneficium*,[89] which reveals that by this time cases like his that involved magic not explicitly tied to the use of drugs could also be prosecuted under the Cornelian law.[90]

In addition to Apuleius' rhetorical skill, this last example affords us a glimpse of one of his favorite tactics. As we have noted, on the one hand Roman authors as early as the 50s BCE down to the first century CE continuously used the term *magus* to refer to Persian magi, for whom they reserved respect just as the Greeks had before them. On the other hand, the self-serving man who styled himself as a *magus* and preyed on the superstitious had been regarded by many civilly minded Greeks and Romans as contemptible. Apuleius does not deny that he is a *magus*; instead, he highlights the positive and most traditional interpretation of the term. Then he says that the same kind of invidious claims made against vulgar magi were also commonly made against philosophers – among whom, of course, he numbers himself – men who were not, contrary to popular opinion, irreligious.[91] Here Apuleius uses a key term in Latin: these philosophers were not *irreligiosi* – which means they were *religiosi*, the term for those who were properly observant of the traditional gods and cults and the diametrical opposite of magical practitioners, or the *superstitiosi*. Apuleius allies himself with these earlier philosophers, among whom he names traditional philosophers – including Anaxagoras and Democritus – along with several other legendary men – including Epimenides of Crete, Orpheus, Pythagoras, Empedocles – who were strongly associated with magic but remained above moral reproach. Among them he adds, curiously, Ostanes, who was a notorious magician,[92] and Socrates and Plato, names that were so distinguished in philosophy that either Apuleius hoped they would extinguish all doubt about the character of the preceding figures or introduce a red herring that would lead his listeners astray. All of these were men who inquired into nature with greater care and honored the gods more intensely, Apuleius says, but who were wrongly called 'magicians' *magi* by the people.[93]

As we learn through Apuleius' defense speech, his accuser Aemilianus had based his charges of *maleficia* on several instances of questionable behavior. They included Apuleius' attempt to purchase certain kinds of fish; his enchantment of a slave boy who collapsed and then recovered; his keeping of certain secret objects wrapped in linen and kept among the household gods of his friend, Pontianus; his performance of nocturnal sacrifices; his commissioning and veneration of a wooden figurine; and his marriage to Pudentilla accomplished through incantations (*carmina*) and magical drugs (*venena*). For each of these charges Apuleius provides a non-magical explanation, which turns instead on his interest in philosophy, natural investigation, or pious religious observance. Moreover, all of the charges can be seen as concocted in the face of Aemilianus' and Rufinus' true motives, which were according to Apuleius to lay claim through their children to Pudentilla's dowry.

An examination of the charges against Apuleius will show how each instance admitted of more than one explanation, even against the backdrop of Aemilianus' and Rufinus' questionable motives. Among the rare fish Apuleius was supposedly seeking was the *lepus marinus* 'sea-hare', which was actually not a fish but a poisonous mollusk.[94] In typical fashion Apuleius readily admits to having his slave (Themison) seek to acquire this mollusk as well as rare fish in an effort, as he claims, to further his naturalistic investigations as Aristotle and Theophrastus had done before him.[95] However, the *lepus marinus* was well known to Pliny the Elder from Italian and Indian waters as poisonous to the touch, and doing so immediately caused vomiting and disorders of the stomach.[96] Pliny adds elsewhere that the *lepus marinus* used as a 'poison' *venenum* can be served in food or drink, and a man who has died from this poison reeks of the mollusk's smell, which gives observers the first hint that his death was caused by *veneficium*. At the very sight of the mollusk, pregnant women are seized with nausea and vomiting and their pregnancies inevitably end in abortion.[97] Thus whatever Apuleius' actual motives in seeking to acquire this mollusk, it is doubtful that he could have claimed ignorance of the mollusk's well-known pharmacological properties. Indeed, Apuleius never addresses these properties directly; instead, his defense switches gears and focuses on two other fish he supposedly sought whose names carried sexually suggestive meanings. He dismisses out of hand his accusers' claim that he sought these fish, based on their names alone, to use as erotic magic – and yet contemporary uses of fish and other sea creatures in Roman magic, including erotic magic, were well known.[98]

The enchanted slave boy who collapsed in Apuleius' presence, supposedly after Apuleius had recited a charm, is explained away with a perversely generous amount of magical detail. To the claim that Apuleius enchanted the boy, he asserts that his accusers should have added the charge that he also used him for divination.[99] He further acknowledges the depth of his reading in magic and divination by citing several examples of the very common practice in late antiquity of using children as mediums.[100] Typically a suitable child, usually a young boy, was blindfolded while a divinity was invoked, then the blindfold was removed and the boy gazed either into a lamp's flame or a bowl of water, which was sometimes infused with oil. The divinity then appeared in the flame or on the surface of the liquid and reported the prophecy.[101] More remarkable than Apuleius' knowledge of this procedure, however, is that his explanation for why the boy (named Thallus) collapsed was that he was an epileptic – more in need of a doctor than a *magus*, quips Apuleius.[102] But to readers familiar with Greek magical tradition this point should raise more questions than it answers. For as we have seen in the Hippocratic treatise *On the Sacred Disease*, epileptics in particular were the favored patients of itinerant religious specialists, including *magoi*. We then learn that Apuleius was sought out by others on behalf of epileptics – later in the defense we hear that a freeborn epileptic woman had also been brought to him for help and that she too collapsed.[103] He claims that his knowledge of epilepsy was again derived from reading the philosophers – Plato, Aristotle, and Theophrastus, in particular – although he acknowledges having read the medical writers and poets on the subject too.[104] Most suspicious of all, however, in my view is that Apuleius says that the freeborn woman was brought to him for treatment by her physician (*medicus*).[105] Now however learned a philosopher Apuleius might have been, he was decidedly not a physician. Furthermore, the rivalry between academic physicians and *magoi* runs back at least to the late fifth and early fourth centuries BCE, as we saw in chapter 2, and is attested memorably in *On the Sacred Disease*. Roman-era physicians, such as Soranus, Galen, Rufus, and Marcellus, certainly had knowledge of magic and occasionally offered it as a remedy for a given illness (as we saw in chapter 4). But one conceivable reason why a physician would have brought an epileptic patient to Apuleius was that the physician had exhausted all of the traditional medical options at his disposal. We may note here the common saying in antiquity that when the remedies of the physicians fail, everyone resorts to sacrificers and seers, incantations and amulets[106] – with the unexpected twist that here we have the physician himself appealing to Apuleius' unconventional services. Whether the epileptic woman was thought to suffer from demonic possession, which was a phenomenon well known to Apuleius and his contemporaries,[107] is plausible, and it fits with the prevailing popular understanding of epilepsy as a divine or demonic invasion.[108] Nevertheless, it is hard to escape the conclusion that it was for Apuleius' magical, and not his medical, services that he was approached, even if his accusers mistakenly connected incantations with the epileptics' collapse.

The charges of possessing objects wrapped in linen are also dismissed by Apuleius in less than transparent terms. Aemilianus claimed that Apuleius kept some unknown objects, wrapped in linen, with the *lares* or household gods of his friend, Pontianus. On the grounds that he had not seen them, Aemilianus unfortunately asserted that the objects were magical.[109] He thus leaves himself wide open to attack by Apuleius as a result, because Apuleius had left the wrapped objects in plain view in Pontianus' home, and yet no one had bothered to unwrap them. When it comes to explaining what the objects were, however, they appear to have been votives. In a famous passage, Apuleius explains that he has been initiated into many mystery cults in Greece, and had been given many souvenirs and symbols by various priests.[110] He then alludes to initiates of the cult of Dionysus present in his audience, who within the privacy of their homes silently venerate objects, performing a ritual obeisance which they are bound by the strictures of the mystery cult not to reveal.

He is no different than them in their worship, and he adds importantly that out of his ardor for truth and duty to the gods he has learned many cults, rites, and ceremonies – actions evocative of *religio* and nothing more.[111]

But then, in one of the most interesting passages of the *Apology*, because its implications reverberate for his accusers, audience, and judge, as well as for modern readers, Apuleius directly and consciously embroils the proper observance of *religio* with magic. The issue is what may seem to others as magical:[112]

> Thus, in a case of magic, anything at all that people have done can be held against them. You have attached a written vow (*votum*) to the thigh of a statue: so you are a magician (*magus*), or else why did you do so? You have made a silent prayer in a temple to the gods: so you are a magician, or else what did you ask for? Or, conversely, you have *not* made a prayer in a temple: so you are a magician, or else why did you *not* ask the gods? The same could be said if you have deposited a gift, made a sacrifice, or taken home a sacred branch.

In the same way, he concludes, objects sealed or stored someplace or wrapped inside the house could be called 'magical' and be transferred from the storeroom to the forum and into the courtroom. The balance that has to be struck here is no less than monumental, and it speaks to the range of practices with which every Roman was intimately familiar. To be more precise, it is not just a matter of one person's magic or superstition being another person's religion, but rather that the ritual practices which they share are inherently ambiguous. This is a point on which I have insisted throughout this book, insofar as, terminology aside, we have concentrated on understanding how 'magical' practices have to be situated within a larger ritual and cultural context. Apuleius' strategy is to call attention to the underlying normative judgment of what is acceptable in the realm of *religio* as the deciding factor in what is therefore judged unacceptable, superstitious, and magical. To anything that is contrived by his accusers as magical, Apuleius adds that he will counter that it is either fraudulent, serves as a remedy (*remedium*), fulfills a religious purpose, or that it has been commanded in a dream.[113] Common practice and the most widespread custom will be his benchmark. But in all this there is more than a little prevarication, because in the end Apuleius chooses to insist that his objects have sacred meanings derived from the mystery cults in which he has participated – meanings which he is therefore *religiously* bound to keep secret.

As to the performance of nocturnal sacrifices, the written testimony was offered by a landlord, Julius Crassus, who alleged that Apuleius and his friend Quintianus had repeatedly celebrated the sacrifices in Crassus' home, where Quintianus rented a room. At the time, Crassus himself was in Alexandria, but when he returned home to Oea he found bird feathers in the hall and the walls defaced by soot. His slave informed him that Apuleius and Quintianus were responsible.[114] Nocturnal sacrifices made for private rather than public purposes, especially in the context of mysteries, had been a source of concern for Roman legislators since the Republic and they remained subject to imperial prohibition well into the fourth century CE.[115] Generally the concern was that such sacrifices contributed to *superstitio*, not *religio*, with implications for the maintenance of order in the body politic, and thus the state had an interest in maintaining its monopoly over public sacrifice. Apuleius' defense in this instance is aided by the fact that Crassus was a known tippler, who notoriously accepted small fees from clients to lie on their behalf, and thus his argument is an attack on Crassus' character, as well as on Aemilianus who suborned him. As in the case of some of the other charges, the details about what really happened are hazy, nor do we know exactly which type of bird feathers were found.[116] Nonetheless, Apuleius' defense once again puzzlingly rests on the shortcomings of his accusers, not on a clear explanation of why soot and feathers were found in Crassus' house.

We turn finally to Apuleius' wooden figurine, which he commissioned to have carved by a known artisan, Cornelius Saturninus. Apparently in direct answer to questions about the figurine posed by the judge, Maximus, Apuleius testifies that he asked Saturninus to carve a figurine of any god he wanted, from any material he wanted provided it was wood, to which Apuleius would address his regular prayers.[117] It is important to stress at the outset that Apuleius couches this whole request in the context of his customary (*ex more meo*) – and therefore *religiosus* – prayers, to which no one should attach any suspicion. We learn that Saturninus first tried to carve the figurine from boxwood, but meanwhile, Apuleius' stepson Pontianus, desiring to have the figurine made for him, acquired some ebony – a wood known for its durability – from an unknown lady, and asked Saturninus to use that instead. The god Saturninus supposedly chose to make was Mercury (Hermes).[118]

Further claims made against Apuleius in the episode include secretly having the figurine made, which of course he denies since Saturninus was known and summoned to court; requesting a special wood, which he attributes to Pontianus; and thirdly that the figurine resembles a frightful corpse or skeleton, which he disproves by presenting the little Mercury to the judge Maximus for his inspection. But we must be cautious here for several reasons. First, it is not at all clear that the Mercury presented to Maximus is the same figurine in question.[119] But even if it is a substitute, we have seen in chapter 3 the extensive role Mercury (Hermes) plays in Greek magic, and not only as an underworld figure who can be addressed in curse tablets and binding spells. More significantly the Greek magical papyri prescribe erotic binding spells addressed to Hermes, as well as recipes for fashioning figurines of Hermes from beeswax or dough to be used as magical aides in business or in divination, as we saw in chapter 3.[120] The correspondences between these magical recipes and Apuleius' figurine are too close to be accidental.[121] It is probable that Apuleius revealed these details knowing that his audience would fail to grasp their magical significance. The first and most significant detail is that in an erotic binding spell in *PGM* addressed to Hermes, it is said that Hermes' preferred wood is ebony,[122] the very wood which Apuleius claims his stepson Pontianus sought for the artisan to make the figurine. The next is that the Mercury figurine presented to Maximus wears a mantle,[123] which corresponds to the description in *PGM* for fashioning a prophetic Hermes figurine, which must also wear a mantle.[124] More interesting is that Apuleius says he usually carries his Mercury with him wherever he travels, and that on feast days he offers incense, wine, and occasionally an animal victim, to the figurine.[125] The audience is to infer from Apuleius that these offerings and especially the sacrifice are made publicly, lest his actions attract the taint of *superstitio*, but this is never clearly stated. In *PGM* we find a Hermes spell for increasing business – since Hermes governs all commercial transactions – which requires that after a beeswax figurine of the god is fashioned, a cock is to be sacrificed to him, a drink offering made of Egyptian wine is to be poured, and a lamp that is not colored red is to be burned.[126] These details are strikingly close to those given by Apuleius and make it virtually certain that his Mercury figurine was used in magical rites. Moreover, to seal the Hermetic link between Apuleius' figurine and the Greek magical papyri, Apuleius allegedly addressed his figurine as *basileus* 'king', which recalls a demonic figure by the same name that appears in several magical spells.[127]

There is no need to insist on the general point that figurines were venerated by Romans, as they had been by the Greeks before them – sometimes in the context of pious observance, as with their household gods (*lares, penates*), and sometimes in notoriously magical contexts, as when the emperor Nero toward the end of his life acquired the figurine of a girl, which he venerated and to which he made sacrifices in the belief that it could divine the future for him.[128] The main issue, as Apuleius would have his audience believe, was that his treatment of the Mercury figurine, along with all of his other activities, was conducted in the context of proper, and even banally normal, religious observance. However, the evidence as I have presented it weighs heavily against this interpretation, and renders all the more rational the judgment of later authors that Apuleius was, indeed, a skillful and capable *magus.*

Among the most important of these later authors was Augustine, who accepted that Apuleius practiced 'magic arts' (*magicae artes*) and showed 'no desire to be innocent except by denying actions that cannot be performed by an innocent man'.[129] Consistent with his own theory of magical operation, to Augustine Apuleius could only have accomplished his magic through demons.[130] In the *Apology*, Apuleius himself argues for the existence of *daemones* (Greek *daimones*), as Plato had before him,[131] as intermediary divine powers situated between gods and men that govern divination and the miracles of magicians.[132] But the Greek *daimōn* and Augustine's Christian demon with its theological implications for the spread of evil are two distinct entities, and can only be superficially compared.[133] Nevertheless, Augustine devotes a chapter to refuting what he calls Apuleius' worship of demons (*cultus daemonum*), arguing instead that demons are bent on harm and that the less educated multitude has cultivated their worship out of a longstanding tradition of *superstitio.*[134] Moreover, we know that in Augustine's lifetime Apuleius was still highly regarded as a magician among pagans, and was often compared to the notorious magician and miracle-worker Apollonius of Tyana. The magic of both men was compared by pagan writers, to the horror of Augustine, to the miracles of Jesus.[135] Apuleius' reputation both for magic and for his storytelling abilities only grows throughout the Middle Ages – two of his stories, for example, are translated into Italian by Boccaccio (1313–75) in his *Decamerone* – but it is not to his literary talent that I wish primarily to point. A detailed study of Apuleius' treatment by medieval and early modern demonologists – men who may be broadly defined as canon lawyers, theologians, jurists, philosophers, physicians, and magistrates who wrote about demons in the context of magic and witchcraft[136] – has not been written. Nor is such a task before us. But it is of more than passing interest that Augustine's judgment of Apuleius as a fully fledged magician stands the test of time. As late as the sixteenth century, for example, we find Apuleius still cited by authorities on witchcraft as proof for the existence of magic in Roman antiquity.[137]

The Opinions of Paulus and Later Law Codes

We turn finally to a major example of how the scope of the *Cornelian law on assassins and poisoners* was extended by Roman jurists in the third century CE to incorporate a wider range of magical activity.[138] This shift in interpretation, which can be attributed to a multitude of factors including actual trials, senatorial decrees, imperial rescripts (viz. points of legal clarification, relevant to ad hoc cases, that were officially issued by sitting emperors), and the updating and further elucidation of the Cornelian law by lawyers and legal scholars, took time to develop and can already be partially glimpsed in the trial of Apuleius in 158/9 CE. But it was in the formulation of the early third-century CE jurist Julius Paulus, in his *Sententiae* or *Opinions*, or in works attributed to him, that the groundwork was laid for all future prosecutions for magic under Roman law. After citing the Cornelian law, Paulus adds an extensive set of further considerations, of which I quote only the most relevant:[139]

> 14. Those who give abortifacients or love philtres, even if they do not act with malice aforethought, nevertheless because it sets a bad example: *humiliores* are relegated to the mines, *honestiores* to an island with partial forfeiture of their property; but if as a result a woman or a man has died, they are punished with the supreme punishment. 15. Those who perform, or arrange for the performance of, impious or nocturnal rites, in order to enchant (*obcantare*), magically bind (*defigere*), or restrain (*obligare*) someone, shall be crucified or thrown to the beasts. 16. Those who sacrifice a man or obtain omens from his blood, or pollute a shrine or a temple, shall be thrown to the beasts, or, if *honestiores*, be capitally punished. 17. It is agreed that those guilty of the magic art (*magicae artis*) be inflicted with the supreme punishment, i.e. to be thrown to the beasts or crucified. Actual magicians (*magi*), however, shall be burned alive. 18. No one is permitted to have in their possession books of the magic art; and if anyone is found to have them in their possession, the books shall be publicly burnt and their property confiscated; *honestiores* shall be sent to an island; *humiliores* capitally punished. Not only the profession of this art, but also its knowledge (*scientia*) is prohibited. 19. If a man has died from a medicine (*medicamen*), which was given for health or as a remedy (*remedium*), the one who gave it, if *honestior*, is relegated to an island; a *humilior*, however, is punished capitally.

By way of background, it is first important to note the Roman legal distinction between *honestiores*, or persons of upper class, and *humiliores*, or persons of lower class. Although no legal definition of these terms has been found, we can clearly see how marked the differences are in criminal law with milder penalties for *honestiores*, often involving the partial confiscation of property and relegation to islands, in comparison with the variously brutal death penalties meted out to *humiliores*.

Paulus brings several important strands of legal thinking together in this opinion, beginning with the use of love philtres and abortifacients, two common *venena*.[140] Note here that intent is less at issue than the outcome, as in Greek law: if a person dies, the act is treated as a capital crime with the supreme penalty for both *honestiores* and *humiliores*, whereas if no death results milder sanctions differentiated by class apply. Intent is considered in section 19, on the other hand, when death results from the administration of medicine. In contrast to abortifacients and philtres, here the law acknowledges the inherent utility of *medicamina* and is thus in a case of death less punitive in its treatment of *honestiores*. In section 15, nocturnal rites of the kind for which Apuleius was accused are now explicitly coupled with other classes of magic, including incantations and binding magic. This means that by the third century, the array of binding spells accomplished through the writing of lead tablets, papyri, and fashioning of figurines discussed in chapter 3 were all punishable by death. The matter of human sacrifice is somewhat harder to clarify, and probably attached to the activities of numerous Jewish and Christian sects, upon which Roman emperors had for some time looked with suspicion.[141] The reason for the prohibition of divination through human blood is also not entirely transparent, although such charges are not unknown. There is the case of the first-century CE holy man and miracle-worker, Apollonius of Tyana, who was charged before the emperor Domitian (emp. 81–96 CE) with sacrificing human beings – and notably one Arcadian boy – for purposes of divination; however, the authenticity of this charge cannot be proven.[142]

Roman authorities had fervently managed popular divination since the time of Augustus, when he is said to have burned all Greek and Roman prophetic books that were not considered to contain genuine Sibylline oracles. The true Sibylline oracles were thenceforth preserved in state-controlled oracular books.[143] The Roman state protected its monopoly on divination, and especially forbade any divination that predicted the death of an emperor. There are many examples found in the law codes that attest an almost zealous concern with restricting divination (*haruspicina*), the activities of prophets (*hariolus*), astrologers (*mathematicus*), and those of the caster of natal horoscopes (*genethliacus*).[144] By the third and fourth centuries, magic and divination had become more closely aligned and the restrictions placed on both activities were often grouped together under one rubric in the law codes.[145] We can observe this alignment even in Paulus, insofar as the same strict prohibition is applied to the possession of magical books, which like divinatory books are also to be burned.

Of the punishments specifically directed toward *magi* – that they are to be burned alive like their books – we come to one of the most important capital sentences issued with respect to the legislative history of magic. In the second century CE, we do find an obscure reference to burning a *pharmakis* in the only surviving rhetorical exercise of Hadrian of Tyre, which accords in some respects with the *sententiae* of Paulus given above.[146] However, the exact legal context to which the speech refers is obscured by the fact that the hypothetical scenario – that of a woman who was convicted of 'magic' (*pharmakeia*) but could not be burned, and another woman who undertook to burn her and succeeded, with Hadrian justifying the burning – finds no parallels to my knowledge in any other source. Still, the general emphasis of Hadrian's speech on acquiring the *tekhnē* of *pharmakeia* as implying ill intentions on the part of the acquirer seems to align with Paulus' mention of *scientia* of the *ars magica* above.[147] Neverthless, because Hadrian's exercise predates Paulus, our ability to identify the relevant legal precedent that would have formed the context of his speech is hampered.

Burning alive was not an uncommon punishment in itself, and, as we might expect, we also find it levied against seers in later legislation, as in the *Theodosian Code*,[148] which was published by the emperor Theodosius II in 438 CE, and in the *Code* of Justinian,[149] which was promulgated in 529. The emperor Diocletian (emp. 284–305), who proscribed the Manichaeans as a subversive foreign cult, also specified burning alive for the leaders of that sect, with lesser penalties for their followers.[150] It goes without saying that burning alive was reserved for individuals in the state who were perceived to be a serious threat to the maintenance of order, and who were believed, as we find in another imperial rescript issued by Constantius Augustus (d. 361) in 357, to disturb the course of nature and to ruin the lives of innocent people.[151]

Interpretationes Christianae

Constantius was the third son of Constantine I ('The Great', emp. 306–37 CE), by whom the official imperial religion of Rome was unified in Christianity in 325, at the council of Nicaea. Under the Christian emperors, the demonic underpinnings of pagan magic and divination are given a more substantial base in the law codes, and in the fifth century we begin to find anonymous Christian interpretations attached to earlier, pagan Roman laws. Formally called an *interpretatio* 'explanation, signification', each explanation usually adds operational detail to the magic or divination proscribed in a given law. As one example, consider an *interpretatio* in the *Theodosian Code* found in section 3, in book 9, title 16, which bears the general rubric: *On Magicians (maleficus) and Astrologers (mathematicus) and others suchlike*. We begin with the law itself, in which can be found some of the same emphases in the opinion of Paulus, given above, as for instance the equally vehement focus on punishing the knowledge (*scientia*) of magic arts as well as the practice of them. This particular law is also interesting because it makes a distinction, which was not to last, between harmful and beneficial (agrarian) magic:[152]

> The knowledge (*scientia*) ought to be punished and deservedly avenged with the severest laws of those who, supported by magic arts (*magicae artes*), have either threatened the safety of someone or are found to have turned chaste minds to lust. However, no criminal charges are to be attached to remedies (*remedia*) sought for human bodies, or for rural districts for fear of protecting the mature grape harvests from rainstorms or from violent hailstorms. By these remedies neither the safety nor the reputation of anyone is harmed, but their activities bring it about that neither divine gifts nor the labors of men are destroyed.

This is a remarkable passage. On the one hand, a clear distinction is made between harmful and libidinous magic – the latter of which was a charge frequently directed toward any group, and notably toward non-Christian religious sects, whose activities took place in secret – and agrarian magic. Concern with protecting the grape harvest – since wine remained an important Roman commodity – can be found in many Roman and medieval Greek agricultural handbooks, such as in the tenth-century *Geoponica* mentioned in chapter 4.[153] Similarly, as early as Cato 'The Censor' (234–149 BCE), we find in his treatise on agriculture the mention of helpful incantations used to heal dislocations or fractures, presumably in farm animals.[154] On the other hand, such a distinction in magic – which is not found in our Greek sources – does not last within the law codes, and this suggests that the *Theodosian Code* here preserves an older, Roman attitude toward traditions of agrarian magic that were viewed as relatively harmless.

In any case, this section of the law is immediately followed by an *interpretatio*:

> Interpretatio: Let magicians (*malefici*) or enchanters (*incantatores*) or instigators of storms, or those who through the invocation of demons (*invocatio daemonum*) disturb the minds of men, be punished with every kind of penalty.

For the anonymous author of this *interpretatio*, the prevailing theory of how magic is accomplished could not be more at odds with what the law code itself says. A new operational dimension to magic has been added that depends on demons, which as we saw in Augustine represents the most significant shift in the Christian effort to explain the efficacy of pagan magic. More examples like this can be found: in later sections of the same rubric on magicians and astrologers, we find *interpretationes* that specify demons as either the agents for divination or as the honorees of nocturnal sacrifices.[155] Although a detailed examination of this transition as it is reflected in the law codes would extend beyond the scope of this study, these anonymous *interpretationes* give us direct insight into how Christian authorities adapted a demonic worldview to pagan Roman law. They deserve further research, not only on the grounds of legal history, but especially with regard to the agency and perceived human abilities these constructions of demons exhibit.

The Medieval Inheritance

I want finally to turn to the key implication of Roman laws as they were accumulated and applied across the eastern and western parts of the formerly unified empire. By tradition Roman law was accretive, and earlier compilations were subsumed within later ones, often after due purging of inconsistencies and rectification of conflicting provisions. Some 90 years after the appearance of the *Theodosian Code*, the emperor Justinian (emp. 527–65 CE) ordered the preparation of a comprehensive collection of all imperial laws, including those in the three major existing codices, of which the *Theodosian Code* was one,[156] as well as more recent laws. Written in Latin, his *Digesta* or *Digest* was issued in 529,[157] and revised and reissued in 533, and its practical aim was to reduce the number of lawsuits and to be used in the famous law schools of Beirut and Constantinople. In the eastern, Byzantine empire less use was made of the laws until a Greek version appeared between the ninth and tenth centuries (called the *Basilica*). In the western part of the empire, however, Justinian's laws held force for two centuries, in parts of both Italy and North Africa. After the expansion of Islam in the seventh century, the *Digest* was lost for a time until it was rediscovered in the eleventh century. From then, the *Digest*, now more broadly known as the *Corpus Juris Civilis* (Corpus of Civil Law), was gradually accepted, subject to local variations, as the basis of legal education, and criminal and civil jurisprudence throughout Europe, with the exception of Britain where a different tradition of common and statutory law prevailed. In the later Middle Ages, within the Catholic church the *Corpus* greatly influenced the development of canon law, which unlike criminal and civil law dealt primarily with ecclesiastical rules for the regulation of faith, morals, and discipline.

The implications for magic were profound. In a history that has been treated by many authors, magic remained a source of, at times, intense concern for both religious and civil institutions throughout the Middle Ages and the early modern period. With the *Digest* and its specific interpretations of and proscriptions against magic – magic which we have seen in its outlines to be quintessentially Greek – having settled into the sediment of continental European law, it was no longer possible to deny its existence or to doubt its harm. Instead, it became incumbent upon those individuals and institutions charged with the responsibility to strive in every possible way to continue extirpating magic from the fabric of society. Demonic magic had become the ultimate threat to civil and religious society alike.

CHAPTER 6

Conclusion

捕捕捕捕

Despite my attempts in the preceding chapters to convey both some general outlines for, and suggestive methodological approaches to, ancient Greek magic, I still believe the subject is inexhaustible. I have been reading and thinking about magic the better part of twenty years, and in that time I have yet to find an absolutely airtight explanation for any given magical object or practice. Instead, as more attention is paid to the ritual context, cultural and historical background, and the interpretive possibilities for understanding a magical object or action, it seems that a grasp of its essential qualities recedes. A more modest concluding statement is thus in order: what I hope to have shown in this book is that by asking questions not only about what Greek magic is, but in particular about how magic does whatever it does and who is affected by it, we may gain some insight into what its practitioners thought it was. After all, magic remains perennially interesting to scholars and lay persons alike not because they believe it to be true, but precisely because they fail to understand how others could believe it to be true. And this very attitude characterizes in different ways the attacks on magic by the Hippocratic author of *On the Sacred Disease* and Plato. If my interpretations of Greek magic have at all been persuasive, however, I hope to have offered several alternative approaches to this issue. For a historian of magic, it is less important whether magic is true or real than which cultural constructs allow it to exist. Only within that framework can we approach an understanding of what magic looks like and how people interact with it in a given culture, at a particular time and place.

We paid a good deal of attention in chapter 1 to general cultural constructs that bear on magical practices and magical thinking. These constructs, drawn for the most part from disparate cultures, help us to see how key notions of sympathy, analogy, agency, and participation inform how an outsider ought to approach magical practice in any culture, not just in an ancient one. The task then becomes to identify, in the present case, which specifically Greek constructs of sympathy, agency, and so forth are at issue in a given magical practice. These are generalizable constructs that can be applied to any culture's magical practices. With the particular example of the Azande offered by Evans-Pritchard, I hope to have shown that as outsiders to a magical tradition more often than not we ask questions about causality and efficacy, which from a native point of view are for the most part irrelevant to their practices and concerns. Instead, it is the key notions outlined above that invite one, as close as the evidence will allow, "inside" the heads of magical practitioners. And it is noteworthy to recall that even when Evans-Pritchard directly asked his informants about their rationale for a given practice or belief, they were unable to articulate it much beyond the Zande constructs which he already knew to be active.

Understanding specific Greek constructs then becomes crucial, as it would for any given cultural and historical context, and the example of Homeric incantations is a case in point. Homer was arguably the most significant archaic Greek poet from the point of view of both Greeks and Romans, but this in itself does not explain why his verses were used as incantations. Vergil was equally significant to imperial Romans, yet his verses tend only to have been used for divination. To offer an explanation for this difference, as we have seen, we need to situate Homer in a late antique, Greco-Egyptian context, in which both the rhythm of the hexameter and key terms within individual verses were believed to have therapeutic properties. But as to why Homer and not other epic poets were the preferred source of incantations, we need also to grasp how Neoplatonist authors elaborated on the sympathetic connections between his verses and the divinity they sought to reach through them.

Other examples are the binding and animation of figurines, which I see as flowing from the set of ritual attitudes generally toward statuary shared by both Greeks and Romans. Not that they are exactly alike, but it is such ritual interactions that regard statues as social agents – as humans, or at least as partaking of human qualities – which inform the magical use of figurines. I do not claim to have exhausted the interpretive possibilities of binding figurines, and while some readers will take issue with my claim that binding them is to anger them which in turn motivates retributive action on their part, I am nevertheless certain that magical figurines inhabited the same moral universe as statues and inanimate objects generally. Hence we should be able to translate some of the moral attributes from one realm of activity to the other, and vice versa, because it is culturally consistent to do so. In the same way, the rites for animating *erōtes* can be better understood as transferring the affection of a lover to the figurines, which in turn transfers that affection to the beloved, because the figurines themselves are social agents. The lavish gifts, flowers, fruit, and winged offerings are needed not only because they invoke analogies with Eros, but also because *erōtes* are in effect young boys who need to be persuaded to do one's bidding. Like children, they have a mind of their own.

Conceptions of Greek magic in its main forms and language used to describe it were developed in the fifth and fourth centuries BCE, especially in the hostile writings of the Hippocratic author of *On the Sacred Disease* and Plato. We have seen how the Hippocratic author, as well as other writers interested in magic before him, such as Gorgias, strongly imbues magic with a purificatory strain. The issue of correct purification, with an acceptable theology, seems to have lain at the heart of the dispute between the Hippocratic author and the itinerant specialists with whom he likely competed for business. However, I do believe the Hippocratic author's arguments are misplaced to the extent that he fails to recognize that epilepsy, his main subject, was thought to result from magical binding. Plato, who is for the most part uninterested in magic, nevertheless uses it as a vehicle to admonish Athenian citizens who fall prey to the envy of their neighbors in believing magic to be real. As an extension of his concern for tranquility in the body politic, his ideal state enacts laws that check these private disputes on the one hand, and check the ambitions of educated men who purvey magical remedies on the other.

Where definitions of magic and its effects are most at issue is in Greek, and then later Roman, law and jurisprudence. The ambiguity of terms like *pharmakon* and *venenum* plagued defendants and jurists alike, as whether by trial or careful reasoning attempts were made to distinguish intent from the nature of 'drugs' generally. In later centuries, the emphasis on determining intent recedes into the background as both the drugs themselves and a broadened and negative conception of magic more generally take center stage. In order to have a fuller grasp of this shift in perspective, we delved into late Roman law both to show how it relied on earlier Greek precedents in its interpretation of magic and to foreshadow, through compilations like Justinian's *Digest*, the hardening of medieval Christian minds toward pagan magic. While the definition of magic would change – not least owing to the puzzling case of Apuleius – and eventually be grafted onto myriad forms of medieval heresy, for late Roman jurists it was ostensibly in the service of protecting the people that private, nocturnal sacrifices, impious rites, the charming away of crops, poisoning, divination from human blood, and magic's power to disturb the minds of the masses which made magic imperative to punish.

The key point to take away is that ancient Greek magic was an expressive and creative realm of human activity, and to that extent it remains open to new scholarly interpretation. The methodological approach to magic adopted in this book tries to appreciate magic's basic cultural metaphors, as well as how those metaphors can change as circumstances and users dictate, without falling prey to the temptation to regard magic as a primarily rhetorical or symbolic exercise. Part of coming to terms with individual Greek practices involves accepting that magic was not static, that such practices necessarily changed over time, and that they were operative within the same understandings of causality and agency that informed daily ancient life. Depositing a curse tablet in a grave with instructions for an invisible entity, for example, simply made no sense in a world in which such invisible entities did not already play a significant role as respondents to human needs. They were part of the extended community, with due obligations and responsibilities, even if some Greeks themselves expressed ambivalence about dealing with them. But it is ultimately modern audiences, with their often deeply felt but little understood anxieties about "magic," that refuse to accept how helpful a hand from the grave could be at times. Yet if the reader can now sympathize, even reluctantly, with that perspective, then this book will have gone some way toward revealing how Greek magic speaks to basic and timeless human needs – because, like the Greeks, we all need help from the grave now and then.

Notes

INTRODUCTION

1 An excellent overview of recent scholarship can be found in Fowler and Graf 2005, with bibliography at pp. 286–87. My own review of some key debates can be found in Collins 2003, with bibliography at n. 1.

1 MAGIC: WHAT IS IT AND HOW DOES IT WORK?

1 See Kieckhefer 1994: 817–20 and generally Kieckhefer 1989.
2 The role of demons in medieval magic has been well emphasized by Flint 1991: 101–8 and Flint 1999.
3 Tambiah 1990: 72.
4 Malinowski 1954: 70–84.
5 Cf. Skorupski 1976: 155, "a great mass of everyday explanations link one event or state of affairs with another, without ever moving from the question: Why did it happen? to: Who *did it* or *made it* happen, and why? Within the terms of the underlying conceptual scheme, however, the thinker is naturally led in this direction if he presses for further or deeper understanding" (italics in original).
6 Gell 1998: 101.
7 Lévy-Bruhl 1979: 65.
8 Johnston 1999: 127–60.
9 Lévy-Bruhl 1979: 302.
10 The term "Azande" identifies the ethnic group and "Zande" is the adjective.
11 Evans-Pritchard 1937: 387.
12 A divination procedure in which branches from two separate trees are placed in a termite hill. The "answer" to whatever question is addressed to the oracle depends on which of the two, or whether neither or both, branches are eaten. See Evans-Pritchard 1937: 352–57.

13 A divination procedure in which answers are determined by rubbing two small boards together, which have been anointed with medicines. Whether the boards stick together or slide determines the answer. See Evans-Pritchard 1937: 359–74.

14 The most prestigious of Zande oracles (*benge*). A strychnine-based poison derived from a creeper plant is given to domestic fowl, often causing convulsions. Whether the fowl live or die determines the answer. See Evans-Pritchard 1937: 258–351.

15 E.g., Wax and Wax 1962.

16 Evans-Pritchard 1937: 65–66.

17 Evans-Pritchard 1937: 82.

18 Evans-Pritchard 1937: 82–83.

19 Frazer 1917: 52.

20 The time dimension of the sympathetic relation is an understudied area in its own right, since often the time horizon in magic, in contrast to witchcraft or divination, is usually short and sometimes immediate. Moreover, magic typically looks ahead in time, even if it is aimed at undoing a situation that was brought into being in the past.

21 Evans-Pritchard 1937: 11 and 320–21.

22 Lévy-Bruhl 1979: 327.

23 See the summary of views presented in Gell 1998: 137–43.

24 See Hansmann and Kriss-Rettenbeck 1966: 123–25.

25 Further examples of sacred geography can be found in Tambiah 1990: 106–8.

26 Cf. *DTA* 66 and 84.

27 Taussig 1993: 47–48.

28 Taussig 1993: 51.

29 Gell 1998: 135 (italics in original).

30 Skorupski 1976: 125–59.

31 See the summary of Wittgenstein's criticism of Frazer in Tambiah 1990: 54–64.

32 His two most important essays on magic, "The Magical Power of Words" and "Form and Meaning of Magical Acts," are reprinted in Tambiah 1985.

33 Tambiah 1985: 75–76.

34 The classic study in this regard is Lévi-Strauss 1966.

35 See the summary of Tambiah's work in Bell 1992: 41–42 and 111–12.

36 Tambiah 1985: 53.

37 The word 'religion' comes from Latin *religio*, which the Romans themselves defined largely in terms of the traditional honors that the state paid to its gods. On this see, Beard, North, and Price 1998.I: 214–27. The Greeks did not have an equivalent term for *religio*. By contrast both Greeks and Romans had terms for the perverse or excessive worship of the gods, *deisidaimonia* and *superstitio* respectively, both of which can be translated as 'superstition'.

38 Thomas 1971: 51–77 and *passim*.

39 Thomas 1971.

40 Clark 1997.

41 Discussed in detail by Phillips 1986 and 1991.

2   A FRAMEWORK FOR GREEK MAGIC

1   E.g., Dickie 2001: 23.
2   Johnston 1999: 85.
3   Scarborough 1991: 139 with n. 24.
4   Hopfner 1928.
5   E.g., Edelstein 1967: 222 n. 53.
6   See further Scarborough 1991: 139–42.
7   Translation by Foley 1994. Unless otherwise attributed, as here, all translations are by the author.
8   Richardson 1974 *ad* 228–29.
9   Faraone 2001.
10 Collins 2003.
11 *On the Nature of Animals* 2.14.
12 Collins 2001: 491.
13 11 A 1 D-K, 11 A 3 D-K.
14 12 A 15 D-K.
15 13 A 10 D-K and 13 A 7 D-K.
16 22 A 1 D-K.
17 24 A 12 D-K.
18 Fr. 199 Kassel-Austin.
19 31 A 32 D-K.
20 Weyer's views in *De praestigiis daemonum* are summarized in Clark 1997: 198–203.
21 Weyer's text can now conveniently be found in English in Mora 1991. The pages that quote *On the Sacred Disease* are in Mora 1991: 158–60.
22 *On the Sacred Disease* 1.10–12 Grensemann.
23 *On the Sacred Disease* 18.1–2 Grensemann.
24 Collins 2003: 25.
25 *On the Sacred Disease* 1.29–30 Grensemann.
26 See now Laskaris 2002: 73–93.
27 Lloyd 1979: 45–46.
28 Diodorus Siculus, fr. 31.43.
29 See further Lloyd 1987: 26–28.
30 Human and animal dissection are not non-existent in the Hippocratic treatises, but rare. See Lloyd 1975: 130–31 and *passim*.
31 *On the Sacred Disease* 18.6 Grensemann.
32 *On the Sacred Disease* 7.1 Grensemann.
33 Euripides, *Herakles* 930–35, with Bond 1981 *ad* 930–1009.
34 Still useful is Lewis 1989: 40.
35 Collins 2002.
36 One recent exception is Dickie 2001: 62.
37 Ganschinietz 1919.
38 *On the Sacred Disease* 1.40 Grensemann.
39 Ganschinietz 1919: 2527, citing Galen 10.314 Kühn.

40 *DT* 72.17, 79.3.
41 *DT* 161.132.
42 *DT* 52.7, 72.10, 76.10.
43 Ganschinietz 1919: 2532–33.
44 Plato, *Republic* 2.364b–c.
45 Aesop 56 (Perry).
46 *On the Sacred Disease* 1.44 Grensemann.
47 Parker 1983: 232–34.
48 22 B 5 D-K.
49 Parker 1983: 229.
50 See now Laskaris 2002: 68–72.
51 *On the Sacred Disease* 1.45–46 Grensemann.
52 Collins 2003: 25–26.
53 Plato, *Theaetetus* 149c–d.
54 Plato, *Republic* 4.426b.
55 Plato, *Laws* 10.909b.
56 Plato, *Republic* 2.364b–c.
57 Dickie 2001: 60–63.
58 Plato, *Laws* 11.933a.
59 Plato, *Laws* 11.933a–b.
60 Collins 2003: 35–37 and see chapter 5 on Plato's *Laws* as they pertain to magic.
61 Background on mechanical cause in Greek thought can be found in Hankinson 1998: 51–83; Vegetti 1999; and, in relation to magic, Collins 2003: 29–37.
62 See further Hart and Honoré 1959: 81–82 and Collins 2003: 29.
63 See also on this case Hankinson 1998: 71–72.
64 Plutarch, *Pericles* 36.3.
65 The Prytaneum (e.g., Demosthenes 23.76), on which see MacDowell 1978: 117–18.
66 Antiphon, *Second Tetralogy* 3.2.4–5.
67 Antiphon, *Second Tetralogy* 3.3.8.
68 Plato, *Laws* 11.933a–b.
69 Gell 1998: 101 (emphasis in original).
70 For the Greek background to this type of judicial curse, see Faraone 1989: 156–57, with specific reference to the *Brutus* at p. 154.
71 Cicero, *Brutus* 217.
72 Aeschylus, *Agamemnon* 1195, 1273, with Dickie 2001: 65.
73 Dickie 2001: 65–67.
74 Background on Greek seers and their Near Eastern counterparts can be found in Burkert 1992: 41–64. See further on *manteis* and prophetic authority, Dillery 2005.
75 Herodotus 9.33–36.
76 See further Pritchett 1979: 73–90.
77 Herodotus 9.93–94.
78 Plato, *Republic* 2.364e–365a.

79 Dickie 2001: 72–73.
80 Diphilus, fr. 125 Kassel-Austin, with Hoessly 2001: 162–63 and Parker 1983: 207–9.
81 *FGrH* 457. On Epimenides, see now Hoessly 2001: 175–81.
82 Aristotle, *Rhetoric* 1418a.23–26.
83 For the argument and background, see Kingsley 1995: 363–65.
84 Diogenes Laertius 8.58.
85 Diogenes Laertius 8.63; Athenaeus 14.620d.
86 Diogenes Laertius 8.66.
87 *On the Sacred Disease* 1.29–30.
88 Empedocles, fr. 111.
89 Translation by Kirk et al. 1983: 286, modified.
90 As in a *katabasis*, so Kingsley 1995: 41 with n. 17 and 225–27.
91 Aristophanes, *Clouds* 749–55.
92 Plato, *Laws* 10.909b.
93 So Kingsley 1995: 217–32, esp. 225–27, followed by Hoessly 2001: 192.
94 For these, see Obbink 1993: 90.
95 Diogenes Laertius 8.69.
96 See Lloyd 1979: 37–39 and Hoessly 2001: 239–40.
97 *Pace* Parker 1983: 210–11.
98 Diogenes Laertius 8.61 and 67.
99 See Kingsley 1994.
100 Cf. Diodorus Siculus' description of the Telchines (5.55.3), the mythical smiths who could produce clouds, rainstorms, hail, and snow when they wanted 'like the *magoi*', on which see Kingsley 1995: 224–25.
101 De Jong 1997: 387, with further bibliography at n. 1.
102 See, e.g., Nock 1972; Bremmer 1999; and see further below.
103 Heraclitus, fr. 22 B 14 D-K.
104 Dickie 2001: 28.
105 Sophocles, *Oedipus Tyrannos* 387–89.
106 Bremmer 1999: 3.
107 Sophocles, *Oedipus Tyrannos* 382.
108 Bernand 1991: 85–105.
109 De Jong 1997: 76–120.
110 Herodotus 7.113, with De Jong 1997: 400–1.
111 On this see Bremmer 1999: 5.
112 Herodotus 7.114; cf. 3.35 on the twelve Persians who were buried alive up to the neck by command of Cambyses.
113 De Jong 1997: 314–15.
114 Cf. Plutarch, *On Superstition* 13.171d, where only twelve victims are mentioned.
115 Herodotus 7.188–92.
116 Herodotus 2.119.
117 Cf. Dickie 2001: 34.
118 Bremmer 1999: 8.

119 Satyrus *apud* Diogenes Laertius 8.59.
120 Burkert 1962: 43–44.
121 Plato, *Laws* 10.909b (*goēteuontes*).
122 For a detailed examination of *goēs* and *goēteia*, see Johnston 1999: 100–23.
123 As at Aeschines 3.137.
124 Gorgias, *Encomium of Helen* 14.
125 See Scarborough 1991.
126 Plato, *Laws* 11.933a.
127 The four humours are discussed in several Hippocratic treatises, including *On the Nature of Man*, *On Breaths*, and *On Humours*, and they prevailed in ancient medicine well into the sixteenth century through the special status accorded to them by Galen (second century CE), the famous court physician in the Rome of Marcus Aurelius.
128 Gorgias, *Encomium of Helen* 16–17.
129 Furley 1993: 85–87.
130 [Hippocrates], *Aphorisms* 1.20, 1.24, 2.36 (*pharmakeia*); 1.22 (*pharmakeuein*).
131 See Hoessly 2001, esp. 247–313.
132 For more on this see Hoessly 2001: 310–13, especially her contrast between the largely 'external' purification involved in religion, and the largely 'internal' purification utilized in medicine. Nevertheless, she demonstrates that, since the basic medical idea of disease as pollution, manifested in the body as a harmful humour, which therefore has to be purged, can be found in conventional Greek religion, medical *katharsis* must have derived from religious or magical purification (see p. 312, with further bibliography at n. 300).
133 Laskaris 2002: 69.
134 This point is also made by Dickie 2001: 34–35.
135 Plato, *Theaetetus* 149c–d.
136 E.g., Euripides, *Hippolytus* 1038.
137 Phrynichus, *Praeparatio Sophistica* 56.8 de Borries. Phrynichus lived in the second century CE.
138 Bremmer 1999: 9.
139 Rives (forthcoming, pp. 12–15) has recently documented that Latin prose authors (with the exception of the elder Pliny) use *magus* to refer to Persian priests more often than poets, in a manner that is consistent with the use of *magos* by earlier Greek historians, ethnographers, and philosophers.
140 Catullus, *Carmina* 90.1.
141 E.g., Cicero, *Laws* 2.26, *On the Nature of the Gods* 1.43.
142 Vergil, *Eclogue* 8.66.
143 Vergil, *Aeneid* 4.493. Cf. Ovid, *Amores* 3.7.35, *Ars* 2.425, *Rem.* 250, with further references to classical Latin authors in Rives (forthcoming, p. 26 n. 43). For *ars magica* in late antique and medieval authors, see the references in Abt 1908: 104–5.
144 Graf 1997: 30–35.
145 31 B 112 D-K.

3   BINDING MAGIC AND EROTIC FIGURINES

1   Plato, *Republic* 2.364b–c.
2   The term *defixio* comes from the Latin verb *defigere* 'to bind with a curse/bewitch'.
3   For an overview of the competitive context of Greek binding spells, see Faraone 1991a.
4   For an overview of judicial prayers, see Versnel 1991.
5   See Gager 1992: 3. Lead alloys included other metals such as tin and copper.
6   Gager 1992: 4–5.
7   Forsdyke 2005: 157–58.
8   For Demosthenes and Lycurgus, Gager 1992: 129, no. 42 (=*DT* 60).
9   See Gager 1992: 31 n. 5.
10   The most comprehensive treatment of the Greek magical papyri (*PGM*) to date remains Brashear 1995.
11   See the ostraca, no. 1–5 in *PGM*, vol. 2, pp. 233–35. For an example of a love spell which needs to be written on an ostracon, see *PGM* XXXVI.187–210.
12   *DTA* 27.
13   *DTA* 26.
14   As, e.g., in *DTA* 67, with Faraone 1991a: 7–8.
15   *DTA* 43.
16   See Gager 1992: 67–72, no. 13 (=*DT* 140–87) with figure 9 and no. 14 (=Wünsch 1898, no. 29) with figure 10.
17   See Gager 1992: 98, figure 13, often reprinted.
18   So Faraone 1991b: 167, although his examples differ somewhat from those presented here.
19   *Homeric Hymn to Apollo* 127–29.
20   The noun is heteroclite, on which see *LSJ* s.v.
21   *Homeric Hymn to Dionysus* 12–14.
22   *Homeric Hymn to Hermes* 156–58.
23   *Homeric Hymn to Hermes* 409–13.
24   *Iliad* 1.401.
25   *Iliad* 15.18–24, also alluded to at 1.590–93.
26   Aeschylus, *Prometheus* 97 and 113.
27   E.g., *DT* 68.
28   Johnston 1999.
29   *Odyssey* 11.72–73.
30   E.g., in Sophocles' *Antigone* and *Oedipus at Colonus*.
31   *DTA* 85.
32   See *LSJ* s.v. πρός C.7 and further, Johnston 1999: 73 with n. 112.
33   Curbera and Jordan 1998, with pl. 32.
34   E.g., Xenophon, *Memorabilia* 1.2.31; Demosthenes 7.33; Plato, *Apology* 28a.
35   Hesiod, *Theogony* 411–52.
36   Hekate plays an important role in mediating the return of Persephone from the underworld to her mother Demeter in the *Homeric Hymn to Demeter*.

37 For some examples of tablets addressed to Demeter, both from the Greek islands and Asia Minor, see Gager 1992: no. 75 (= *SGD* no. 60) and no. 89 (= *DT* 1, 4, and 13).

38 Tomlin 1988: 262.

39 The third-century BCE Cypriot tablets, e.g., *DT* 22–37, commonly begin '*Daimones* under the earth and *daimones* whoever you are . . . and whoever lies (buried) here. . . .'

40 Johnston 1999: 72–73.

41 See Johnston 1999: 90–95, with further bibliography.

42 *DTA* 102.

43 *DTA* 103.

44 *DT* 189.

45 Tomlin 1988: 247, with reference to texts 112–16.

46 Graf 1997: 130–31.

47 Cf. Faraone 1991a: 4 and Versnel 2002b: 62.

48 *DT* 52.

49 *DT* 52.7–8.

50 *DT* 43 and 44. *DT* 44 substitutes the names Akestōr for Neophanes, and Eratophanes and Timandridas for Aristandros.

51 E.g., Graf 1997: 130, *contra*, e.g., *DTA* 43–44 (p. 79) where Pasianax is taken to be the name of the lord of the underworld.

52 So Versnel 2002b: 61.

53 *Pace* Versnel 2002b: 61. I do not agree with Versnel that the reference to Pasianax's lack of sensation in the last line "unequivocally proves" that the corpse should not read the message. The line finds parallels in typical *similia similibus* 'like to like' formulae of the type, 'so as this corpse lies useless, so too may everything for Theodora be useless' (*DT* 68b.1–3; cf. *DTA* 105, 106, 107), and may therefore not imply anything about the preceding sentence.

54 Caches of tablets written by the same person have been found in an Athenian well, on which see *SGD* 160. Roman-era tablets more strongly attest professionalization, on which see Tomlin 1988: 99, with further bibliography.

55 See Gager 1992: 10–11.

56 E.g., *PGM* VII.795–845.

57 A picture of a manuscript page with characters can be found in Gager 1992: 8, figure 1. For more on magic and astrology in the *Picatrix*, see Thorndike 1915: 126–33.

58 See further Kieckhefer 1989: 133.

59 *Apologia* 26.6.

60 E.g., Origen (ca. 184–ca. 254 CE), *Against Celsus* 1.25.

61 Iamblichus, *On the Mysteries of Egypt* 3.14.

62 Augustine, *De Doctrina Christiana* 2.74.

63 Augustine, *De Doctrina Christiana* 2.87–95, with Harmening 1990: 75.

64 Augustine, *De Doctrina Christiana* 2.75. Translation by Green 1995: 92–93.

65 See Kotansky 1991: 107 and *passim*.

66 Augustine, *De Doctrina Christiana* 2.111. Translation by Green 1995: 109.
67 Plato, *Laws* 11.933a–b (and see chapter 2).
68 For more on this, see Graf 2002: 93–98 and Markus 1994.
69 *PGM* XXXVI.178–87, *kharaktēres* are to be drawn around a figure.
70 Gager 1992: 169–70 no. 78 with figure 19.
71 See Gager 1992: 56–58, no. 6. Translation by Gager et al., modified.
72 These could be the names of the chariot-drivers or the horses, both of which
    appear frequently in tablets found in hippodromes.
73 Gager 1992: 57 n. 41.
74 Gager 1992: 57 n. 41.
75 *PGM* VII.417–22.
76 Moulokh = Moloch?, on which see Brashear 1995: 3593 s.v.; Khre = Gk. χρή
    'destiny'?; Maskelli = μασκελλι μασκελλω binding (?) formula, Brashear 1995:
    3592 s.v.; Iabezebuth = Hebrew *Jahweh Sabaoth*, Brashear 1995: 3587 s.v.
77 *PGM* XXXVI.178–87.
78 The judicial curses in the tablets from Selinus, Sicily, which date to the begin-
    ning of the fifth century, already single out the tongue and intellectual body
    parts. See Gager 1992, nos. 49–51.
79 *DTA* 51.
80 *DTA* 90.
81 Cicero, *Brutus* 217.
82 A good starting point for the treatment of body parts in curse tablets is
    Versnel 1998.
83 *DTA* 96, 97; citation from 96.
84 Sophocles, *Oedipus Tyrannos* 718.
85 *DTA* 96.14, 97.25–26.
86 Faraone 1991b: 182 n. 62 and 194 n. 103; also Ogden 1997: 29.
87 Garland 1995: 14–15.
88 *Gynaecology* 2.10.5.
89 Ogden 1997: 24–28.
90 For the account, see Gager 1992: no. 165 (= Sophronius, *Account of the
    Miracles of Saints Cyrus and John*, in *PG* 87.3, cols. 3541–48), with Faraone
    1991b: 193.
91 Gager 1992: no. 166 (= Sophronius ibid., *PG* 87.3, col. 3625).
92 For Roman practices, see, e.g., Dionysius of Halicarnassus 2.15.1–2, with
    Garland 1995: 16–18.
93 On which see Ogden 1997: 9–14.
94 Plutarch, *Lycurgus* 16.1–3.
95 Plutarch, *Lycurgus* 16.2.
96 *SGD* nos. 24–35, 37–38.
97 *SGD* no. 38.
98 Tomlin 1988: 70–71.
99 *DT* 74. cf. *DT* 75.
100 Translation by Versnel 1998: 236.
101 *DT* 190.

102 Versnel 1998: 246.
103 *P. Colon.* inv. T 4. On this tablet, see Versnel 1998: 224 with n. 21. Cursing the 365 members of the body has Coptic parallels (e.g., *PGM* IV.149–53), and 365 is the numerical value of the Greek letters of the important magical demon, Abrasax (Ἀβρασάξ). See further Betz 1992: 40 n. 43.
104 Weiner 1983. Her research population lives on the island of Kiriwina, one of the Trobriand islands, in Papua New Guinea.
105 R. Gordon, *Spells of Wisdom* (forthcoming). His model is discussed by Versnel 1998: 224 with n. 22.
106 Weiner 1983: 705.
107 Gordon, *Spells of Wisdom* (forthcoming), cited in Versnel 1998: 224–25 n. 22. Cf. Gordon 1999: 268 for a similar formulation.
108 *DT* 155–56, cited in Versnel 1998: 244.
109 Versnel 1998: 244–46.
110 Meyer and Smith 1999: no. 66 (= *P. Mich.* 1190).
111 Translation by Meyer and Smith 1999.
112 See now on Greece, Burkert 2005: 6–8 and, on Rome, Maggiani 2005: 56–59.
113 See Lloyd 1975: 116.
114 See van Straten 1981; Beard, North, and Price 1998.I: 12–13.
115 Van Straten 1981: 149.
116 Tomlin 1988: 230–31. Translation by Tomlin.
117 Tomlin 1988: 231 n. 6.
118 Henig et al. 1988: 6.
119 See Potter 1985.
120 Henig et al. 1988: 8.
121 See again Skorupski 1976: 149–59, and Faraone 1992: 9–10.
122 E.g., *PGM* XVI and XIXa were found folded around hair. See further, Gager 1992: 16–18.
123 See Faraone 1999: 25–30.
124 Brashear 1995: 3419.
125 For more on Egyptian magical practice, see Ritner 1995: 3353–71.
126 See most recently Daniel and Maltomini 1990–92, no. 47.
127 Translation by Daniel and Maltomini, modified.
128 On exorcism, Bonner 1943 is still useful.
129 Faraone 1999: 34–35.
130 The Antinous in this spell may be the same Antinous, famous lover of the emperor Hadrian, whom we are told was sacrificed in 130 CE by the emperor who then founded the city of Antinoupolis on the site of his death (Dio Cassius 69.11). The numerous statues Hadrian dedicated in Antinous' honor suggest magical appeasement of his restless soul, on which see Ogden 2002: no. 241. Moreover, the spell and figurine were found near Antinoupolis, on which see Daniel and Maltomini 1990–92: 179 n. 1.
131 As, for example, is the case with Lucan's superwitch, Erichtho. In return for summoning a corpse through necromancy, Erichtho promises that once she hears the relevant prophecy it will be free from any further magical requests

and will be allowed permanently to die (Lucan, *Pharsalia* 6.768–70 and 822–25).

132 Winkler 1991 and Faraone 1999: 43–95.

133 E.g., the Cyrenean foundation decree, in Meiggs and Lewis 1988: 5–9, no. 5, lines 44–49. See Faraone 1993.

134 Theocritus *Idyll* 2.24–25; cf. Horace, *Satire* 1.8.43–44.

135 Faraone 1999: 45.

136 See Faraone 1991b: 200–5, with figures.

137 E.g., Schlörb-Vierneisel 1966: 38 n. 6 with plate 51.1; image reprinted in Gager 1992: 17, figure 3. For the Mnesimachos doll, see Gager 1992: no. 41 with figure 17.

138 E.g., Faraone 1991b: 200.

139 Schlörb-Vierneisel 1966: 38 n. 6 with plate 51.1. For the dating, see Schlörb-Vierneisel 1964: 99–101.

140 Representations of male genitalia in Greece and Rome were widely used as magical defenses and "lucky charms."

141 Text and translation from Jordan 1988: 276.

142 Jordan 1988: 276.

143 Plato, *Apology* 33e.

144 Jordan 1988: 276.

145 Faraone 1991b: 168–72.

146 Faraone 1991b: 169 n. 11, but cf. Faraone 1992: 9–10.

147 Adapted from Collins 2003: 44.

148 Pausanias 6.11.2–3.

149 Pausanias 6.11.6.

150 Demosthenes 23.76.

151 Cf. Plato, *Laws* 9.873d–874a on the prosecution of animals and inanimate objects in his ideal state.

152 Pausanias 6.11.6–9.

153 Adapted from Collins 2003: 37–44.

154 Gell 1998: 66–68. Cf. Skorupski 1976: 155, "The primary idea required here is not the complex notion of religion, with 'magic' as a residual category, but that of a mode of understanding and acting on the world whose fundamental rationalising concept is the notion of *agency*" (italics in original).

155 For a good overview, see Elsner 1996 and Gordon 1979.

156 Aristophanes, *Wealth* 594–97.

157 Aeschylus, *Eumenides* 242; Herodotus 6.61.

158 E.g., Lucian, *On the Syrian Goddess* 36–37; Pausanias 3.16.7–11.

159 Euripides, *Alcestis* 1097–158.

160 Ovid, *Metamorphoses* 10.243–97.

161 Athenaeus 605f–606b; Pliny, *Natural History* 36.21.

162 Gell 1998: 134.

163 *Palatine Anthology* 6.280; Persius 2.70.

164 Persius 5.31.

165 Clerc 1915.

166 Clerc 1915: 16 and 61.
167 Clerc 1915: 77–78. In a memorable characterization (p. 78), Clerc refers to magical figurines as *petits drames souterrains et muets* ("little subterranean and silent dramas").
168 See Felton 2001.
169 Apuleius, *Metamorphoses* 4.28–6.24.
170 *PGM* XIII.378–79.
171 Dodds 1951: 292–95.
172 See Struck 2004: 210–13 and Steiner 2001: 119–20.
173 *Asclepius* 24, 38.
174 See Geffcken 1916–19: 309.
175 See, e.g., Anacreon 55.6–7 West; Theognis 1275–79; and Greifenhagen 1957: 7–34.
176 Galen 18.2.19 Kühn.
177 E.g., Felton 2001.
178 E.g., *DT* 234.14–17, 235.9–10, 237.8–11, all from Carthage, probably third century CE.
179 So Versnel 1998: 246.
180 Notably Faraone 1999.
181 Daniel and Maltomini 1990–92, no. 47
182 E.g., Daniel and Maltomini 1990–92, no. 46.23, 50.64.
183 But cf. Attic *DT* 75b.2 (ἔν[τερα]), restored.
184 *PGM* IV.2622–707, at 2658.
185 Durkheim 1915. See the overview of Durkheim by Bell 1992: 23–25 and Skorupski 1976: 18–35.
186 Cf. Collins 2003: 45.
187 For a recent overview of the concept of magic, with bibliography, see Fowler and Graf 2005.

4 HOMERIC INCANTATIONS

1 See Renehan 1992 (though I advise caution with regard to his distinction on p. 2 between 'rational' medicine and 'irrational' magic).
2 See Faraone 1999: 97–102.
3 E.g., the kiln curse, [Homer] *Epigram* 14.
4 Philostratus, *Heroicus* 43.12 (= 195 Kayser). Homer's knowledge of necromancy is also implied in Philostratus, *Life of Apollonius of Tyana* 4.16 and Apuleius, *Apology* 31. See further Ogden 2001: 259–60.
5 For a potsherd that contains fragments of *Iliad* 12.442–44 (Elephantine, Upper Egypt, second century CE), see Wessely 1886. For a stone amulet, described as '*serpentinus forma rotunda*' that contains most of *Iliad* 5.291 (provenance unknown), see *IG* 14.2580.2. For a gold *lamella* inscribed with *Iliad* 2.95 (provenance unknown), see the discussion below.
6 Documented by Thiers 1984. Cf. the Greek hexameter detected by Daly 1982: 96 in an eighth-century English spell in Latin, which is based on *Iliad* 24.451.

7   For more on *PGM* XXIII, see Wünsch 1909: 2–19.
8   See Puschmann 1963 and Daremberg and Ruelle 1963.
9   *De Med.* 15.108, and see further below.
10 Heim's (1892: 514–19) survey is the standard reference.
11 Iamblichus, *De Vit. Pyth.* 25.111 and 29.164. Note that in these passages both verses from Homer and Hesiod are mentioned, yet no verses from Hesiod survive in the magical papyri. Cf. Dio Chrysostom 33.61.1, where we find the query 'What Homer or what Archilochus is strong enough to dispel (lit. 'sing away' ἐξᾳδειν) these evils?'
12 E.g., Aristophanes, *Frogs* 1032–33; Plato, *Republic* 364e.
13 Iamblichus, *De Vit. Pyth.* 2.11.
14 Porphyry, *Vit. Pyth.* 1; Iamblichus, *De. Vit. Pyth.* 2.11.
15 Iamblichus, *De Vit. Pyth.* 14.63.
16 Cf. Porphyry, *Vit. Pyth.* 32–33.
17 In Pythagorean circles, hearing the *aulos* was cause for purifying oneself, as mentioned in Aristides Quintilian, *On Music* (2.19.28): 'Pythagoras advised his disciples after hearing the reed to wash off the sound since it was defiled by a breath, and through favorable melodies on the lyre purify the irrational impulses of the soul.'
18 For the Phrygian mode, see Plato, *Republic* 398e–399a.
19 Iamblichus, *De Vit. Pyth.* 25.113.
20 Heim 1892: 518.
21 Faraone 1996: 85 and 87.
22 E.g., Frankfurter 1995. While I am sympathetic to Frankfurter's *historiola* model for many types of magical spells, I do not think it is specific enough to explain the particular tradition of using Homeric verses.
23 Versnel 2002a.
24 See further Boyancé 1937: 126.
25 See *LSJ* s.v.
26 Dickie 2000: 570–71. As examples he cites *PGM* V.330–1 and *PGM* XXXVI.144–53.
27 On the magnet in women's medicine, see Scarborough 1991: 158–59.
28 They were, however, reading Homer and other Greek authors, as emphasized by Schwendner 2002.
29 So Faraone 1996: 84.
30 Faraone 1996: 84 n. 24.
31 Celsus, *De Re Med.* 6.18.9.
32 *Epid.* 4.58. Cf. *Aph.* 6.11–12.
33 *Epid.* 6.3.23.
34 Galen, *Nat. Fac.* 2.8.109.
35 Further research is still needed on the understanding of disease among medical writers in comparison with what is implied in magical texts. For the purposes of the present study, I assume that the boundary between professional medical knowledge and popular interpretation of disease was porous.
36 Note that functionally the blood here is a social agent that is directly addressed by the practitioner.

37 Hippocrates, *Airs, Waters, Places* 4.29.

38 See Dean-Jones 1989.

39 King 1998: 29.

40 Hippocrates, *Airs, Waters, Places* 21, with Dean-Jones 1989: 181–82. The expected amount was two Attic *kotulai*, or one pint, excessive by any modern standard, on which see King 1998: 30.

41 See King 1998: 29.

42 Hippocrates, *Diseases of Women* 1.6, with King 1998: 30.

43 [Hippocrates], *Aphorisms* 5.50.

44 Barring any magical use of menses. In the first century CE, for example, the elder Pliny knew that smearing menses on doorposts served as an antidote to magic (*tactis omnino menstruo postibus inritas fieri Magorum artes, Natural History* 28.85), but this can hardly be relevant here.

45 See Brashear 1995: 3547.

46 Namely *Iliad* 8.424, 10.193, and 5.385. The question of whether all six verses at *PGM* IV.468–74 form a set is made problematic by the *paragraphoi* that appear above verses 469, 471, and 474. However, the three verses in which we are interested (*Iliad* 10.521, 564, and 572) do reappear with one additional verse at *PGM* IV.821–24 and then alone at 2146–50, making it likely that they were regarded in some sense as a unit. Heim 1892: 518 calls these three verses '*potentissimi*'.

47 See Betz 2003: 226 with n. 804.

48 Cf. the literal and metaphorical meanings of Latin *fossa* 'trench/ditch', on which see *OLD* s.v.

49 See further Bradley 1994: 117–21.

50 Some Greek examples are *Iliad* 16.843–61; Sophocles, *Oedipus at Colonus* 605–28, 1370–96, 1516–55, etc. For the Roman sources, see the account of Callanus and the Rhodian in Cicero, *De Div.* 1.23, 1.30. Cf. *PGM* IV.2140–44 in which a flax leaf is to be inscribed with *voces magicae* and inserted into the mouth of a corpse to make it prophesy. See further Ogden 2001: 212–13.

51 *Iliad* 1.314; [Hippocrates], *On the Sacred Disease* 1.42 Grensemann.

52 Consider again the discussion in chapter 2 on the relationship between epilepsy, magic, and purification already outlined in *On the Sacred Disease*.

53 Tambiah 1985: 53.

54 E.g., *Geoponica* 1.12.37. Cf. 1.12.16, which suggests burying the skin of a hippopotamus in the place where one wishes to prevent thunderbolts from falling, and 11.2.7, where thunderbolts are said not to fall where fig trees are planted.

55 Artemidorus, *Oneirocriticon* 2.9.8.

56 Artemidorus, *Oneirocriticon* 2.9.10.

57 See Niedermann 1916.

58 Roeper 1850: 163.

59 See Faraone 1996: 84 n. 24 for further references.

60 *PGM* IV.2136–39.

61 Most strikingly, consider Marcellus' (*De Med.* 8.58) remedy for eye disease that involves writing a verse that conflates *Iliad* 3.277 and *Odyssey* 11.109 and 12.323. The conflation of the Iliadic and Odyssean verses in Marcellus may indicate a desire for the verse to be intelligible on its own.

62 Ross 1965: 29 (no. 29 with plate XXV).

63 Faraone 1996: 84 n. 23.

64 It is worth noting that in the Hippocratic authors the verb *tarassein* can also mean 'to cause relaxation', as of the bowels (e.g., *Nat. Mul.* 12).

65 Marcellus, *De Med.* 36.39 (hot gout) and 36.44 (cold gout).

66 See, e.g., Xenophon, *Cyr.* 1.6.28 and Lucian, *Podagra* 69.188.

67 Lucian, *Podagra* 69.124.

68 Lucian, *Podagra* 69.146–74, *epaoidai* mentioned at 172.

69 Athenaeus 458a–f; Plutarch, *Quaest. Conv.* 737a–c.

70 Robert 1950: 216, no. 233.

71 To date I have only found *Iliad* 5.127 = *PGM* VII.115, which is used in Lucian, *Charon* 7.12–13. It should be noted that *PGM* VII.1–148 is fragmentary and 24 verses (of 216 total) are only partially legible or missing.

72 I thank my colleague, Arthur Verhoogt, for calling this papyrus to my attention. On the Heroninus archive, see Rathbone 1991.

73 E.g., Rathbone 1991: 12–13, with further references. Rathbone (p. 12) notes that five letters from the central administration of the Appianus estate are written on the back of fragments of literary texts, including portions of *Iliad* 3 and 8. However, *P. Flor.* II 259 is not a reused papyrus, making it certain that the Iliadic verses were intended to accompany the letter.

74 This is confirmed by Messeri 1998 (with table CXXVI).

75 On this see Lamberton 1986: 1–43, and his section on Proclus, pp. 162–232. Further considerations of Homer's place in Greek education are summarized by Van der Horst 1998: 159–63.

76 See again Struck 2004: 210–13.

77 Lamberton 1986: 183–97.

78 Dillon 1976: 255.

79 See Struck 2004: 210–18, and Van den Berg 2001: 70 and 79–81.

80 Van den Berg 2001: 86–111.

81 For this interpretation I follow Van den Berg 2001: 182. The term 'noeric' refers to spiritual enlightenment.

82 Marinus, *Vita Procli* 22. On Helios, see Van den Berg 2001: 145–47.

83 As already noted, *Iliad* 5.127, for example, also appears in the 'Homer oracle', *PGM* VII.115.

84 So Van den Berg 2001: 99–100 and 182.

85 For more on biblical verses, see Van der Horst 1998: 143–73.

86 On the fabricated tradition of the *sortes Vergilianae*, most of which derive from *Aeneid* 6, see Kisch 1970.

87 The classic instance is Augustine, *Epist.* 55.20.37, on which see Klingshirn 2002: 82–84 and 104–14.

88   Hamilton 1993: 313–17. On the *sortes Sangallenses*, which derive in part from the Greek *sortes Astrampsychi*, see Klingshirn 2005.
89   See Grodzynski 1974.
90   Augustine, *Confessions* 8.12.29.
91   Augustine, *Confessions* 4.3.5.
92   See O'Donnell 1992 *ad* 4.3.5.
93   Rose 1874: 48.
94   Hence the majority of our evidence survives in the Greek magical papyri and in the Byzantine *Geoponica*.

5   MAGIC IN GREEK AND ROMAN LAW

1   Lucian, *On Salaried Posts* 27.23.
2   The testimonia can conveniently be found in Ogden 2002: 275–76.
3   Notably at Thucydides 2.48, where *pharmaka* refers to the 'poisons' the Peloponnesians allegedly put into the cisterns in Peiraieus, which was first to experience the outbreak of the Athenian plague in 430 BCE.
4   As in Euripides' *Hippolytus,* where 'enchanting philtres' (509) are also referred to as a *pharmakon* (516).
5   See further, Scarborough 1991.
6   See further Collins 2001.
7   Demosthenes 23.22 and Aristotle, *Athenian Constitution* 57.3. See further MacDowell 1978: 39–47.
8   Demosthenes 23.22.
9   Meiggs and Lewis 1969: no. 30 A1, with Graf 1997: 35.
10   Meiggs and Lewis 1969: no. 30 A6.
11   Antiphon, *Against the Stepmother* 1.14–20.
12   [Aristotle] *Magna Moralia* 16 = 1188b29–38.
13   See further Faraone 1999: 110–19.
14   This is the plot of Sophocles, *Women of Trachis.*
15   Examples can be found in Faraone 1999: 116–17.
16   See further Collins 2001, with further bibliography at p. 478 n. 7.
17   Cf. recently Parker 2005a: 132–34 and 2005b: 67–68 with n. 17, and Dickie 2001: 50–54.
18   Demosthenes, *Against Aristogeiton* 25.79–80.
19   Plato, *Meno* 80a–b.
20   Philochorus, *FGrH* 382 F 60.
21   Plutarch, *Demosthenes* 14.4.
22   See Collins 2001: 491–92.
23   Scholia to Demosthenes 19.281; Josephus, *Against Apion* 2.267. See further Dickie 2001: 52–53.
24   Dickie 2001: 54.
25   56 Perry. See Dickie 2001: 51–52 and Collins 2001: 484 n. 42.

26 Dickie 2001: 52.
27 1.40 Grensemann.
28 2.364b–c.
29 Plato, *Laws* 10.909a–c.
30 Plato, *Laws* 10.909c–d.
31 Cf. Dickie 2001: 60.
32 Plato, *Laws* 11.933d–e.
33 Cf. Plato, *Laws* 9.870d–872c.
34 Plato, *Laws* 10.908b–d.
35 Cf. Dickie 2001: 63.
36 Plato, *Laws* 11.933a–b.
37 In what follows, I rely on Rives' 2002 analysis of the Twelve Tables.
38 *Natural History* 28.10.
39 Rives 2002: 279–87.
40 Augustine, *On the City of God* 8.19, with Rives 2002: 275. It should be noted that Augustine attributes the mention of the Tables in this context to Cicero, but the passage in question has yet to be found.
41 Although they almost certainly discussed *venena* at some point, as Gaius (Justinian, *Digest* 50.16.236) attests.
42 *Natural History* 28.10.
43 Rives 2002: 273–74.
44 In what follows I rely on Graf 1997: 62–65.
45 Pliny, *Natural History* 18.41–43.
46 Graf 1997: 64.
47 For the possible etymological connection of *venenum* with *Venus*, see Walde 1910 s.v. *venenum*, which would yield an original meaning of "Liebestrank."
48 In Latin 'purification', both medical and ritual, can translate *purgatio*, *purificatio*, whereas 'ritual purification' can translate *lustrum*, *lustratio*.
49 Justinian, *Digest* 50.16.236. See Watson 1985. I have used Watson's edited translation, but with modifications.
50 Rives 2002: 276.
51 As when Pliny refers to the *veneficia* that cause an eclipse, *Natural History* 2.54. For *pharmakeia*, see chapter 2.
52 Pliny, *Natural History* 28.
53 See Rives 2003: 318 n. 14.
54 So Ferrary 1991: 422.
55 Rives 2003: 318.
56 The reconstruction is given by J.-L. Ferrary in Crawford 1996: 752, on which see Rives 2006: 49–52.
57 For the importance of this case, see Graf 1997: 48.
58 Livy 8.18.
59 Justinian, *Digest* 50.16.236.
60 Rives 2003: 320–21.
61 Beard, North, and Price 1998.I: 214–27.
62 Beard, North, and Price 1998.I: 217.

63 Beard, North, and Price 1998.I: 218.
64 Tacitus, *Annals* 2.69.3.
65 Cf. Suetonius, *Caligula* 3.3, where we are told that Germanicus was the target of *veneficia* and *devotiones*. Dio (57.18.9) records that Germanicus was killed by a *pharmakon*.
66 But *devotio* had an earlier, narrower meaning that referred to particular rituals in which Roman generals dedicated their enemies to underworld gods in exchange for victory, on which see Rives 2006: 56–57, with n. 39.
67 Tacitus, *Annals* 3.14.
68 Rives 2003: 321 n. 24.
69 Pliny, *Natural History* 28.19.
70 Apuleius, *Metamorphoses* 6.16.
71 See further Rives 2003: 321–22, and 334 n. 65.
72 See Augustine, *On Christian Doctrine* 2.74, where he explains that 'superstition' (*superstitio*) concerns the making or worshipping of idols, and certain kinds of consultations or contracts ratified with demons as in the 'magic arts' (*magicae artes*).
73 Isidore, *Etymologies* 8.9.9.
74 Lucan, *Pharsalia* 6.413–830. This scene depicts Pompey's son, Sextus, consulting the Thessalian witch Erictho on the eve of his father's battle with Julius Caesar. Caesar defeated Pompey at Pharsalus in 48 BCE.
75 Partial histories of this development can be found in Kieckhefer 1989: 19–42 and Flint 1991: 13–35.
76 On the use of *magus* and related terms in Apuleius, see again Rives (forthcoming).
77 Treatments of Apuleius' trial can be found in Harrison 2000: 39–86; Bradley 1997; Graf 1997: 65–88; and MacMullen 1966: 121–24.
78 Apuleius, *Apologia* 82.1.
79 Apuleius' acquittal can be inferred from the fact that he delivered speeches several years later before two proconsuls of Africa: Severianus in 162/3 CE (*Florida* 9.39), and Scipio Orfitus in 163/4 CE (*Florida* 17.1 and 17.18–21). The *Florida* (17.18) also suggests that in 163/4 Apuleius was something of a local celebrity among the Carthaginians.
80 Apuleius, *Apologia* 28.4–5 and 24–25.
81 Apuleius, e.g., *Apologia* 25.14.
82 E.g., Apuleius, *Apologia* 2.5.
83 Apuleius, *Apologia* 103.27.
84 E.g., Apuleius, *Apologia* 9.3.
85 E.g., in Apuleius' *Metamorphoses* (also known as *The Golden Ass*), which is about the magical misadventures of its hero, Lucius (at 3.16, 6.16, etc.). For this point see Rives 2003: 322 and n. 28.
86 Zoroaster (Zarathustra) was a legendary Persian *magus* who lived possibly as early as the eleventh century BCE, whom the Greeks knew about as early as the fifth century BCE. Oromazes (Ahuramazda) is the supreme, benevolent Iranian god and protector of kings, who was traditionally the teacher and/or father of Zoroaster.

87 The logical fallacy to which Apuleius appeals here is reminiscent of the Aesop fable (56 Perry) of the *gunē magos* who was similarly asked how, for one who professed control over the gods, she could not persuade the jury of her innocence (see earlier).

88 Apuleius, *Apologia* 26.9–10.

89 Apuleius, *Apologia* 32.26, 41.13.

90 Rives 2003: 323.

91 Apuleius, *Apologia* 27.18.

92 Ostanes is mentioned later in the context of other infamous magicians at *Apologia* 90.10–13.

93 Apuleius, *Apologia* 27.16–27.

94 Apuleius, *Apologia* 33.8, with Abt 1908: 209.

95 Apuleius, *Apologia* 36.

96 Pliny, *Natural History* 9.155.

97 Pliny, *Natural History* 32.8.

98 Apuleius, *Apologia* 35.7–8. For more on fish and other sea creatures used in Roman and Greco-Egyptian magic, see Bradley 1997: 209–12.

99 Apuleius, *Apologia* 42.9.

100 For this practice, see Johnston 2001. Many such child divination spells are attested in *PGM*, on which see Abt 1908: 236–51.

101 Johnston 2001: 101–2.

102 Apuleius, *Apologia* 43.23–25.

103 Apuleius, *Apologia* 48.1–5.

104 Apuleius, *Apologia* 49–51.

105 Apuleius, *Apologia* 51.18–24.

106 E.g., Diodorus Siculus, fr. 31.43 (Dindorf).

107 E.g., Lucian, *Philopseudes* 16.

108 For this point see Graf 1997: 78–79.

109 Apuleius, *Apologia* 53.26–29.

110 Apuleius, *Apologia* 55.20–22.

111 Apuleius, *Apologia* 55.22–56.2.

112 Apuleius, *Apologia* 54.17–29. Translation by Harrison 2001: 77.

113 Apuleius, *Apologia* 54.26–29.

114 Apuleius, *Apologia* 58.3–8.

115 The case of the Bacchic mysteries in 186 BCE was famous (Livy 39.8–19). See further Cicero, *Laws* 2.21; Paul, *Sententiae* 5.23.15; *Theodosian Code* 9.16.7.

116 So Abt 1908: 295.

117 Apuleius, *Apologia* 61.16–25.

118 Apuleius, *Apologia* 61.1–8 (*Mercuriolus*).

119 Noted by Harrison 2001: 85 n. 156.

120 *PGM* VIII.1–63 (erotic binding spell), IV.2359–72 and V.370–446 (Hermes figurines), with Abt 1908: 300–2.

121 Although Abt 1908: 302 hesitates to accept the connection, he concedes: "Apuleius hat ein Götterbild, einen Merkur, dessen Material und dessen Verehrung durch den Redner die Ankläger nicht ohne Grund darauf

gebracht hat, die Figur diene Zaubereien." Recent authors accept the connection, e.g., Harrison 2000: 74 with n. 91 and Hunink 1997.II: 165.

122 *PGM* VIII.14.
123 Apuleius, *Apologia* 63.25.
124 *PGM* V.379.
125 Apuleius, *Apologia* 63.5–8.
126 *PGM* V.2371–73.
127 *Apologia* 61.2, 64.3, with Harrison 2000: 74, no. 91 and Graf 1997: 81.
128 Suetonius, *Nero* 56.
129 Augustine, *City of God* 8.19.
130 Augustine, *City of God* 8.19.
131 Plato, *Symposium* 202e; *Timaeus* 40a–41e.
132 Apuleius, *Apology* 43.2–5.
133 A good treatment of this topic can be found in Flint 1999.
134 Augustine, *City of God* 8.22.
135 Augustine, *Letters* 136.1 and 138.18–19.
136 The most comprehensive study of early modern demonologists can be found in Clark 1997.
137 E.g., in the French demonologist, Nicholas Rémy 1930 [1595]: 141.
138 A more detailed account of this development can be found in Rives 2003: 328–34.
139 The *Opinions of Paulus* 5.23.14–19. Translation based on Rives 2003: 329, modified.
140 In later laws, in addition to the love philtre (*amatorium poculum*) and abortifacient (*abortionis poculum*), we find further distinctions in *venena*, including contraceptives (*medicamentum ad conceptionem*) and cosmetics (referred to by their dealers, *pigmentarii*). Dealers in cosmetics are liable to be punished under the Cornelian law if they dispense hemlock, salamander, aconite (monkshood), pinegrubs, poisonous beetles, mandrake, and, with the exception of using it for purification, Spanish fly (Marcian, *Institutes* [*Digest* 48.8.3]).
141 A brief treatment of this extensive topic can be found in Russell 1972: 89–92.
142 Philostratus, *Life of Apollonius of Tyana* 8.7.10, 8.7.12–14.
143 Suetonius, *Augustus* 31.1. See further Potter 1994.
144 *Theodosian Code* 9.16.4. See also the texts quoted in Pharr 1932.
145 For more on this development, see Graf 1999.
146 Polemon, *Declamationes* (pp. 44–45 Hinck), with Ogden 2002: no. 295.
147 The *Opinions of Paulus* 5.23.18.
148 *Theodosian Code* 9.16.
149 *Justinian Code* 9.18.
150 *Coll.* 15.3.6.
151 *Theodosian Code* 9.16.6.
152 *Theodosian Code* 9.16.3. For this *Code* I have used the Latin text of Haenel 1837.
153 E.g., *Geoponica* 1.12.37.

154 Cato, *On Agriculture* 160. See the discussion of this charm in Graf 1997: 43–46.
155 *Theodosian Code* 9.16.4 (divination), 9.16.7 (nocturnal sacrifice).
156 The others were the *Gregorianus* (ca. 291) and the *Hermogenianus*, which contained Diocletian's laws from 291 to 294 CE. The *Theodosian Code* contained the laws from Constantine to Theodosius II.
157 Technically, in addition to the *Digest* Justinian also issued two other codes, the *Codex* and *Institutiones*, which over time were gradually integrated into one compilation.

Select Bibliography

Abt, A. 1908. *Die Apologie des Apuleius von Madaura und die antike Zauberei*. Giessen.

Beard, M., North, J., and Price, S. 1998. *Religions of Rome*. 2 Vols. Cambridge.

Bell, C. 1992. *Ritual Theory, Ritual Practice*. Oxford.

Bernand, A. 1991. *Sorciers grecs*. Paris.

Betz, H. D., ed. 1992. *The Greek Magical Papyri in Translation*. 2nd ed. Chicago.

Betz, H. D., ed. 2003. *The "Mithras Liturgy": Text, Translation, and Commentary*. Tübingen.

Bond, G., ed. 1981. *Euripides: Heracles, with Introduction and Commentary*. Oxford.

Bonner, C. 1943. "The Technique of Exorcism." *HThR* 36: 39–49.

Boyancé, P. 1937. *Le Culte des Muses chez les philosophes grecs: Etudes d'histoire et de psychologie religieuses*. Paris.

Bradley, K. 1994. *Slavery and Society at Rome*. Cambridge.

Bradley, K. 1997. "Law, Magic, and Culture in the *Apologia* of Apuleius." *Phoenix* 51.2: 203–23.

Brashear, W. 1995. "The Greek Magical Papyri: An Introduction and Survey; Annotated Bibliography (1928–1994)." *ANRW* II.18.5: 3380–684.

Bremmer, J. 1999. "The Birth of the Term 'Magic.'" *ZPE* 126: 1–12.

Burkert, W. 1962. "ΓΟΗΣ: Zum griechischen 'Schamanismus.'" *RhM* n.s. 105: 36–55.

Burkert, W. 1992. *The Orientalizing Revolution: Near Eastern Influence on Greek Culture in the Early Archaic Age*. Translated by M. Pinder and W. Burkert. Cambridge, Mass.

Burkert, W. 2005. "Divination." *ThesCRA* 3: 1–16.

Clark, S. 1997. *Thinking with Demons: The Idea of Witchcraft in Early Modern Europe*. Oxford.

Clerc, C. 1915. *Les Théories relatives au culte des images chez les auteurs grecs du II-ème siècle après J.-C.* Paris.

Collins, D. 2001. "Theoris of Lemnos and the Criminalization of Magic in Fourth-Century Athens." *CQ* 51.2: 477–93.

Collins, D. 2002. "Reading the Birds: *Oiōnomanteia* in Early Epic." *Colby Quarterly* 38: 17–41.

Collins, D. 2003. "Nature, Cause and Agency in Greek Magic." *TAPA* 133: 17–49.

Crawford, M. H. et al. 1996. *Roman Statutes*. (Bulletin of the Institute of Classical Studies, Suppl. 64). London.

Cunliffe, B., ed. 1988. *The Temple of Sulis Minerva at Bath*. Vol. 2. *The Finds From the Sacred Spring*. Oxford.

Curbera, J. and Jordan, D. 1998. "A Curse Tablet from the 'Industrial District' Southwest of the Athenian Agora." *Hesperia* 67.2: 215–18.

Daly, L. W. 1982. "A Greek Palindrome in Eighth-Century England." *AJP* 103: 95–97.

Daniel, R. W. and Maltomini, F., eds. 1990–92. *Supplementum Magicum* (Papyrologica Coloniensia 16.1 and 2). Opladen.

Daremberg, C. and Ruelle, C., eds. 1963. *Oeuvres de Rufus d'Éphèse*. Amsterdam.

Dean-Jones, L. 1989. "Menstrual Bleeding According to the Hippocratics and Aristotle." *TAPA* 119: 177–92.

Dickie, M. 2000. "Who Practised Love-Magic in Classical Antiquity and in the Late Roman World?" *CQ* 50.2: 563–83.

Dickie, M. 2001. *Magic and Magicians in the Greco-Roman World*. London.

Dillery, J. 2005. "Chresmologues and *Manteis*: Independent Diviners and the Problem of Authority." In Johnston and Struck, 167–231.

Dillon, J. 1976. "Image, Symbol, and Analogy: Three Basic Concepts of Neoplatonic Allegorical Exegesis." In R. B. Harris, ed., *The Significance of Neoplatonism*. Virginia. 247–62.

Dodds, E. R. 1951. *The Greeks and the Irrational*. Berkeley.

Durkheim, E. 1915. *The Elementary Forms of the Religious Life*. London.

Edelstein, L. 1967. "Greek Medicine in Its Relation to Religion and Magic." In O. Temkin and C. Temkin, eds., *Ancient Medicine: Selected Papers of Ludwig Edelstein*. Baltimore. 201–46.

Elsner, J. 1996. "Image and Ritual: Reflections on the Religious Appreciation of Classical Art." *CQ* 46: 515–31.

Evans-Pritchard, E. 1937. *Witchcraft, Oracles, and Magic Among the Azande*. Oxford.

Faraone, C. 1989. "An Accusation of Magic in Classical Athens (Ar. *Wasps* 946–48)." *TAPA* 119: 149–60.

Faraone, C. 1991a. "The Agonistic Context of Early Greek Binding Spells." In Faraone and Obbink, 3–32.

Faraone, C. 1991b. "Binding and Burying the Forces of Evil: The Defensive Use of 'Voodoo Dolls' in Ancient Greece." *CA* 10: 165–205.

Faraone, C. 1992. *Talismans and Trojan Horses: Guardian Statues in Ancient Greek Myth and Ritual*. Oxford.

Faraone, C. 1993. "Molten Wax, Spilt Wine and Mutilated Animals: Sympathetic Magic in Near Eastern and Early Greek Oath Ceremonies." *JHS* 113: 60–80.

Faraone, C. 1996. "Taking the 'Nestor's Cup Inscription' Seriously: Erotic Magic and Conditional Curses in the Earliest Inscribed Hexameters." *CA* 15.1: 77–112.

Faraone, C. 1999. *Ancient Greek Love Magic*. Cambridge, Mass.

Faraone, C. 2001. "The Undercutter, the Woodcutter, and Greek Demon Names Ending in -*TOMOS* (Hom. *Hymn to Dem* 228–29)." *AJP* 122: 1–10.

Faraone, C. and Obbink, D., eds. 1991. *Magika Hiera: Ancient Greek Magic and Religion*. Oxford.

Felton, D. 2001. "The Animated Statues of Lucian's *Philopseudes*." *The Classical Bulletin* 77.1: 75–86.

Ferrary, J.-L. 1991. "Lex Cornelia de Sicariis et Veneficis." *Athenaeum* 69: 417–34.

Flint, V. 1991. *The Rise of Magic in Early Medieval Europe.* New Jersey.

Flint, V. 1999. "The Demonisation of Magic and Sorcery in Late Antiquity: Christian Redefinitions of Pagan Religions." In B. Ankarloo and S. Clark, eds., *Witchcraft and Magic in Europe: Ancient Greece and Rome.* Philadelphia. 279–348.

Foley, H., ed. 1994. *The Homeric Hymn to Demeter: Translation, Commentary, and Interpretive Essays.* Princeton.

Forsdyke, S. 2005. *Exile, Ostracism, and Democracy.* Princeton.

Fowler, R. and Graf, F. 2005. "The Concept of Magic." *ThesCRA* 3: 283–87.

Frankfurter, D. 1995. "Narrating Power: The Theory and Practice of the Magical *Historiola* in Ritual Spells." In M. Meyer and P. Mirecki, eds., *Ancient Magic and Ritual Power.* Leiden. 457–76.

Frazer, J. G. 1917. *The Golden Bough.* 3rd ed. London.

Furley, W. 1993. "Besprechung und Behandlung: Zur Form und Funktion von ΕΠΩΙΔΑΙ in der griechischen Zaubermedizin." In G. Most, H. Petersmann, and A. Ritter, eds., *Philanthropia kai Eusebeia: Festschrift für Albrecht Dihle zum 70. Geburtstag.* Göttingen. 80–104.

Gager, J., ed. 1992. *Curse Tablets and Binding Spells from the Ancient World.* Oxford.

Ganschinietz, L. 1919. "Katochos." *RE* 10: 2526–34.

Garland, R. 1995. *The Eye of the Beholder: Deformity and Disability in the Graeco-Roman World.* London.

Geffcken, J. 1916–19. "Der Bilderstreit des heidnischen Altertums." *ARW* 19: 286–315.

Gell, A. 1998. *Art and Agency: An Anthropological Theory.* Oxford.

Gordon, R. 1979. "The Real and the Imaginary: Production and Religion in the Graeco-Roman World." *Art History* 2: 5–34.

Gordon, R. 1999. "'What's in a List?' Listing in Greek and Graeco-Roman Malign Magical Texts." In Jordan, Montgomery, and Thomassen, 239–77.

Graf, F. 1997. *Magic in the Ancient World.* Translated by F. Philip. Cambridge, Mass.

Graf, F. 1999. "Magic and Divination." In Jordan, Montgomery, and Thomassen, 283–98.

Graf, F. 2002. "Augustine and Magic." In J. Bremmer and J. Veenstra, eds., *The Metamorphosis of Magic from Late Antiquity to the Early Modern Period.* Leuven. 87–103.

Green, R. P. H., ed. 1995. *Augustine: De Doctrina Christiana.* Oxford.

Greifenhagen, A. 1957. *Griechische Eroten.* Berlin.

Grodzynski, D. 1974. "Par la bouche de l'empereur." In *Divination et Rationalité.* Paris. 267–94.

Haenel, G., ed. 1837. *Codices Gregorianus, Hermogenianus, Theodosianus.* Leipzig.

Hamilton, R. 1993. "Fatal Texts: The *Sortes Vergilianae.*" *Classical and Modern Literature* 13.4: 309–36.

Hankinson, R. J. 1998. *Cause and Explanation in Ancient Greek Thought.* Oxford.

Hansmann, L. and Kriss-Rettenbeck, L. 1966. *Amulett und Talismann: Erscheinungsform und Geschichte.* Munich.

Harmening, D. 1990. "Zauberinnen und Hexen: Vom Wandel des Zaubereibegriffs im späten Mittelalter." In A. Blauert, ed., *Ketzer, Zauberer, Hexen: Die Anfänge der europäischen Hexenverfolgungen.* Frankfurt am Main. 68–90.

Harrison, S. J. 2000. *Apuleius: A Latin Sophist.* Oxford.

Harrison, S. J., ed. 2001. *Apuleius: Rhetorical Works.* Translated and annotated by S. Harrison, J. Hilton, and V. Hunink. Oxford.

Hart, A. and Honoré, A. 1959. *Causation in the Law.* Oxford.

Heim, R. 1892. *Incantamenta Magica Graeca Latina.* Leipzig.

Henig, M. et al. 1988. "Objects from the Sacred Spring." In Cunliffe, 5–53.

Hoessly, F. 2001. *Katharsis: Reinigung als Heilverfahren. Studien zum Ritual der archaischen und klassischen Zeit sowie zum Corpus Hippocraticum.* Göttingen.

Hopfner, T. 1928. "Μαγεία." *RE* 14. Pt. 1: 301–93.

Hunink, V., ed. 1997. *Apuleius of Madauros Pro Se de Magia (Apologia).* 2 Vols. Amsterdam.

Johnston, S. I. 1999. *Restless Dead: Encounters Between the Living and the Dead in Ancient Greece.* Berkeley.

Johnston, S. I. 2001. "Charming Children: The Use of the Child in Ancient Divination." *Arethusa* 34: 97–117.

Johnston, S. I. and Struck, P. eds. 2005. *Mantikê: Studies in Ancient Divination.* Leiden.

Jong, A. de. 1997. *Traditions of the Magi: Zoroastrianism in Greek and Latin Literature.* Leiden.

Jordan, D. R. 1988. "New Archaeological Evidence for the Practice of Magic in Classical Athens." *Praktika tou XII Diethnous Synedriou Klasikēs Archaiologias: Athēna, 4–10 Septembriou 1983.* Vol. 4. Athens.

Jordan, D. R., Montgomery, H., and Thomassen, E., eds. 1999. *The World of Ancient Magic: Papers from the First International Samson Eitrem Seminar at the Norwegian Institute at Athens, 4–8 May 1997.* Bergen.

Kieckhefer, R. 1989. *Magic in the Middle Ages.* Cambridge.

Kieckhefer, R. 1994. "The Specific Rationality of Medieval Magic." *American Historical Review* 99.3: 813–36.

King, H. 1998. *Hippocrates' Woman: Reading the Female Body in Ancient Greece.* London.

Kingsley, P. 1994. "Greeks, Shamans and Magi." *Studia Iranica* 23: 187–98.

Kingsley, P. 1995. *Ancient Philosophy, Mystery, and Magic: Empedocles and Pythagorean Tradition.* Oxford.

Kirk, G. S., Raven, J. E., and Schofield, M. 1983. *The Presocratic Philosophers: A Critical History with a Selection of Texts.* 2nd ed. Cambridge.

Kisch, Y. de. 1970. "Les *Sortes Vergilianae* dans l'Histoire Auguste." *Mélanges d'archéologie et d'histoire* 82: 321–62.

Klingshirn, W. E. 2002. "Defining the Sortes Sanctorum: Gibbon, Du Cange, and Early Christian Lot Divination." *Journal of Early Christian Studies* 10: 77–130.

Klingshirn, W. E. 2005. "Christian Divination in Late Roman Gaul: The *Sortes Sangallenses.*" In Johnston and Struck, 99–128.

Kotansky, R. 1991. "Incantations and Prayers for Salvation on Inscribed Greek Amulets." In Faraone and Obbink, 107–37.

Lamberton, R. 1986. *Homer the Theologian: Neoplatonist Allegorical Reading and the Growth of the Epic Tradition.* Berkeley.

Laskaris, J. 2002. *The Art is Long: On the Sacred Disease and the Scientific Tradition.* Leiden.

Lévy-Bruhl, L. 1979. *How Natives Think.* Translated by L. A. Clare. New York.

Lévi-Strauss, C. 1966. *The Savage Mind.* Chicago.

Lewis, I. M. 1989. *Ecstatic Religion: A Study of Shamanism and Spirit Possession.* 2nd ed. London.

Lloyd, G. E. R. 1975. "Alcmaeon and the Early History of Dissection." *Sudhoffs Archiv* 59.2: 113–47.

Lloyd, G. E. R. 1979. *Magic, Reason and Experience: Studies in the Origin and Development of Greek Science.* Cambridge.

Lloyd, G. E. R. 1987. *The Revolutions of Wisdom: Studies in the Claims and Practice of Ancient Greek Science.* Berkeley.

MacDowell, D. 1978. *The Law in Classical Athens.* Ithaca.

MacMullen, R. 1966. *Enemies of the Roman Order: Treason, Unrest, and Alienation in the Empire.* London.

Maggiani, A. 2005. "La divinazione in Etruria." *ThesCRA* 3: 52–78.

Malinowski, B. 1954. *Magic, Science and Religion and Other Essays.* Edited with an introduction by R. Redfield. New York.

Markus, R. 1994. "Augustine on Magic: A Neglected Semiotic Theory." *Revue des Études Augustiniennes* 40: 375–88.

Meiggs, R. and Lewis, D., eds. 1969. *A Selection of Greek Historical Inscriptions to the End of the Fifth Century* BC. Oxford.

Meiggs, R. and Lewis, D., eds. 1988. *A Selection of Greek Historical Inscriptions.* Oxford.

Messeri, G. 1998. "136. P. Flor. II 259." In G. Cavallo et al., eds. *Scrivere Libri e Documenti nel Mondo Antico.* Florence. 208–9.

Meyer, M. and Smith, R., eds. 1999. *Ancient Christian Magic: Coptic Texts of Ritual Power.* Princeton.

Mora, G., ed. 1991. *Witches, Devils, and Doctors in the Renaissance.* Binghamton.

Niedermann, M., ed. 1916. *Marcelli De Medicamentis Liber* (*CML* 5). Leipzig.

Nock, A. D. 1972. "Paul and the Magus." In id., *Essays on Religion and the Ancient World.* Vol. 1. Oxford. 308–30.

Obbink, D. 1993. "The Addressees of Empedocles." *MD* 31: 51–98.

O'Donnell, J. 1992. *Augustine: Confessions.* 3 Vols. Oxford.

Ogden, D. 1997. *The Crooked Kings of Ancient Greece.* London.

Ogden, D. 2001. *Greek and Roman Necromancy.* Princeton.

Ogden, D. 2002. *Magic, Witchcraft, and Ghosts in the Greek and Roman Worlds: A Sourcebook.* Oxford.

Parker, R. 1983. *Miasma: Pollution and Purification in Early Greek Religion.* Oxford.

Parker, R. 2005a. *Polytheism and Society at Athens.* Oxford.

Parker, R. 2005b. "Law and Religion." In M. Gagarin and D. Cohen, eds., *The Cambridge Companion to Ancient Greek Law.* Cambridge. 61–81.

Pharr, C. 1932. "The Interdiction of Magic in Roman Law." *TAPA* 63: 269–95.

Phillips, C. R. 1986. "The Sociology of Religious Knowledge in the Roman Empire to AD 284." *ANRW* II.16.3: 2677–773.

Phillips, C. R. 1991. "Nullum crimen sine lege: Socioreligious Sanctions on Magic." In Faraone and Obbink, 260–76.

Potter, D. 1994. *Prophets and Emperors: Human and Divine Authority from Augustus to Theodosius.* Cambridge, Mass.

Potter, T. 1985. "A Republican Healing-Sanctuary at Ponte di Nona near Rome and the Classical Tradition of Votive Medicine." *Journal of the British Archaeological Association* 138: 23–47.

Pritchett, W. K. 1979. *The Greek State at War*. Part III. Berkeley.

Puschmann, T., ed. 1963. *Alexander von Tralles*. 2 Vols. Amsterdam.

Rathbone, D. 1991. *Economic Rationalism and Rural Society in Third-Century AD Egypt*. Cambridge.

Rémy, N. 1930. *Demonolatry*. Translated by E. A. Ashwin. London. (Originally published as *Demonolatreia*, 1595.)

Renehan, R. 1992. "The Staunching of Odysseus' Blood: The Healing Power of Magic." *AJP* 113: 1–4.

Richardson, N. J., ed. 1974. *The Homeric Hymn to Demeter*. Oxford.

Ritner, R. 1995. "Egyptian Magical Practice under the Roman Empire: The Demotic Spells and their Religious Context." *ANRW* II.18.5: 3333–79.

Rives, J. 2002. "Magic in the XII Tables Revisited." *CQ* 52.1: 270–90.

Rives, J. 2003. "Magic in Roman Law: The Reconstruction of a Crime." *CA* 22.2: 313–39.

Rives, J. 2006. "Magic, Religion, and Law: The Case of the *Lex Cornelia de sicariis et veneficiis*." In C. Ando and J. Rüpke, eds., *Religion and Law in Classical and Christian Rome*. Stuttgart. 47–67.

Rives, J. (forthcoming). "*Magus* and its Cognates in Classical Latin." In R. Gordon and F. Marco, eds., *Magical Practice in the Latin West: Papers from the International Conference held at the University of Zaragoza, 30th Sept.–1st Oct. 2005*. Leiden.

Robert, J. and L. 1950. "Bulletin Épigraphique." *REG* 63: 121–220.

Roeper, G. 1850. "Homerischer Talisman." *Philologus* 5: 162–65.

Rose, V. 1874. "Über die Medicina Plinii." *Hermes* 8: 18–66.

Ross, M. C. 1965. *Catalogue of the Byzantine and Early Mediaeval Antiquities in the Dumbarton Oaks Collection*. Vol. 2. Washington, DC.

Russell, J. 1972. *Witchcraft in the Middle Ages*. Ithaca.

Scarborough, J. 1991. "The Pharmacology of Sacred Plants, Herbs, and Roots." In Faraone and Obbink, 138–74.

Schlörb-Vierneisel, B. 1964. "Zwei klassische Kindergräber im Kerameikos." *MDAI* 79: 85–104.

Schlörb-Vierneisel, B. 1966. "Eridanos-Nekropole, I. Gräber und Opferstellen hS 1–204." *MDAI* 81: 4–111.

Schwendner, G. 2002. "Under Homer's Spell." In L. Ciraolo and J. Seidel, eds., *Magic and Divination in the Ancient World*. Leiden. 107–18.

Skorupski, J. 1976. *Symbol and Theory: A Philosophical Study of Theories of Religion in Social Anthropology*. Cambridge.

Steiner, D. 2001. *Images in Mind: Statues in Archaic and Classical Greek Literature and Thought*. Princeton.

Struck, P. 2004. *Birth of the Symbol: Ancient Readers at the Limit of Their Texts*. Princeton.

Tambiah, S. 1985. *Culture, Thought, and Social Action: An Anthropological Perspective*. Cambridge, Mass.

Tambiah, S. 1990. *Magic, Science, Religion and the Scope of Rationality*. Cambridge.

Taussig, M. 1993. *Mimesis and Alterity: A Particular History of the Senses*. New York.

Thiers, J.-B. 1984. *Traité des superstitions: croyances populaires et rationalité à l'Age classique*. 4th ed. Paris. (Originally published in 1741.)

Thomas, K. 1971. *Religion and the Decline of Magic*. New York.

Thorndike, L. 1915. "Some Medieval Conceptions of Magic." *The Monist* 25: 107–39.

Tomlin, R. S. O. 1988. "The Curse Tablets." In Cunliffe, 59–277.

Van den Berg, R. M. 2001. *Proclus' Hymns: Essays, Translations, Commentary*. Leiden.

Van der Horst, P. W. 1998. "*Sortes*: Sacred Books as Instant Oracles in Late Antiquity." In L. V. Rutgers et al., eds., *The Use of Sacred Books in the Ancient World*. Leuven. 143–73.

Van Straten, F. T. 1981. "Gifts for the Gods." In H. Versnel, ed., *Faith, Hope and Worship*. Leiden. 65–151.

Vegetti, M. 1999. "Culpability, Responsibility, Cause: Philosophy, Historiography, and Medicine in the Fifth Century." In A. A. Long, ed., *The Cambridge Companion to Early Greek Philosophy*. Cambridge. 271–89.

Versnel, H. S. 1991. "Beyond Cursing: The Appeal to Justice in Judicial Prayers." In Faraone and Obbink, 60–106.

Versnel, H. S. 1998. "An Essay on Anatomical Curses." In F. Graf, ed., *Ansichten griechischer Rituale: Geburtsags-Symposium für Walter Burkert*. Stuttgart. 217–67.

Versnel, H. S. 2002a. "The Poetics of the Magical Charm: An Essay on the Power of Words." In P. Mirecki and M. Meyer, eds., *Magic and Ritual in the Ancient World*. Leiden. 105–58.

Versnel, H. S. 2002b. "Writing Mortals and Reading Gods: Appeal to the Gods as a Dual Strategy in Social Control." In D. Cohen, ed., *Demokratie, Recht und soziale Kontrolle im klassischen Athen*. Munich. 37–76.

Walde, A. 1910. *Lateinisches etymologisches Wörterbuch*. 2nd ed. Heidelberg.

Watson, A., ed. 1985. *The Digest of Justinian*. 2 Vols. Philadelphia.

Wax, M. and Wax, R. 1962. "The Magical World View." *Journal for the Scientific Study of Religion* 1: 179–88.

Weiner, A. B. 1983. "From Words to Objects to Magic. Hard Words and the Boundaries of Social Interaction." *Man* 18: 690–709.

Wessely, K. 1886. "Neue griechische Ostraka." *Wiener Studien* 8: 116–18.

Winkler, J. 1991. "The Constraints of Eros." In Faraone and Obbink, 214–43.

Wünsch, R., ed. 1898. *Sethianische Verfluchungstafeln aus Rom*. Leipzig.

Wünsch, R. 1909. "Deisidaimoniaka." *ARW* 12: 1–45.

Index